# THE ULTIMATE

# ART OF WAR

## BY THE SAME AUTHOR

*Fundamental Samurai Teachings* (Book of Samurai Series Book I)
*Samurai Arms, Armour & the Tactics of Warfare* (Book of Samurai Series Book II)
*Book of Ninja: The First Complete Translation of the Bansenshukai*
*Ninja Skills: The Authentic Ninja Training Manual*
*The Dark Side of Japan: Ancient Black Magic, Folklore, Ritual*
*Iga and Koka Ninja Skills: The Secret Shinobi Scrolls of Chikamatsu Shigenori*
*The Illustrated Guide to Viking Martial Arts*
*In Search of the Ninja: The Historical Truth of Ninjutsu*
*The Lost Samurai School: Secrets of Mubyoshi Ryu*
*The Lost Warfare of India: An Illustrated Guide*
*Modern Ninja Warfare: Ninja Tactics and Methods for the Modern Warrior*
*Old Japan: Secrets from the Shores of the Samurai*
*Samurai and Ninja: The Real Story Behind the Japanese Warrior Myth that Shatters the Bushido Mystique*
*Samurai War Stories*
*The Secret Traditions of the Shinobi: Hattori Hanzo's Shinobi Hiden and other Ninja Scrolls*
*Secrets of the Ninja: The Shinobi Teachings of Hattori Hanzo*
*True Path of the Ninja: The Definitive Translation of the Shoninki*

# THE ULTIMATE

# ART OF WAR

## A STEP-BY-STEP ILLUSTRATED GUIDE TO SUN TZU'S TEACHINGS

ANTONY CUMMINS

# THE ULTIMATE ART OF WAR

## ANTONY CUMMINS

First published in the UK and USA in 2019 by
Watkins, an imprint of Watkins Media Limited
Unit 11, Shepperton House, 83–93 Shepperton Road
London N1 3DF

enquiries@watkinspublishing.com



Commissioning Editor: Fiona Robertson
Managing Editor: Daniel Culver
Editor: James Hodgson
Head of Design: Georgina Hewitt
Designer: Karen Smith
Production: Uzma Taj

Commissioned artwork: Jay Kane
Calligraphy: Yamamoto Jyuhō

A CIP record for this book is available from the British Library

ISBN: 978-1-78678-271-7

10 9 8 7 6 5 4 3 2 1

Typeset in Adobe Garamond Pro and Brandon Grotesque
Colour reproduction by XY Digital
Printed in China

www.watkinspublishing.com

## WARNING

The information contained within this book is for historical research purposes only and should not be recreated nor re-enacted in any way. Watkins Media Limited, the author and any other persons who have been involved in working on this publication cannot accept responsibility for any injuries or damage incurred as a result of applying the information in this book.

# CONTENTS

# FOREWORD

As I write this foreword for *The Ultimate Art of War*, I am working on a new article interpreting the concepts and evolution of Chinese military dialectics. One may consider the two works belong to different realms – one aimed at a mainstream readership, the other at an academic audience – but it occurs to me that their importance is linked. The harder I try to advance the scholarship of Chinese strategic thought in the West, the more I fear my efforts might be in vain, as the current foundation of the scholarship remains flimsy. Groundwork is needed for the academic scholarship to stand firm.

*The Ultimate Art of War* gives me some hope with regard to this longstanding problem. As a classic that is often heard of and read but seldom understood in the West, Sun Tzu's *Art of War* has thus far remained in the translation phase. And we know this translation approach has reached its limits. Antony Cummins has made an important first step in going beyond mere translation by offering readers a modern reading that takes a step-by-step, graphical approach. By breaking down the *Art of War* into individual, easy-to-understand teachings, it helps clarify the chapters of the original that are hard to digest for most non-academic readers. Such use of lessons is an enhanced form of studying Sun Tzu by the means of maxims, yet it is more helpful than merely trying to learn from the maxims alone. I believe Antony Cummins has developed a new and systematic way of studying the *Art of War* for the Western world.

I am impressed by Antony's devotion and enthusiasm in his studies of the *ninja* and the *samurai*, and taking on the transmission of Chinese strategic thought to the West is another tremendous task that requires the same courage and determination. I am glad that Antony Cummins is on board with this project. His cross-cultural literacy and clever illustrations make *The Ultimate Art of War* an ideal companion book to Sun Tzu's original text.

As I suggested in my book *Deciphering Sun Tzu*, in addition to the historical and philosophical approach that I have been advocating and pursuing, the next essential step to be taken in the scholarship of Sun Tzu and broader Chinese strategy is a more extensive study of Chinese military and strategic history. I am hopeful that Antony Cummins will continue his great work and through his illustrated books help reignite the study of Chinese strategy in the West.

Derek M.C. Yuen
Author of *Deciphering Sun Tzu: How to Read the Art of War*

**BIO**

Derek M.C. Yuen has a PhD in Strategic Studies from the University of Reading. He is the author of *Deciphering Sun Tzu: How to Read the Art of War* (New York: Oxford University Press; London: Hurst). Based in Hong Kong, he has been researching and publishing on the synthesis of Chinese and Western strategic thought and the strategic thinking of Sun Tzu, Lao Tzu and Mao Zedong. He is currently working on a book about the strategic thought and military dialectics of Mao Zedong.

孫子兵法

# INTRODUCTION

The *Art of War* is a military text believed to have been written by an ancient Chinese strategist known as Sun Tzu during the late Spring and Autumn Period (fifth century BC). Its continued influence in all parts of the modern world is a testament to the timeless and universal wisdom of its teachings. There are myriad translations, interpretations, expansions and inspirations based on the original, all of which hold merit. However, this book focuses on Sun Tzu's core teachings and explores each lesson in greater depth than has been done before. By breaking the *Art of War* down into individual, easy-to-understand teachings, this book aims to inspire readers to delve deeper into the weightier writings on war and strategy.

## WHY WE NEED AN ILLUSTRATED GUIDE

The *Art of War* has been in existence for over 2,000 years, yet it remains a text that is often read but seldom explored. New translations and treatments of the work continue to spring up year after year. From comic book interpretations to business models and leadership guides, there is seemingly no end of uses for the *Art of War*, but none of these books fully explores the teachings themselves. Previous illustrated editions have contained only the translated text lavishly adorned with gorgeous pictures of old China and related artefacts to help give a flavour of the subject matter. In contrast, this edition presents not only the translation itself, but also in-depth explanations supported by illustrations and diagrams specifically conceived to clarify Sun Tzu's concepts.

## THE STRUCTURE OF THIS BOOK

This book divides Sun Tzu's original text into separate sections, signalled by the heading "Sun Tzu says". Each section is followed by a number of individual lessons based on the content of that section.

Where applicable, lessons have an accompanying illustration that conveys the essence of the teaching. Some are abstract, others are directly instructional. Lessons that are particularly abstract or that echo earlier teachings do not have an illustration. Take note of the following points:

- When only circles are used, black circles represent the allied troops while red ones represent the leadership.
- When hexagons, squares or blocks are used, black represents the allies and red the enemies.
- The formations are not actual historical examples; they are there to provide an idea only.

The lesson commentary expands on the core point or points that Sun Tzu is making. Where there is disagreement among the various ancient Chinese commentators and modern translators, I discuss the different interpretations, giving equal weight to the different versions.

Each lesson concludes with a "war tip", which summarizes the essence of the lesson in a sentence or two.

## WHO WAS SUN TZU?

Sun Tzu (sometimes rendered as Sunzi) is an enigmatic figure. Most people will jump to the answer that he was a military strategist who wrote the

*Art of War*. However, even this is not completely certain. His very name is incomplete – Sun Tzu just means "Master Sun", Sun being a Chinese surname. Some scholars believe he did not actually exist.

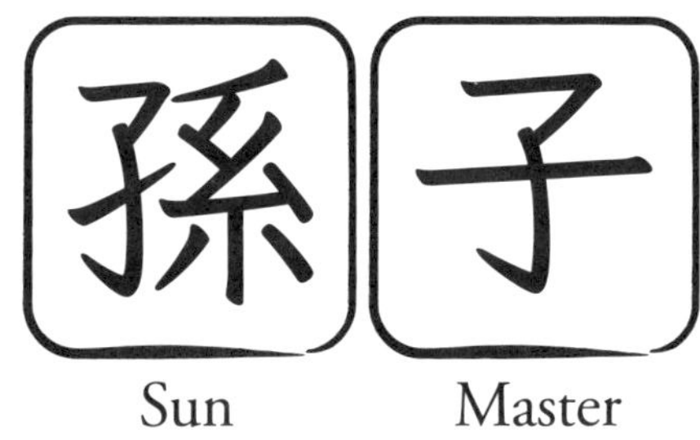


**ABOVE:** You should never say "Master Sun Tzu" because it is like saying "Master, master Sun". Instead say either "Master Sun" or just "Sun Tzu".

Sun Tzu's birth and death dates are unknown – he does not appear in any census or writings of his supposed time and all transcriptions of the *Art of War* are from a much later date. The original is now lost. The lack of firm biographical information has led to a debate that has raged for over a thousand years. Theories about Sun Tzu include the following:

- He presented the *Art of War* to the King of Wu in 512 BC.
- He may be the historically identifiable person called Sun Wu of the fifth century BC.
- He may be an unrecorded man dating to somewhere between the last half of the fifth century BC and the third century BC.
- He may be a fake construct invented sometime between 200 BC and AD 200 to give the text credibility.

In this book I have assumed that Sun Tzu is a historical figure and that he wrote the text known as the *Art of War*.

## WHAT IS THE *ART OF WAR*?

Some people claim that Sun Tzu *created* military ways in old China. This is not true, he merely recorded and perfected them. Warfare existed before the *Art of War*, but the text is notable for capturing military principles in concise, down-to-earth terms without recourse to the lengthy dialogues on esoteric matters that characterize other ancient Chinese writings. It has been famous for its whole existence and, if anything, its fame is actually increasing.

**ABOVE:** The original ideograms for the book and its author's name. A literal translation would be "Military Matters by Master Sun", but the text became widely known as the *Art of War*.

## A HISTORY OF THE TEXT

One of the main problems in dating ancient Chinese texts is that the first emperor of China, Qin Shi Huang, held a mass book-burning crusade during his reign (220–210 BC), which destroyed most of the books that predated him. Until fairly recently, the earliest known transcription of the *Art of War* was from around AD 1000.

However, in 1972 excavators unearthed a pair of tombs in the eastern Chinese province of Shandong. In one tomb they found bamboo strips on which the *Art of War* had been transcribed. The burial of the tomb was found to date to the Han dynasty (206 BC to AD 220), but the transcription could of course be even older than that. What is clear is that the structure of the text had been fixed in place by this time.

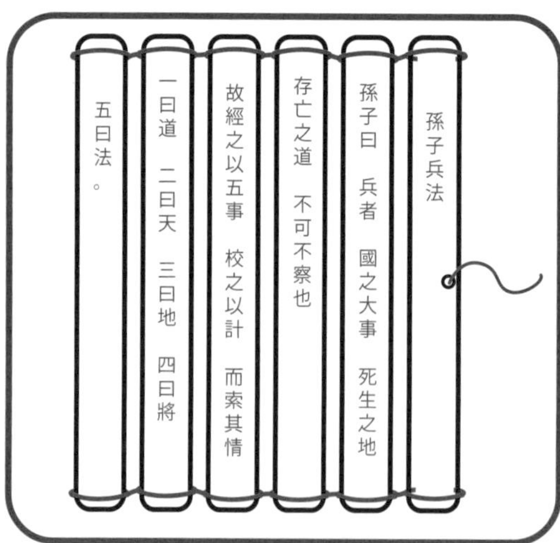


**LEFT:** The ideogram 篇, usually translated as "chapter" or "scroll", originally represented a bamboo book. The *Art of War* would have been written on 25cm (10in) bamboo strips laced together.

Sadly, however, translators and historians agree that sections of the original text have been lost, moved out of place or added during later transcriptions (although they disagree as to which parts may have been moved or added). But take heart, all agree that most of the text is there and that later ideogram changes are minimal.

The manual was passed down the ages, making its way around mainland Asia (also Russia) and into Japan where it was a core text of study for the samurai class. It was not until 1772 that it first appeared in Europe, with sections being presented in French by a Jesuit missionary. It allegedly found its way to Napoleon (or so say certain Chinese scholars) and then on to military theorists like the Prussian general Carl von Clausewitz (1780–1831). The first English translations (*see* page 12) appeared in the early 20th century and since then the *Art of War* has been translated many times into most of the major world languages.

### DATING THE TEXT

Sun Tzu and the *Art of War* are commonly placed in the fifth and sixth centuries BC, but this may not be accurate. For a detailed current understanding, see Ames, R.T., *Sun Tzu: The Art of War*, Folio Society, London, 2017.

## A NOTE ON TRANSLATIONS

This book reproduces the first full English translation, by the British sinologist Lionel Giles (1875–1958), which was published in 1910. However, in the lessons contained within this book I have also analysed and compared all the other leading translations to form a complete understanding of each teaching. I have referred particularly extensively to the 1993 translation by American writer Ralph D. Sawyer, which is one of the most accessible for modern-day Western readers. Therefore, you will find in a few places that my commentary does not match up exactly with the Giles version, but all is explained in the text.

All of the translations are great works by accomplished authors who deserve praise for their outstanding efforts in bringing the writings of Sun Tzu to the English-speaking world. Everard Ferguson Calthrop's partial 1905 translation is often criticized by later academics. However, his version is still included here but with caution because he was working from

Japanese texts and, as an army officer himself, his focus was on conveying the essentials of Asian warfare to the modern Western military rather than on maintaining complete linguistic accuracy.

Here is the full list of texts used for this edition:


- Ames, R. T., Sun Tzu: *The Art of War*, Folio Society, London, 2017
- Calthrop, E. F., *The Art of War*, Capstone, West Sussex, 2010
- Cleary, T., *The Art of War: Complete Texts and Commentaries*, Shambhala, Boston 1988
- Clements, J., Sun Tzu: *The Art of War*, Macmillan, London, 2017
- Denma Translation Group, *The Art of War: A New Translation*, Shambhala, Boston, 2001
- Giles, L., *The Art of War: Sun Tzu*, Arcturus, London, 2017
- Griffith, S. B., Sun Tzu, *The Art of War: A New Illustrated Edition*, Watkins, London, 2002
- Minford, J., Sun Tzu: *The Art of War*, Penguin Books, London, 2005
- Sawyer, R. D., *The Seven Military Classics of Ancient China*, Westview Press, Colorado, 1993
- Trapp, J., *The Art of War: A New Translation*, Amber, London, 2011
- Yuen, D. M., *Deciphering Sun Tzu: How to Read the Art of War*, Hurst and Company, London, 2014


## OTHER VERSIONS OF THE *ART OF WAR*

As we have seen, there are numerous translations of the *Art of War*, but there are also documents that are considered as new "versions" of the work. These include Thomas Cleary's translations of the documents *Mastering the Art of War*, *The Lost Art of War* and *The Silver Sparrow Art of War*, all of which are historical documents concerned with Sun Tzu's text or alternative versions of it. Another important work is the *Art of War* by Sun Bin (died 316 BC), which was also discovered in the 1972 Shandong excavation. To date, only Sun Tzu's standard text is regarded as the *Art of War* proper, and the extra discussions and sentences found in these other documents are seen as additions or complements to the original. This book has focused on the standard text and stayed within its boundaries, but has taken into account additions from other versions.

## TRANSLITERATION SYSTEMS

There are two main systems for transliterating Chinese characters into the Roman alphabet to enable non-Chinese speakers to pronounce them. The original Wade-Giles system, established in the 19th century, gives us the classic spelling of "Sun Tzu". The Hanyu-Pinyin system was developed in the 1950s and has been adopted by international organizations such as the United Nations. Using this system we get the alternative spelling of "Sunzi", which is becoming popular among modern translators.

Almost every name, title and concept in this book will have variations in its Roman spelling. The main problem comes with the names of the ancient Chinese commentators, which do not match across the different versions of the translated commentaries. For example, Tu Mu, Wade-Giles, becomes Du Mu in Hanyu-Pinyin and Ts'ao Ts'ao becomes Cao Cao. Rather than standardizing, I have decided to stick to the spelling that each author used in their text, so that anyone researching further using the source translations will be able to quickly locate the information they are looking for. For simplicity, I have removed all long vowel markers.

## CHINESE MILITARY STRUCTURE

A number of Sun Tzu's teachings rely on an understanding of Chinese military structure, an enduring feature of which was the division of the whole into three separate parts, which when brought together created a massive force. The system is based on multiples of five, starting with the smallest unit, which then builds as shown in the table (*below*):

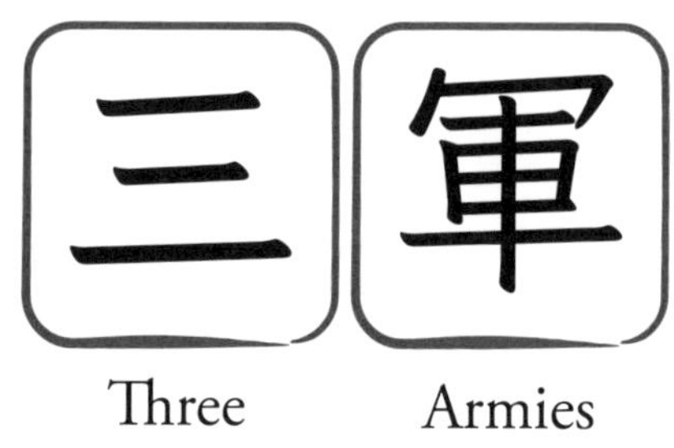


**ABOVE:** The original ideograms for "the three armies", meaning a full military force.

| ENGLISH | CHINESE | IDEOGRAM | Number of troops | Number of squads |
|---|---|---|---|---|
| Army | *Chun* | 軍 | 12,500 | 2,500 |
| Regiment | *Shih* | 帥 | 2,500 | 500 |
| Battalion | *Lu* | 旅 | 500 | 100 |
| Company | *Tsu* | 卒 | 100 | 20 |
| Platoon | *Liang* | 両 | 25 | 5 |
| Squad | *Wu* | 伍 | 5 | 1 |

See Ralph D. Sawyer's *Seven Military Classics of Ancient China* for further details.

## *YIN* AND *YANG* AND PARADOX IN CHINESE CULTURE

Often Eastern wisdom seems mystical and beyond our comprehension with apparent paradoxes such as formless form and far being near and so on. Western minds see these concepts as problems to be solved, whereas in Eastern culture it is not a question of resolving but of merging and flux. *Yin* and *yang* are not static; they form into each other. *Yang* moves into *yin* and *yin* into *yang* in a perpetually productive relationship. In the West we may point to a closed box and say, 'Is there a cat or no cat in that box?' Then we use reason to decide whether there is a cat in there or not. In the East they will say that sometimes there will be a cat in the box and sometimes there will not – it all depends when you look. This is the route to understanding Eastern paradox. Each situation changes and, therefore, form becomes formless and returns to form again and whether something is near or far depends on the perception of the enemy and the movements an army makes. The orthodox needs the unorthodox to exist and they move in and out of phases. They are not, in fact, paradoxical at all; that's just the way they have been presented to us in the past. Therefore, to explore Sun Tzu's text is to enrich yourself with an understanding of ancient Chinese culture and the schools of thought from that time.

## DIFFERING INTERPRETATIONS

This book aspires to be the most comprehensible and comprehensive version of Sun Tzu's original text, built on the great efforts of translators over the past 100 years and more, with additional reference to Chinese commentators old and new. However, at times these translators and scholars disagree over what Sun Tzu was trying to say. Sometimes the ancient Chinese commentators, some of whom were themselves successful generals of their time, may even have used his words to support their own way of warfare. So it is hard to know which, if any, of the interpretations of a given concept matches his original intention. If Sun Tzu were to read this book, there would undoubtedly be some parts of it he would not recognize as his own work. What I hope he would recognize is my genuine endeavour to convey his ideas as faithfully as possible.

# THE ART OF WAR

孫子兵法

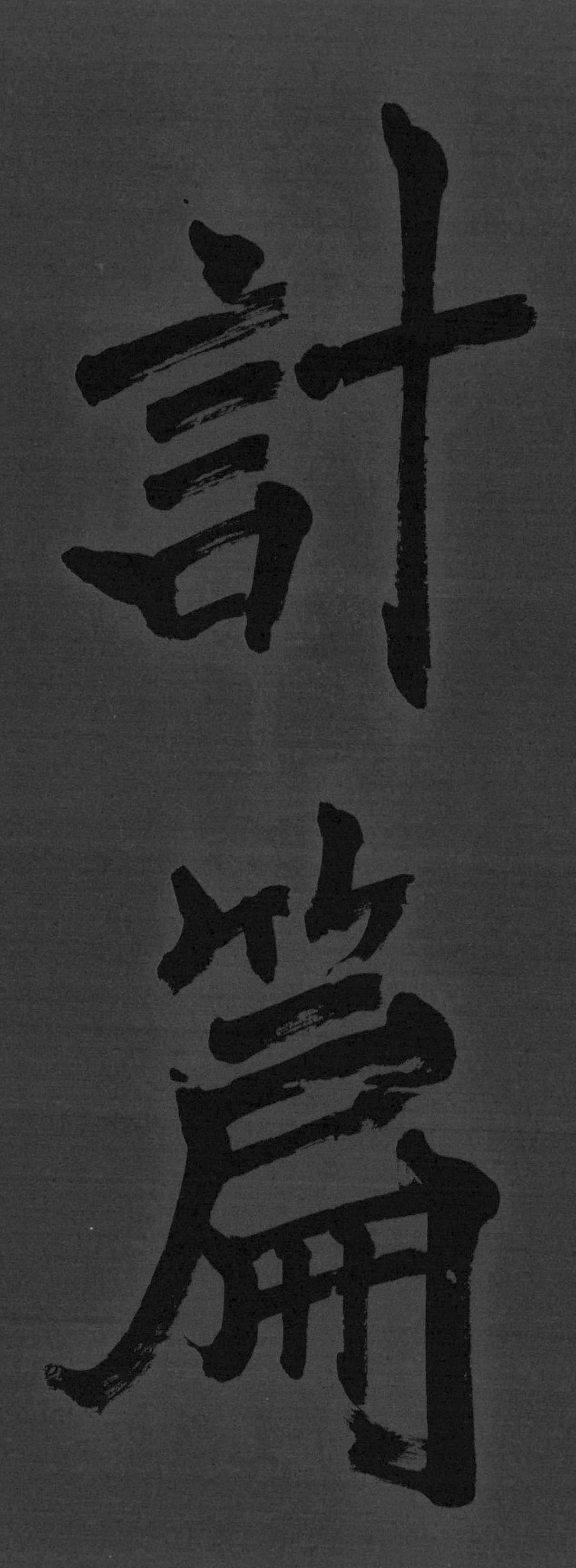
計篇

# CHAPTER 1

# THE SCROLL OF PREPARATION AND PLANS

# THE SCROLL OF PREPARATION AND PLANS

Sun Tzu's opening chapter title features the ideogram 計, meaning "plans". The chapter is divided into three main sections:

1 The five constant factors
2 The seven considerations
3 The 14 ways of deception

The scroll starts with a discussion of the importance of war and the elements that need to be considered before going to war. Sun Tzu lists five factors that military commanders should focus on when preparing an army for war. This is followed by seven points of comparison that commanders should use to weigh up their forces against those of the enemy. The final section consists of a set of 14 types of deception that a military commander can employ to outwit the enemy.

## SUN TZU SAYS

*The art of war is of vital importance to the state. It is a matter of life and death, a road either to safety or to ruin. Hence it is a subject of inquiry which can on no account be neglected. The art of war, then, is governed by five constant factors, to be taken into account in one's deliberations, when seeking to determine the conditions obtaining in the field.*

*These are:*
*1 The moral law*
*2 Heaven*
*3 Earth*
*4 The commander*
*5 Method and discipline*

- *The moral law causes the people to be in complete accord with their ruler, so that they will follow him regardless of their lives, undismayed by any danger.*
- *Heaven signifies night and day, cold and heat, times and seasons.*
- *Earth comprises distances, great and small; danger and security; open ground and narrow passes; the chances of life and death.*
- *The commander stands for the virtues of wisdom, sincerity, benevolence, courage and strictness.*
- *By method and discipline are to be understood the marshalling of the army in its proper subdivisions, the graduations of rank among the officers, the maintenance of roads by which supplies may reach the army, and the control of military expenditure.*

*These five heads should be familiar to every general: he who knows them will be victorious; he who knows them not will fail.*

# LESSON 1

## THINK CAREFULLY BEFORE GOING TO WAR

War decides the future of entire nations and peoples. On war may hang their livelihoods and even their survival. The way of the military commander is to bring about victory without incurring high levels of casualty or major loss of wealth. The state must be certain it can afford a war and see it through to the end; it must also consider whether the war is just. Excellent military leaders dedicate their lives to the study of war and its tactics.

**WAR TIP Approach the study of war as a profession, become an expert in all its elements and never go to war without considering all things from beginning to end.**

# LESSON 2

## NEVER NEGLECT THE FIVE CONSTANT FACTORS OF WAR

- The way
- Heaven
- Earth
- The commander
- Organization

The five constant factors are the main focus of Sun Tzu's teachings and, alongside the seven considerations, they form the backbone of his entire work. Always apply the following processes to all five factors:

• ASSESSMENT – collect and record all the factors for both the enemy and allied forces.
• COMPARISON – decide who has advantage in all the areas for which information has been collected.
• DELIBERATION – using these factors, make plans with a war council.

A military commander cannot be worthy of the name without absorbing the five constant factors. Leaders who truly understand them will gain victory in all conflicts; if they do not study them and assimilate their teachings, they will achieve only defeat.

The translators and ancient Chinese commentators generally agree on the basic outline of the five constant factors.

**WAR TIP: The five constant factors are the building blocks for war.**

# LESSON 3

## THE WAY

*This is the first of the five constant factors.*

Way

**ABOVE:** The way means troops and leaders being in accord and harmony with each other.

The ideogram for "way" (道) can be used to represent the Taoist Way, the primary force of the universe which holds reality together, but here its connotations are more to do with morality, harmony, politics, unity of the force and state, and the relationship of troops and the general populace with their leaders. Giles translates the term as "moral law", which goes some way toward encapsulating these ideas. From a student of war's standpoint, it involves identifying corruption or injustice in both the allied and enemy forces. Consider whether the laws are correct and there is true justice and well-being in the society as a whole, both enemy and allied. If rulers are corrupt, unjust or inhumane, those they command will hate them and their authority will be weakened. The best situation is to command a force that is defending a home that is filled with justice and harmony.

When moral harmony is in place, the following conditions will result:

- Troops join together and have one mind.
- Troops are supportive of their rulers.
- Troops will live and die for the state.
- Troops will stand firm together.

**WAR TIP: Any force under a bad ruler will crumble and fall. Therefore, maintain harmony and unity above all else.**

# LESSON 4

## HEAVEN

*This is the second of the five constant factors.*

Heaven

In the *Art of War*, Sun Tzu uses the ideogram for heaven (天) to refer to climate and weather; in other contexts it can mean divine order. A good knowledge of weather forecasting and an understanding of the effect weather has on terrain and troops is essential. Soldiers who are too hot, too wet or too cold underperform. Too much heat can mean a lack of water, too much rain can mean being bogged down in muddy terrain and a frozen landscape can render equipment useless. When entering enemy territory a good military leader must understand the prevailing weather patterns and equip accordingly.

Heaven can also mean:

- *Yin* and *yang* (considered to be dark and light in this context)
- Hot and cold
- Thxging of the seasons

**WAR TIP: Always be aware of the weather conditions in the area where you will be going to war and learn to predict the weather as accurately as possible.**

# LESSON 5

## EARTH

*This is the third of the five constant factors.*

Earth

Earth (地) in the *Art of War* means geography and topography. Without detailed information on the battleground, the surrounding area and potential escape routes, a functioning plan cannot be put together. A military commander must know the different types of terrain and how they will affect both the allied and the enemy forces. Details for this are found in chapters 10 and 11.

Earth means to have an understanding and knowledge of the following:

- The highest mountains and the lowest valleys
- Distances, both short and long
- The ground – is it difficult or easy to pass through; is it open and free or tight and confined?

Earth has the following implications:

- Forces may have to climb steep mountains.
- Forces may be vulnerable in valleys.
- If far away the forces are safe.
- If the enemy is close there is danger.
- Difficult ground will stop vehicles, mounted troops and equipment.
- "Tight places" increase the risk of ambush and restrict the passage of troops.
- Forces that find themselves on ground where they cannot move or escape are destined for death or defeat.

**WAR TIP: Obtain a detailed map of enemy territory and be realistic about how easily troops will be able to manoeuvre.**

# LESSON 6

## THE COMMANDER

*This is the fourth of the five constant factors.*

A strong military commander (將)is key to success in warfare. Such a leader will have mastered the *Art of War* on behalf of the people and the troops. A proper military leader upholds the following five virtues at all times with an unbreakable determination:

Commander

• WISDOM AND INTELLIGENCE – the ability to make detailed plans and be flexible enough to change them if required
• INTEGRITY AND TRUSTWORTHINESS – so that the forces know their commander is fair
• COMPASSION – understanding the plight of each soldier, sensing when the forces are in discomfort and pain and acting accordingly
• COURAGE – mastering fear in order to be formidable
• DISCIPLINE – enforcing a strict but fair code that rewards the right people and punishes wrongdoers, without any hint of favouritism

**WAR TIP: Train your mind, act in a way that inspires trust, understand the feelings of your troops, conquer your fear and treat everyone fairly.**

# LESSON 7

## ORGANIZATION

*This is the last of the five constant factors.*

The ideogram 法 is often translated as "organization", "discipline", "routine", "codes", "laws" or "way of". The original title of the *Art of War* in Chinese uses the ideograms 兵 and 法, which together mean "codes, matters, or ways of the military and soldiers". Here in the text it refers specifically to systems of punishment, reward and discipline within the ranks.

Organization

**ABOVE:** The ideogram 法 is part of the original title for the *Art of War*: 孫子兵法.

Discipline means to take control of the following:

- ORGANIZATION. The army must be divided into appropriate parts, these parts must have a station and position and a detailed roster of tasks that is easy for all to understand. All soldiers must know where they should be, when they should be there and what they should be doing. Equally, they must know where they should *not* go and which activities they should not involve themselves in.
- CHAIN OF COMMAND. There should be a defined military hierarchy with established protocols. If there is an issue, each soldier must know who to inform and those informed must know who to consult to get the issue resolved.
- LOGISTICS. Supplies and equipment must flow reliably. Troops need food and equipment, so there should be a proper procedure for obtaining, looking after and storing equipment and rations, and replacing them when necessary.

**WAR TIP: A military encampment has to be regulated and the whole army must be aware of the correct protocol for all situations.**

## SUN TZU SAYS

*Therefore, in your deliberations, when seeking to determine the military conditions, let them be made the basis of a comparison, in this wise:*

1. *Which of the two sovereigns is imbued with the moral law?*
2. *Which of the two generals has more ability?*
3. *With whom lie the advantages derived from heaven and earth?*
4. *On which side is discipline more rigorously enforced?*
5. *Which army is stronger?*
6. *On which side are officers and men more highly trained?*
7. *In which army is there the greater constancy both in reward and punishment?*

*By means of these seven considerations I can forecast victory or defeat.*

*The general that hearkens to my counsel and acts upon it will conquer: let such a one be retained in command! The general that hearkens not to my counsel nor acts upon it will suffer defeat: let such a one be dismissed! While heeding the profit of my counsel, avail yourself also of any helpful circumstances over and beyond the ordinary rules. According as circumstances are favourable, one should modify one's plans.*

# LESSON 8

## WEIGH UP THE SEVEN CONSIDERATIONS BEFORE COMMITTING TO WAR

In order to gauge the chances of victory, a military leader has to honestly compare the allied forces to those of the enemy. Gather together the command group to discuss and assess the following points in great detail, using information obtained through intelligence networks.

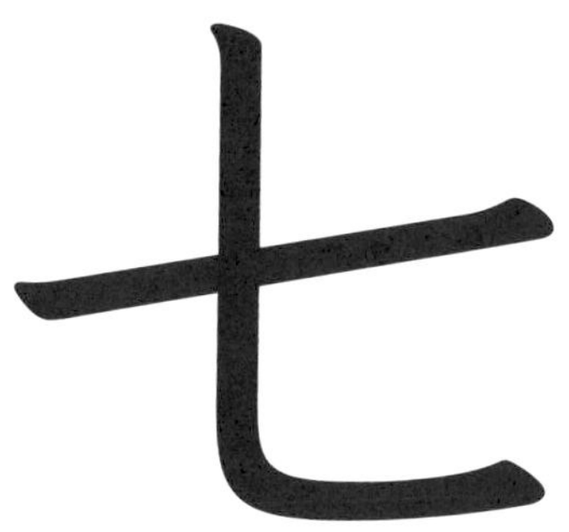

**ABOVE:** The ideogram for seven, referring to the seven considerations used to compare two opposing armies.

1 Which side has more positivity and fewer difficulties? The side whose population is more content and enjoys greater health, wealth and positivity and whose military organization is more harmonious, with no internal rivalry, will have a more efficient military force.

2 Which side has better leaders? The side where the command team is more highly skilled and professional, and whose overall leader has more victories, skill and ability in warfare will have a greater chance when going to war.

3 Which side is in the better position and has the weather working for them? Here, two of the five constant factors, heaven (weather conditions) and earth (terrain), are combined. Compare the landscape to judge who is more likely to be hampered by natural obstacles (details on this are in chapters 10 and 11). Also compare forces in terms of the weather: which army has the wind against them, which army faces the sun, which army is in an area that may flood. These considerations and more affect the chances of victory.

4 Which side has better routines and discipline? The force with the more disciplined soldiers – those who follow orders and react better – will be able to move their troops with more speed and skill. They will be able to make and break camp with little effort, march in line and cross great distances, because their troops will know what to do and when to do it.

5 Which side is more powerful? Strength in numbers should never be underestimated. Do not be seduced by the story of the "heroic underdog" coming out on top; in reality, the larger army usually wins. Assess which force has more troops, better equipment and more advanced technology. Think very carefully before going to war against an army that is stronger in these respects.

6 Which side has better-trained troops? More professional soldiers who are continually updated with the most innovative military techniques will perform better on the field of battle.

7 Which side has the better set of internal rules? The force which has the clearer system of reward and punishment, whose troops know that their efforts to succeed will be recognized just as their misdeeds will be punished, will hold an advantage.

Those who do not consider the above are not true commanders and should not be in a position of leadership.

**WAR TIP: The side that has the majority of the seven considerations in its favour will hold the advantage in war. This means superior political leadership that allows people to live contented lives with greater equality under the law; a larger, better-trained and better-led military force that promotes the worthy and expels the unworthy; and a better position in terms of terrain and weather conditions.**

# LESSON 9

## BE ADAPTABLE TO THE SITUATION

With a full assessment of the five constant factors and the seven considerations, a military commander can now understand the situation, if they have perceived it truthfully, and identify the advantages and disadvantages of each side. After this they can field an army in the most appropriate way for the situation. However, you must be flexible. Too rigid an approach will make it easy for the enemy to read your intentions, so be ready to change any elements that need changing according to the situation.

**WAR TIP: An incorrect understanding of the situation will lead to bad strategy, so a good military commander must see the truth of the situation and plan or respond accordingly. Never lie to yourself.**

### SUN TZU SAYS

*All warfare is based on deception. Hence, when able to attack, we must seem unable; when using our forces, we must seem inactive; when we are near, we must make the enemy believe we are far away; when far away, we must make him believe we are near. Hold out baits to entice the enemy. Feign disorder, and crush him. If he is secure at all points, be prepared for him. If he is in superior strength, evade him. If your opponent is of choleric temper, seek to irritate him. Pretend to be weak, that he may grow arrogant. If he is taking his ease, give him no rest. If his forces are united, separate them. Attack him where he is unprepared, appear where you are not expected. These military devices, leading to victory, must not be divulged beforehand.*

# LESSON 10

## KNOW THAT WAR IS THE PATH OF DECEPTION

One of the most influential ideas in the *Art of War* is that warfare is the path of deception. The original ideograms used are 詭 ("deception") and 道 ("way"). Some people believe that war should be fought in a dignified, sporting manner, but Sun Tzu is not one of them. On the contrary, he believes that each side should try to deceive the other in order to connive its way to victory. To this end, he lists 14 types of deception, which are explained in the remaining lessons of this chapter.

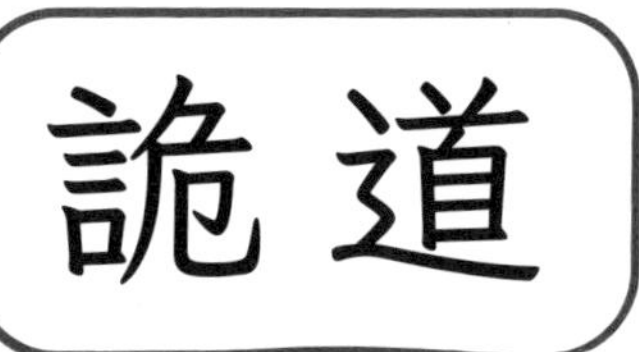


**ABOVE:** The original ideograms meaning "the way of deception" as used in the *Art of War*. Notice the famous character for "way", 道.

**WAR TIP: Warfare should not be upfront, honourable and without deceit. Individual soldiers seek recognition for honour and bravery in combat; good military leaders seek victory by all means necessary.**

# LESSON 11

## PRETEND TO BE INCOMPETENT

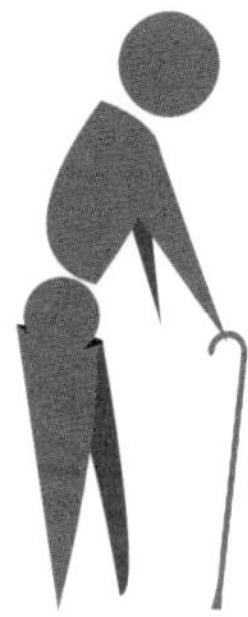

*This is the first of the 14 deceptions.*

The enemy is always watching, so do not "play your hand" before you have to. Hide the fact that you are ready to engage; make the enemy think your force is unprepared. If the enemy perception of your forces is wrong then their strategy will also be wrong.

**WAR TIP: A well-trained army will always be ready but act like it is not.**

# LESSON 12

## DISGUISE WHEN TROOPS ARE ABOUT TO BE DEPLOYED

*This is the second of the 14 deceptions.*

Before an army departs for a new position, there are routines that it must go through, including packing up equipment, assembling troops and sending out scouts. A well-trained force can perform such activities at speed and without arousing suspicion. If the enemy observes your routine it can estimate where you will be and can then pre-empt you. The less warning the enemy receives about the redeployment of troops the better.

**WAR TIP: Enemy spies will be watching your camp. Do not give them anything to report until it is too late or alternatively give them something false to report.**

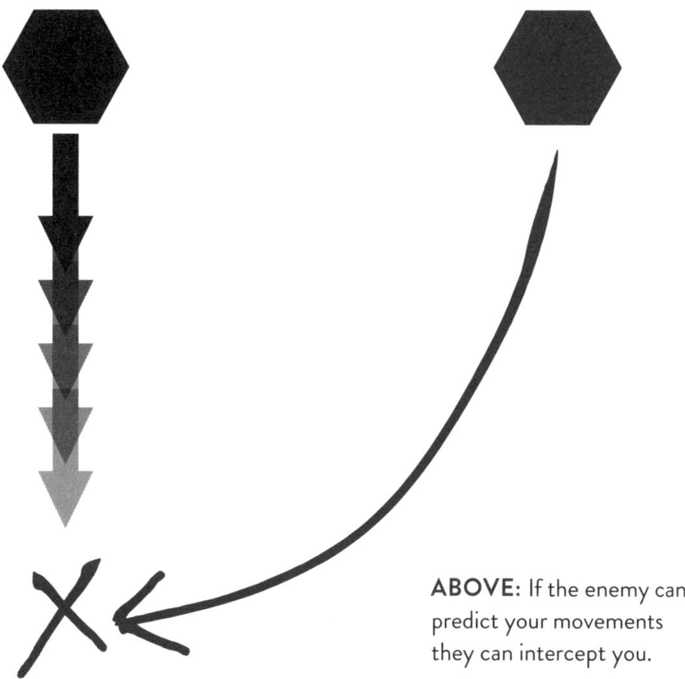

**ABOVE:** If the enemy can predict your movements they can intercept you.

# LESSON 13

## WHEN NEAR APPEAR FAR, WHEN FAR APPEAR NEAR

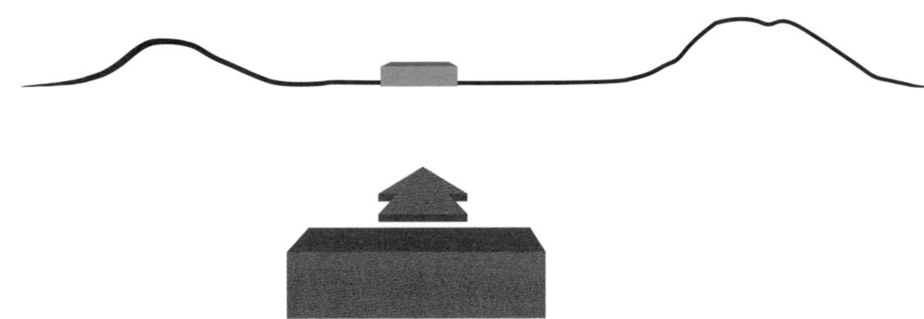

*These are the third and fourth of the 14 deceptions.*

Most translators hold this teaching as the ability to hide an army so that an enemy thinks the army is at a distance from them or to station a small group of troops near the enemy to make the enemy believe that all your forces are close by. Use spies to spread rumour among the enemy that your forces are nearby or far away, depending on which deception you wish to engineer. If the enemy thinks that your forces are further away or nearer than they actually are, it will change its tactics to the advantage of your forces.

However, Sawyer and Cleary believe that this is about *intent* and that when military commanders wish to move their troops far away they should act as if they are going to head toward the enemy or if they want to move close by they should make it look as if they are preparing to move far away. Scouts, rumours, and army routines are all ways to misrepresent your intentions.

**WAR TIP: Hide your army from enemy view or appear to be preparing to move to a place where you are not, either further away from or closer to the enemy than you actually intend.**

# LESSON 14

## OFFER THE ENEMY WHAT IT WANTS

*This is the fifth of the 14 deceptions.*

Discover what the enemy lusts for and offer that particular thing. Alternatively, offer something that would be a temptation to anyone. When the enemy moves to take it, a good military commander should take advantage of any gaps that arise from this movement.

The following are common examples of temptation:

- Leave a position undefended.
- Leave a small force of troops exposed.
- Leave riches to be collected.
- Fake a retreat.

**WAR TIP: Induce an enemy force to move from a strong position to a weaker one so that you can take advantage of the changed situation.**

# LESSON 15

## CREATE DISORDER AND STRIKE

*This is the sixth of the 14 deceptions.*

Perform an action that will cause the enemy to move from order to disorder. This can come from the enemy's own incompetence or actions that a military commander has put into place to create movement. Translators disagree as to whether this teaching should be combined with the previous lesson. Some translations say "offer bait and strike in the confusion", which connects the two. The aim is to take advantage of any movement.

**WAR TIP: Create movement in the enemy: movement means disorder, and disorder means gaps in defence.**

# LESSON 16

## WHEN THE ENEMY IS PREPARED FOR ATTACK, PREPARE TO DEFEND

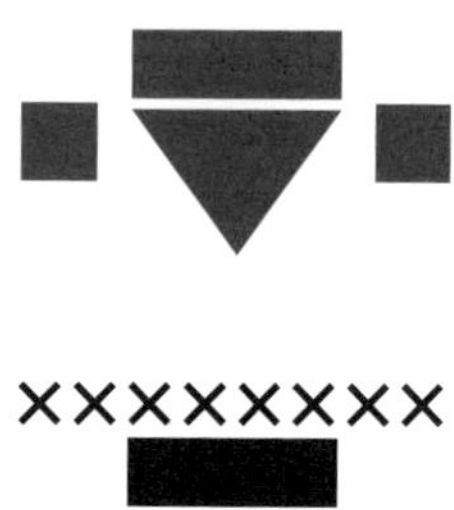

*This is the seventh of the 14 deceptions.*

When an enemy is efficient and well disciplined, with no gaps in its defence and no apparent way to create gaps, do not move against the enemy but instead prepare for any assault it may make.

**WAR TIP: Do not attack when the enemy is in a phase of strength.**

# LESSON 17

## AVOID ENGAGING AN ENEMY THAT IS STRONGER THAN YOU

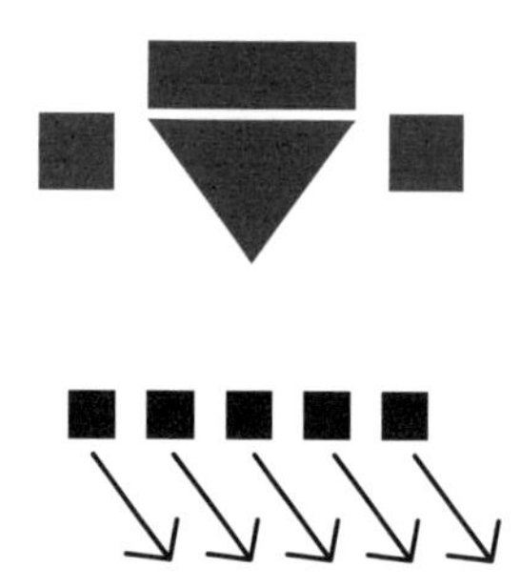

*This is the eighth of the 14 deceptions.*

A smaller force that is tactically weaker and functioning at a lower rate of efficiency will always lose. Therefore, if you are facing an enemy that is stronger than you are, whether numerically, positionally or tactically, do not engage them. If the enemy cannot be overcome, then keep mobile and out of its way until you can change the situation. This also holds true for attacking cities. If a city is well governed and has good systems of punishment and reward, back off and wait for or create change. Alternatively, pick another target.

**WAR TIP: When facing a larger, better and more equipped force, stay mobile and do not engage them.**

# LESSON 18

## ENRAGE THE ENEMY INTO MAKING MISTAKES

*This is the ninth of the 14 deceptions.*

If the enemy commander is prone to emotion – something that may be discovered through previous engagements or reports from spies – then take actions that will cause them embarrassment to raise their anger level. The aim is to provoke the enemy so that they are controlled by anger and not by intellect. An irritated opponent makes mistakes and mistakes give you the opportunity to attack.

This lesson is concerned with creating weak points in the opponent's formation so that a military commander can exploit them. There are three stages to the plan:

1. Attack a relatively soft enemy target in order to cause embarrassment. The idea is to provoke the enemy into making a "revenge move".
2. Allow the enemy to win a small victory in return, so that it gains revenge and builds its momentum.
3. Finally, look for the gap created by this enemy movement and strike a decisive blow there.

The key is that this action creates non-tactical movement within the enemy. It may mean sacrificing some of your troops or a position, but victory will result in the end. There are other ways to needle the enemy commander. For example, you could spread an embarrassing rumour about them to prick their ego.

**WAR TIP: An enemy who thinks many moves ahead is dangerous. Knock them out of this patient way of thinking by provoking them into tit-for-tat retaliation.**

# LESSON 19

## FEIGN INACTIVITY TO PUT THE ENEMY OFF GUARD

*This is the tenth of the 14 deceptions.*

Instead of showing strength, give the impression of inactivity or weakness. Allow the enemy to prod and test your forces without reacting. They will develop a false sense of security and become convinced that you are not going to move. This is the time to switch tack and go on the full offensive.

Another way to interpret this teaching is in terms of humility and arrogance; when the enemy is humble, you need to make them arrogant.

**WAR TIP: Just as you try to provoke the enemy into a reaction, make sure they do not succeed in provoking you. Let them think you are dormant and they will become complacent – and vulnerable.**

# LESSON 20

## WHEN THE ENEMY IS AT FULL STRENGTH, TIRE THEM OUT

*This is the 11th of the 14 deceptions.*

If the enemy forces are relaxed, well fed, well prepared and at ease, make moves to send them on long distances and from point to point to tire them out. When they try to move one way, give them reason to go in the opposite direction. For example, threaten one of their allies or another of their positions, or provoke them with a bait team. Continue this until they are tired and their morale, rations, equipment and health are used up. Then it is time to strike.

**WAR TIP: Keep the enemy moving to tire them out and deplete their stores.**

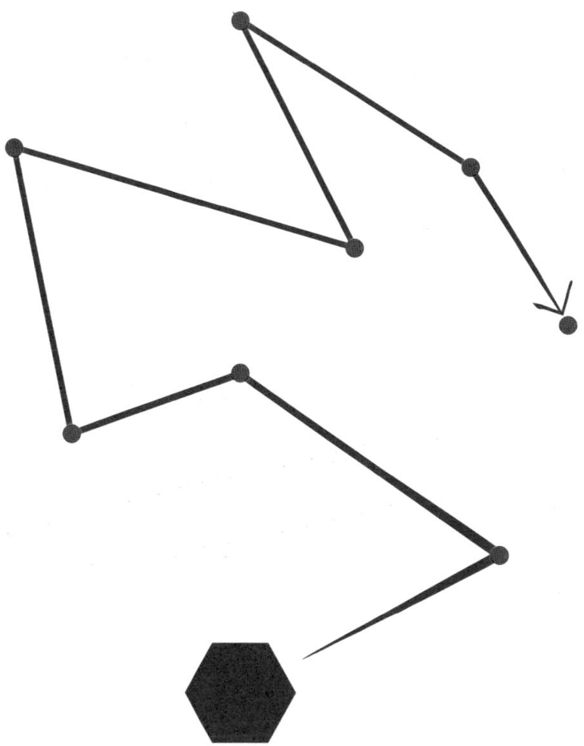

# LESSON 21

## WHERE THERE IS UNITY, SOW DISCORD

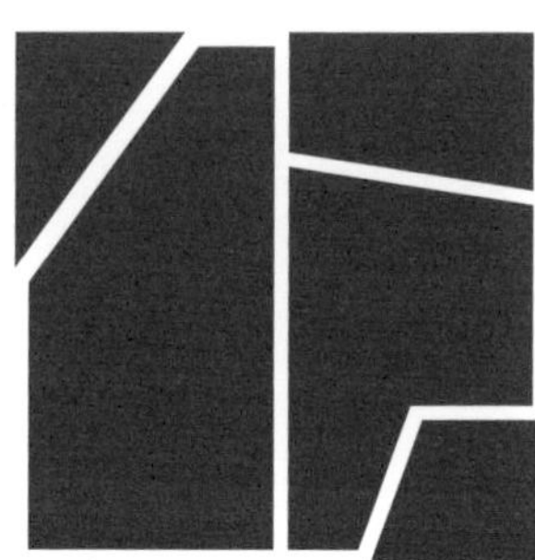

*This is the 12th of the 14 deceptions.*

An enemy may appear to be united, but it will be made up of different factions or clans that can be divided. You should also seek to divide the people from their leaders to undermine popular support for the war and make the common soldiers hate their superiors. Civil leaders do not always see eye to eye with military leaders – find ways to exploit these rivalries.

Division can be achieved through:

- Bribing malleable members of the enemy
- Spreading negative rumours and propaganda about key enemy figures
- Sending secret letters with false information concerning the defection of an enemy general
- Deploying infiltrators to become close friends with key enemy figures
- Convincing enemy troops that your cause is worthier and your soldiers are happier

**WAR TIP: A united enemy is a strong enemy. A good military leader should use deception to cause ill-feeling to fester within the enemy ranks.**

# LESSON 22

## ATTACK WHERE THE ENEMY IS UNPREPARED

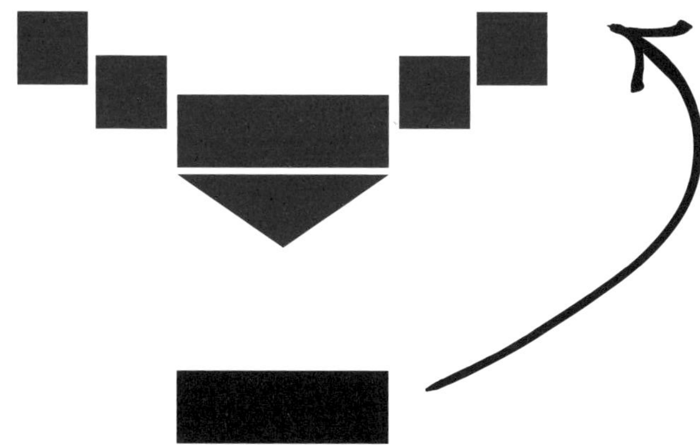

*This is the 13th of the 14 deceptions.*

A large military force can defend a huge expanse of land with multiple positions or fortifications or divisions, but even the most powerful army will have its weak spots. No matter whether the context is an individual battlefield or a whole country, use your intelligence network to identify a target that the enemy does not expect you to attack. This will most likely not be an overly important target, but it will bring you a victory and force the enemy to move or rethink. Hitting these places can have more impact than going for an obvious target.

**WAR TIP: The enemy will defend where they expect you to attack; therefore, attack where they are not prepared.**

# LESSON 23

## APPEAR WHERE AND WHEN UNEXPECTED

*This is the last of the 14 deceptions.*

The distinction between the previous lesson and this one is subtle. The essential difference is between where the enemy *is not prepared* and where the enemy *does not expect* to see an opposing force. The element of surprise can involve appearing from an unexpected direction (for example, from over a mountain) or at a time considered bad for an army to move (such as during winter). Put simply: take the enemy unawares. This will throw them off balance and make them rethink all their plans. However, some positions and timings are unexpected for good reason – in surprising the enemy, do not put your forces in a position of weakness.

**WAR TIP: Move your army to a position and at a time the enemy has not remotely anticipated.**

# LESSON 24

## NEVER DISCLOSE YOUR DECEPTIONS

This lesson marks the end of the 14 deceptions of war. In the Giles translation it states that "These military devices … must not be divulged beforehand." Clearly, it makes sense to keep your plans secret.

However, the second part of the sentence can also be translated as meaning "it is impossible to plan your deceptions in full beforehand," which is another plausible interpretation. Because all the facts of a situation cannot be known in advance, you need to be flexible and able to "think on the fly" to make these deceptions work.

**WAR TIP: When you have made plans to deceive the enemy, keep those plans secret and be ready to adapt them.**

SUN TZU SAYS

*Now the general who wins a battle makes many calculations in his temple ere the battle is fought. The general who loses a battle makes but few calculations beforehand. Thus do many calculations lead to victory, and few calculations to defeat: how much more no calculation at all! It is by attention to this point that I can foresee who is likely to win or lose.*

# LESSON 25

## CREATE A WAR ROOM

In old China war councils were most commonly held in or around religious areas, as war and religion were closely associated with each other.

Opinions differ as to what form the leaders' calculations took. Many commentators say that they would have used pieces to represent the allied and enemy forces and work through the battle, making moves almost as if playing a board game. However, others, including Clements and the Denma Group, believe that the process involved counting up the advantages for each side by putting tokens or rods in two piles – one for the allies, the other for the enemy. The side with the bigger pile was the one judged to have more advantages and, according to Sun Tzu's rationale, would be the victor.

**WAR TIP: Establish a command centre where you can meet with your most trusted advisors to plan an upcoming war or battle.**

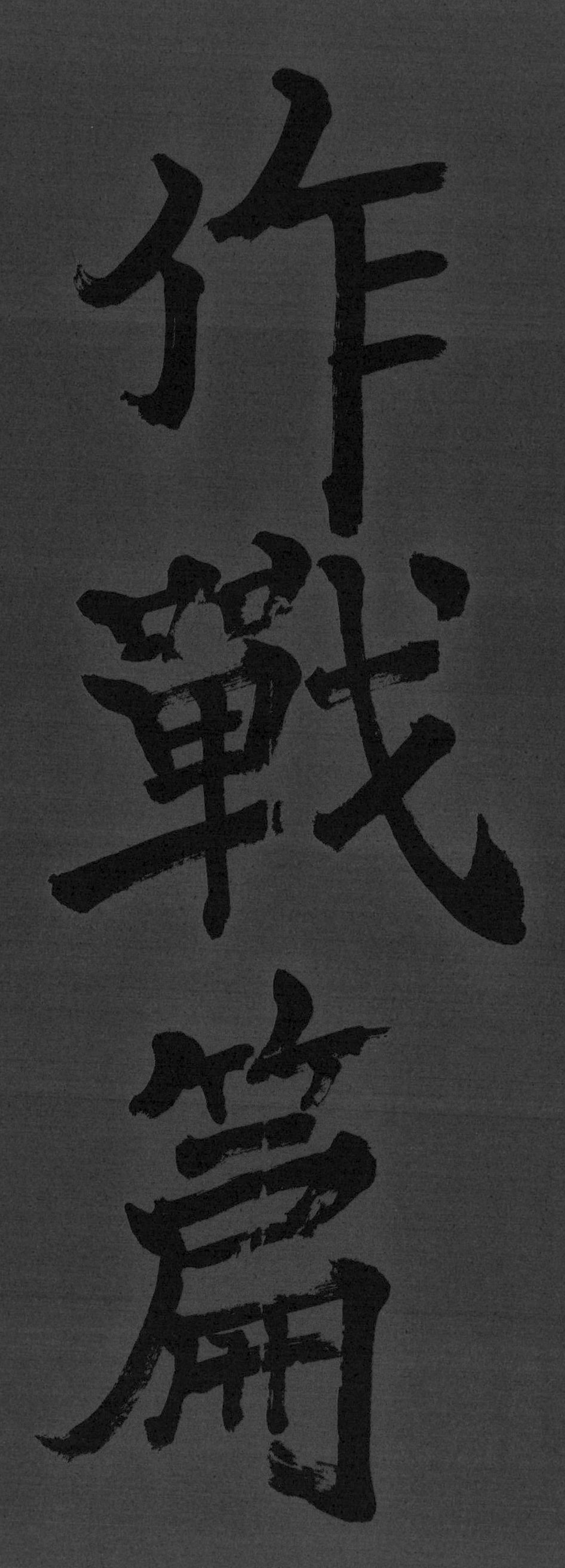
作戰篇

# CHAPTER 2

# THE SCROLL OF BATTLE PREPARATIONS

# THE SCROLL OF BATTLE PREPARATIONS

The title of Sun Tzu's second chapter includes the ideograms 作, meaning "to make", and 戦, meaning "battle" or "conflict", which together represent the idea of "strategic planning for the military". The chapter is divided into three main areas:

1 The raising of an army and its effects
2 The costs of taking an army to war
3 Behaviours, outlook and mindset

The first section deals with the vast expense and disruption involved in raising an army and looks at how that affects not only the soldiers waging the war, but also the people left behind who have to make up for lost workers. It also considers the chaos that an army on the move creates as it passes places of habitation. The second part describes the cost of maintaining an army over a prolonged period at war and emphasizes the sheer scope of military operations. The final part focuses on the troops themselves, on how they should treat enemy soldiers and how they can bring enemy troops over to the allied side, how to capture equipment and stores. It also introduces the idea that the overall military leader is a "master of fate".

Above all, this chapter invites military commanders to consider whether their nation has the money and other resources to afford and endure a war.

## SUN TZU SAYS

*In the operations of war, where there are in the field a thousand swift chariots, as many heavy chariots, and a hundred thousand mail-clad soldiers, with provisions enough to carry them a thousand li [400 km], the expenditure at home and at the front, including entertainment of guests, small items such as glue and paint, and sums spent on chariots and armour, will reach the total of a thousand ounces of silver per day. Such is the cost of raising an army of a hundred thousand men.*

> *When you engage in actual fighting, if victory is long in coming, then men's weapons will grow dull and their ardour will be damped. If you lay siege to a town, you will exhaust your strength.*
>
> *Again, if the campaign is protracted, the resources of the state will not be equal to the strain.*
>
> *Now, when your weapons are dulled, your ardour damped, your strength exhausted and your treasure spent, other chieftains will spring up to take advantage of your extremity. Then no man, however wise, will be able to avert the consequences that must ensue.*
>
> *Thus, though we have heard of stupid haste in war, cleverness has never been seen associated with long delays. There is no instance of a country having benefited from prolonged warfare. It is only one who is thoroughly acquainted with the evils of war that can thoroughly understand the profitable way of carrying it on.*

# LESSON 26

## GATHER YOUR VEHICLES

At this point Sun Tzu briefly alludes to different types of chariots, but this has much deeper connotations. The ancient Chinese military was rigorously organized into squads, companies and divisions, and each type of chariot was accompanied by a specific number of troops. The original text of the *Art of War* gives the following numbers:

- 100,000 troops
- 1,000 four-horse attack chariots
- 1,000 armoured wagons

According to historical analysis, the people accompanying a single vehicle broke down as follows:

- 3 officers
- 72 foot soldiers
- 5 grooms
- 5 attendants
- 10 cooks
- 5 labourers

For this lesson, understand that an army must have many types of vehicles, from lightweight all the way to heavy, to serve its many needs, including attack and defence and also the movement of troops and supplies. Do not forget to enlist mechanics to maintain the vehicles.

**WAR TIP: An army must have a well-established detachment of vehicles with support troops to cover multiple tasks.**

# LESSON 27

## ACCOUNT FOR NON-COMBATANTS

Remember that every army comprises auxiliary staff as well as combatants. Some armies even have more non-combatants than fighters. Cooks, administration staff, drivers, doctors, nurses and so on are all needed to keep an army functioning smoothly.

Note that out of the 100 people listed as accompanying a vehicle in the previous lesson, 25 are non-combatants.

**WAR TIP: There will always be support staff to aid the fighting soldiers. These will move with the main body of the army.**

# LESSON 28

## WAR IS ALWAYS EXPENSIVE

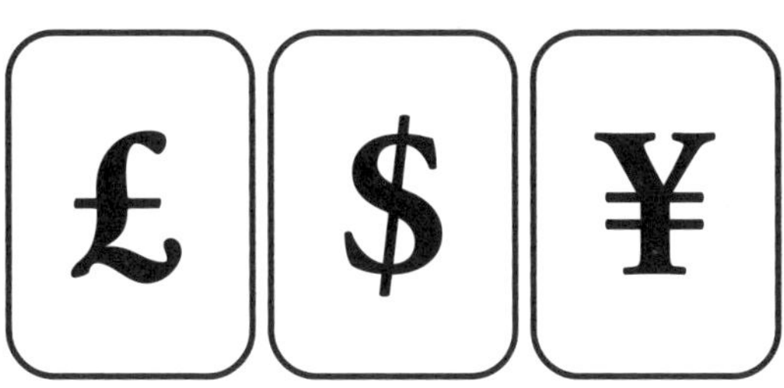

Sun Tzu alludes to various expenses a country at war will incur. To spell these out in a little more detail:

- Expenses both at home and on the frontline will escalate, towns will be destroyed and food will be in short supply.
- Hosting royal guests, envoys and other dignitaries often involves massive costs.
- Acquiring equipment and vehicles is expensive enough, but then you also need to set up workshops to keep them working.

The Giles version gives the cost of running an army of 100,000 to be 1,000 ounces of silver per day, which seems consistent with the colossal amount spent on warfare in modern times. Some other versions say "gold", but either way it means coins of precious metal.

**WAR TIP: Keeping an army in the field is vastly expensive, and the longer the war goes on the more expensive it becomes. Always calculate if you can afford to fight.**

# LESSON 29

## PLAN FOR AS SWIFT A VICTORY AS POSSIBLE

Aiming for a swift victory does not mean rushing into war without planning your tactics carefully. The point here is to use intelligence gathered from spies, scouts and traitors to assess how long it will take to win. There is no standard timescale, but you should not drag out a war any longer than necessary.

**WAR TIP: Always be realistic in your prediction of how long a war will last, then try to beat the deadline you have set with good tactics – but never rush.**

# LESSON 30

## A SLOW VICTORY MEANS TROUBLE

If the war is lasting longer than you had anticipated, then the provisions and taxes allocated to it will start to run dry and the following will happen:

- Equipment will be heavily damaged.
- Troops will become exhausted.
- Your home province will be at risk from attack.
- Troop morale will decline.
- Sieges will form and diminish your forces.
- Strength will be sapped.
- Money will be drained from the homeland.
- The people will become poor.

Avoid this happening by preparing to defeat the enemy swiftly through tactics, intelligence and propaganda. Otherwise it will be as if the life force of the army is drained.

**WAR TIP: If you underestimate the length of a military campaign, you will soon hit problems and your forces will start to break up.**

# LESSON 31

## BE PREPARED FOR OTHERS TO ATTACK YOU WHEN YOU ARE EXHAUSTED

When entering into a military campaign, there will be neutral states or powers that are watching. When your state's energy is depleted, your troops are weak and your equipment spent, these neighbour states may then prey on you. A military leader should understand that the strength of the nation and condition of the force will be much lower by the end of a conflict and plan for this. If you do not understand this, you may push the army too far and achieve victory but end up losing the homeland.

**WAR TIP: Assess the intentions, status and capability of third parties nearby and consider them as threats. Keep enough troops in reserve to defend the homeland. Do not overextend your resources.**

# LESSON 32

## BE SWIFT NOT HASTY

There is a difference between being swift and being hasty. A swift action is a calculated move done with speed but not without thought, whereas a hasty action is not thought out.

Hasty actions often go wrong but even so they are not worse than prolonged or stagnant actions. Acting when you are under extreme time pressure will make for mistakes. Avoid putting yourself under that kind of pressure by anticipating the danger before it arises.

**WAR TIP: Decisive actions are beneficial as long as you take time to think them through. Think first and then move with speed; never move in haste or as a reaction.**

# LESSON 33

## PROLONGED WAR IS ALWAYS A BAD THING

It is never a good idea to purposefully enter into a prolonged military campaign. Your aim as a military commander is to force the enemy to submit without a fight or to create such an advantageous position that a quick victory is inevitable.

**WAR TIP: A strategy based on outlasting the enemy never works well.**

# LESSON 34

## REMEMBER THAT WAR IS HORRIFIC

This lesson is somewhat ambiguous. Some translations convey the idea that without knowing the disadvantages of different weapons, tactics and military formations a leader cannot know how to put them to benefit. In other translations the point is that without experience of the horrors of war, a commander cannot understand how to achieve a positive outcome from it.

Remember that war is only a means to an end. It is expensive and destructive and has negative effects on the state. Therefore, do not promote war as a glorious endeavour, but be mindful of the carnage it brings and conduct it with intelligence and speed.

**WAR TIP: Be fully aware of the horrific nature of war and of its consequences, but also understand that such experiences will produce knowledgeable commanders who know how to use up-to-date weapons and tactics.**

## SUN TZU SAYS

*The skilful soldier does not raise a second levy, neither are his supply-wagons loaded more than twice. Bring war material with you from home, but forage on the enemy. Thus the army will have food enough for its needs.*

*Poverty of the state exchequer causes an army to be maintained by contributions from a distance. Contributing to maintain an army at a distance causes the people to be impoverished. On the other hand, the proximity of an army causes prices to go up; and high prices cause the people's substance to be drained away. When their substance is drained away, the peasantry will be afflicted by heavy exactions.*

*With this loss of substance and exhaustion of strength, the homes of the people will be stripped bare, and three-tenths of their income will be dissipated; while government expenses for broken chariots, worn-out horses, breast-plates and helmets, bows and arrows, spears and shields, protective mantles, draught-oxen and heavy wagons, will amount to four-tenths of its total revenue.*

*Hence a wise general makes a point of foraging on the enemy. One cartload of the enemy's provisions is equivalent to twenty of one's own, and likewise a single picul [shoulder-load] of his provender is equivalent to twenty from one's own store.*

# LESSON 35

## DO NOT CONSCRIPT MORE THAN ONCE

In old China it is believed that at times of war the sons of one in eight families were conscripted to serve in the standing army alongside the full-time military personnel. A state should correctly estimate how many

soldiers they will need for a war, which means if they have to conscript a second wave of troops then their initial calculations were wrong.

**WAR TIP: Send the correct number of troops to war in the first wave. To have to send more people to finish the task is bad management.**

# LESSON 36

## ONLY SEND PROVISIONS TWICE

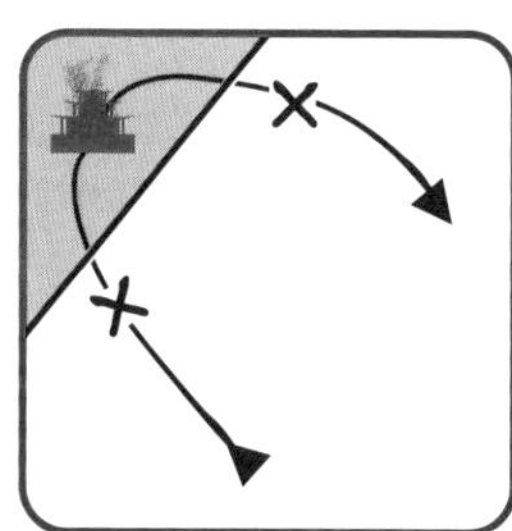

An army should be provisioned only twice, once on its departure and once on its return to home territory. While in enemy territory, a military commander will have troops acquire more provisions and equipment from the enemy by a variety of methods, including stealing them, looting them when capturing towns, equipment dumps and factories, and, where necessary, buying them from the enemy population.

There are numerous reasons for not sending supplies into enemy territory. These include the following:

- Money is taken from the state, leaving the home population impoverished.
- Food is taken from the mouths of the home population.
- The supply lines have to be guarded.
- It gives the enemy a soft target.
- The provisions could fall into enemy hands.

Far better to take supplies from the enemy, as it depletes their stocks and boosts yours.

**WAR TIP: Provide full provisions for an army that is leaving the homeland. When in enemy territory take from the enemy by hostile or peaceful means, then resupply the troops when they pass back into home territory.**

# LESSON 37

## UNDERSTAND THE EFFECTS THAT AN ARMY HAS ON AN AREA

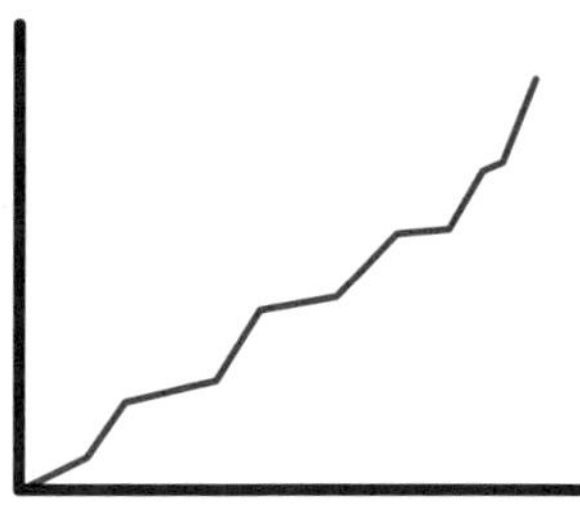

An army is like a fire: if it is not constantly fed it will burn out into nothing. Therefore, wherever an army takes up position it consumes local resources. Demand outstrips supply, causing price spikes that mean the local population goes short. While a few traders will profit from an army encamped near them, the overall effect will be to disrupt normal ways of living. The area will be altered for a certain period of time even after the army has left.

If an allied army is nearby:

- Prices in the area will rise.
- Common people will have to spend their savings on overpriced food.
- Tax and obligations to the government will become difficult to pay.
- The people may become impoverished.
- Everyone's lives are disrupted.

**WAR TIP: When your forces move through an area it will have effects that ripple out and cause changes and problems within the local community. Plan for price rises and disruption in each place the army is stationed.**

# LESSON 38

## REPAIR AND REPLACE EQUIPMENT

A force will dull its weapons, break protective gear and ruin vehicles. A military commander needs to understand that equipment can be repaired within the army by trained personnel, but that this takes time, money and effort. Account for maintenance within your budget and timeframe. Where possible, capture enemy vehicles and equipment to replace your own.

**WAR TIP: Wear and tear is often overlooked – make sure to allow for the cost of replacement equipment and repairs needed for a campaign.**

# LESSON 39

## ONE UNIT OF ENEMY STORES IS WORTH TWENTY OF YOUR OWN

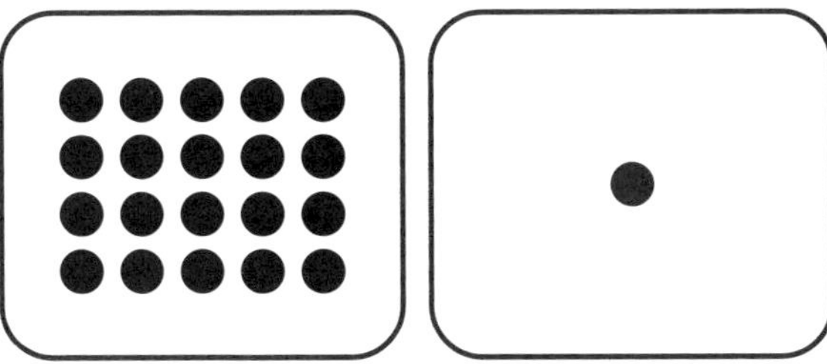

This lesson is about unseen logistics. When sending supplies into enemy territory, they first have to be collected in the homeland, packed and processed, loaded on to vehicles and then carried with the army or behind it, which all costs time, fuel, vehicles and personnel. This means that the collection, processing and transportation of a single unit of food or equipment, costs 20 times its actual worth, highlighting the importance of capturing enemy stores. Never forget that there are unseen costs for most things.

**WAR TIP: Transporting provisions into enemy lands is expensive. Taking them from the enemy is much more economical.**

**SUN TZU SAYS**

*Now in order to kill the enemy, our men must be roused to anger; that there may be advantage from defeating the enemy, they must have their rewards. Therefore in chariot fighting, when ten or more chariots have been taken, those should be rewarded who took the first. Our own flags should be substituted for those of the enemy, and the chariots mingled and used in conjunction with ours. The captured soldiers should be kindly treated and kept. This is called, using the conquered foe to augment one's own strength.*

*In war, then, let your great object be victory, not lengthy campaigns. Thus it may be known that the leader of armies is the arbiter of the people's fate, the man on whom it depends whether the nation shall be in peace or in peril.*

# LESSON 40

## WRATH AND REWARD

If troops feel hatred toward the enemy they will gladly kill them. Therefore, find ways to demonize the enemy and make them appear subhuman. Soldiers who feel compassion toward the enemy become weak and lack fighting determination.

Then if there is also the prospect of reward, troops will fight out of ambition to gain financial benefit. People will take risks for rewards – the higher the reward, the more they will risk. Therefore, the greatest benefits should be given to the troops who put themselves in the greatest danger – the ones who go ahead to achieve feats, such as capturing chariots, before their comrades.

Such rewards cannot be given to every soldier who captures a chariot because there will not be enough wealth to go round. By incentivizing the first to achieve, you will encourage everyone to press forward.

**WAR TIP: A compassionate army is a weak army; troops must hate the enemy. Also, give rewards to the people who achieve before others so that everyone is inspired to act.**

# LESSON 41

## CAPTURE AND ADOPT ENEMY VEHICLES

When you have captured a selection of enemy vehicles, check their status, service them and add them to your own forces. Remove all enemy markings and replace them with allied symbols. Once the captured vehicles have been transformed, mix them in with allied ones so that they do not stand out as an individual troop.

**WAR TIP: Capture enemy vehicles intact, maintain them and change their insignia so that they blend in with your own vehicles.**

# LESSON 42

## TREAT CAPTURED SOLDIERS WITH RESPECT

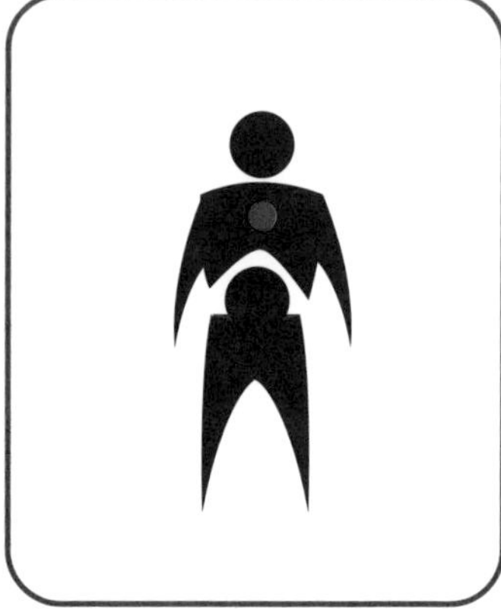

Enemy soldiers should know that if you capture them they will be treated well and may even benefit from changing sides. Always treat enemy soldiers with respect and give them food with the promise of a bright future. Enemy soldiers are often conscripts that have been forced into war so their loyalty can be bought. If word gets back to the enemy ranks that captured comrades have been treated well, others may be encouraged to join your side. Offer them a position in line with their previous station or natural strengths with the added bonus of reward for future achievements.

Both this lesson and the previous one concerning acquiring enemy vehicles can be seen as ways to enlarge your own forces at the cost of the enemy's.

**WAR TIP: Gain a reputation for fair treatment of prisoners of war and for rewarding achievements. This will help weaken enemy bonds and boost your own numbers at a reduced cost.**

# LESSON 43

## THE MILITARY LEADER IS MASTER OF PEOPLE'S FATE

A military leader does not only control the lives of soldiers, but also those of the general population. The future of your whole country can be decided by the strategy they adopt. A military failure can soon become a national failure.

Tactics that bring about swift victory will be of the most benefit to your country.

**WAR TIP: Be aware that your military decisions affect areas far beyond the battlefield. Always plan for the swiftest victory possible.**

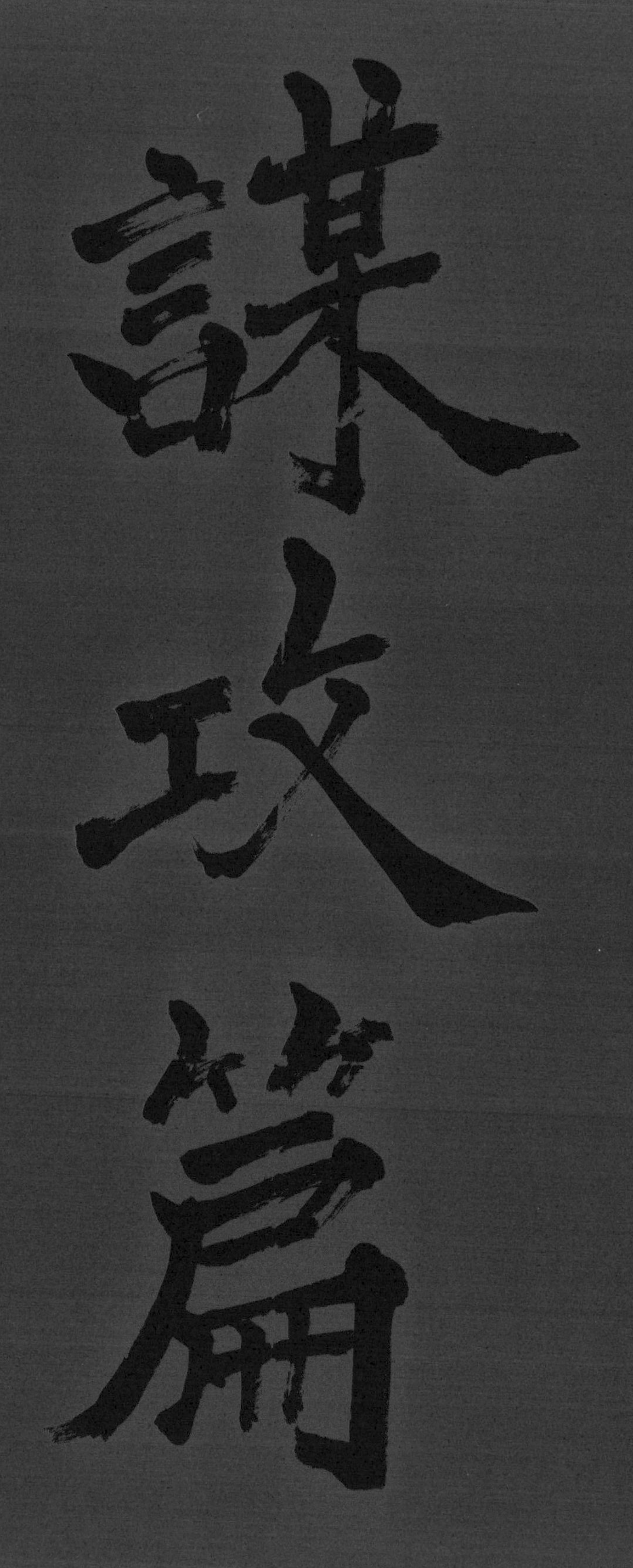
謀攻篇

# CHAPTER 3

# THE SCROLL OF STRATAGEMS FOR ATTACK

# THE SCROLL OF STRATAGEMS FOR ATTACK

The title of Sun Tzu's third chapter includes the ideograms 謀, meaning "plots" or "strategy", and 攻, meaning "attack". The chapter discusses:

1 The importance of planning for victory not destruction
2 Different strategies depending on relative size of opposing forces
3 The role of the military leader

In the first section commanders are urged to think in terms of victory over the enemy, not destruction of the enemy. Victory is different from destruction and there are many ways to bring the enemy to its knees, destruction being one of the lesser methods.

The second section looks at strategies according to numbers of troops. It establishes the best action for when your force outnumbers the enemy, is equal to the enemy, or is outnumbered by the enemy.

The final section investigates the role of the army leader within both military and civil contexts. Here you will learn how to avoid the "three ways of misfortune" and use the "five essentials of victory".

The scroll also covers the use of traps, tricks and stratagems.

## SUN TZU SAYS

*In the practical art of war, the best thing of all is to take the enemy's country whole and intact; to shatter and destroy it is not so good. So, too, it is better to recapture an army entire than to destroy it, to capture a regiment, a detachment or a company entire than to destroy them. Hence to fight and conquer in all your battles is not supreme excellence; supreme excellence consists in breaking the enemy's resistance without fighting.*

*Thus the highest form of generalship is to balk the enemy's plans; the next best is to prevent the junction of the enemy's forces; the next in order is to attack the enemy's army in the field; and the worst policy of all is to besiege walled cities. The rule is, not to besiege walled cities if it can possibly be avoided. The preparation of mantlets, movable shelters, and various implements of war, will take up three whole months; and the piling up of mounds over against the walls will take three months more. The general, unable to control his irritation, will launch his men to the assault like swarming ants, with the result that one-third of his men are slain, while the town still remains untaken. Such are the disastrous effects of a siege.*

*Therefore the skilful leader subdues the enemy's troops without any fighting; he captures their cities without laying siege to them; he overthrows their kingdom without lengthy operations in the field. With his forces intact he will dispute the mastery of the empire, and thus, without losing a man, his triumph will be complete. This is the method of attacking by stratagem.*

# LESSON 44

## PRESERVATION IS BETTER THAN DESTRUCTION

To win 100 battles out of 100 battles is not an achievement; instead to block the plans of the enemy before battle breaks out is a higher skill. It should be the aim of a military leader to take the enemy territory intact. It is far better to use political moves and influence to have the enemy surrender instead of seeking their destruction. If they are destroyed, you have to rebuild; if troops are killed, you have to replace them.

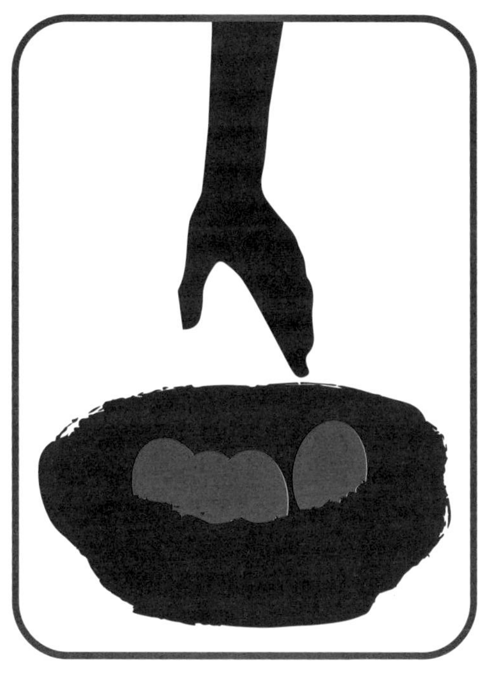

Ames, along with some ancient Chinese commentators, thinks that Sun Tzu is actually referring to the preservation of your own state. However, most translators interpret this as meaning the preservation of the enemy state.

**WAR TIP: To use politics, tactics and strategy to subdue and defeat the enemy before combat takes place is the height of warfare. By preserving their property rather than destroying it you can gain from its capture.**

# LESSON 45

## LEVELS OF WARFARE

- Defeat enemy plans
- Defeat enemy alliances
- Defeat enemy armies
- Defeat enemy cities

As the previous lesson explains, a bloodless victory is best, but if this is not possible then the types of warfare are ranked as follows:

1 Dividing the enemy from its allies and support
2 Engaging in open combat with the enemy
3 Besieging a fortified city

**WAR TIP: Some types of warfare are preferable to others. Siege warfare is to be used only as a last resort.**

# LESSON 46

## WHY SIEGE WARFARE SHOULD BE AVOIDED

Understand that siege warfare is expensive, time-consuming and should be avoided. Sun Tzu warns that it takes three months to get ready for a siege. The Clements translation stipulates that reaching the battlements will take three months. It is unclear where this addition comes from and if it means that the whole siege process takes a total of six months – three months to prepare and three months to advance – or if both stages are done simultaneously. However, the main point that it takes time remains.

Preparing for a siege includes the following:

### MOVEABLE WALL

Siege warfare is to create a temporary wall around a centre of habitation, be it a "wall" of troops or a physical wall. These walls are solid enough to hold but they can be moved closer in, tightening the siege until the enemy is totally cut off.

### SHIELDS

Shields can either be held in the hand or fixed in the ground. Hand-held shields can be brought together to form a line and free-standing shields can be placed together to form a wall.

## SIEGE EQUIPMENT

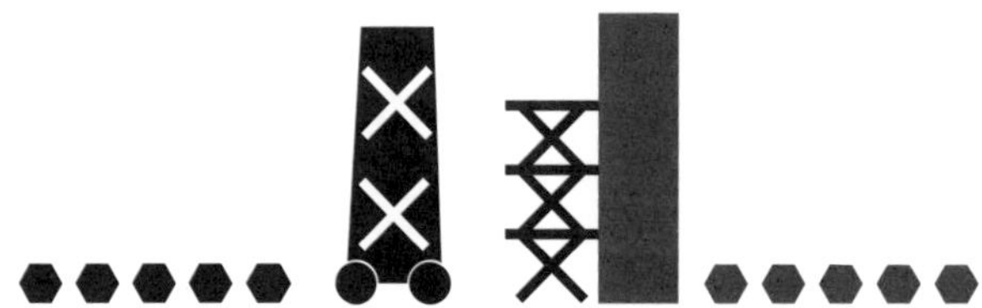

Siege equipment has evolved over time, but the basics remain the same. You will need ladders, towers, scaffolding, armoured troop carriers, mining apparatus, etc. Making siege equipment takes time and resources and you also need a workforce to maintain it.

## EARTHWORKS

When besieging, create a network of defensive structures made of compacted earth to protect against the enemy firing out at you from inside the city. These can include trenches, vantage mounds, camp walls and defences against sally raids.

**WAR TIP: If you have not been successful in other strategies and you have to move to a siege, allow enough time and money to prepare equipment and fortifications.**

# LESSON 47

## NEVER BE IMPATIENT IN SIEGE WARFARE

Laying siege is frustrating, takes a long time, costs a lot of money and may not pay off. A military leader who allows stress to build up will want to order a full charge to the walls to end the stalemate. However, this is a disastrously incorrect thing to do – a third of your troops will perish, the fortification will not break and it will leave you in a worse position.

**WAR TIP: Never give in to anger or impatience during a siege. If you send troops to climb city walls at the wrong time or out of anger you will leave behind a field of dead.**

# LESSON 48

## WAGE THE PERFECT WAR

The perfect war is an ideal, consisting of:

- Perfect political moves
- Excellent alliances
- Proper planning
- Capturing the enemy without hostile action
- Destroying other states
- Taking other cities

- Preserving your own troops
- Preserving and turning enemy troops
- Preserving and using enemy lands and equipment
- Being victorious in all

**WAR TIP: Aim for the perfect war, but be realistic. The further up the scale toward perfection you reach, the greater your chances of victory. Remember, there is no such thing as a fair fight – make sure the odds favour you.**

SUN TZU SAYS

*It is the rule in war, if our forces are ten to the enemy's one, to surround him; if five to one, to attack him; if twice as numerous, to divide our army into two. If equally matched, we can offer battle; if slightly inferior in numbers, we can avoid the enemy; if quite unequal in every way, we can flee from him. Hence, though an obstinate fight may be made by a small force, in the end it must be captured by the larger force.*

# LESSON 49

## TEACHINGS FOR WHEN OUTNUMBERING THE ENEMY

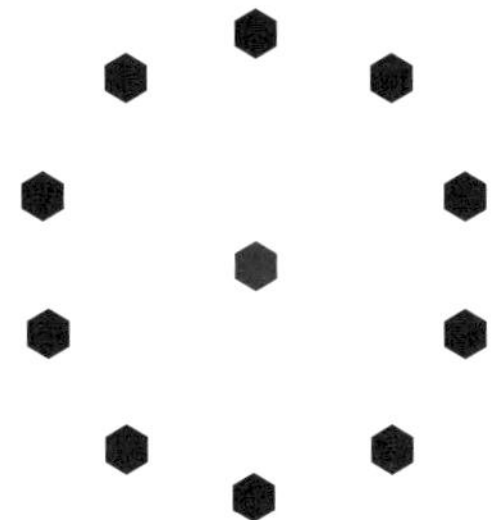

If your forces outnumber the enemy by ten to one you will be able to totally and successfully surround them. Then, depending on the situation, the troop types and the geography, you should be able to move in and defeat them.

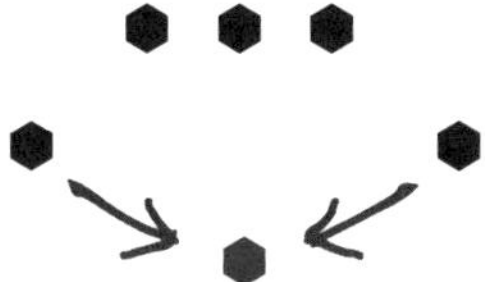

If you outnumber the enemy by five to one you can attack them with full force as your superiority in numbers will ensure victory. Some Chinese commentaries state that your force should be divided into five parts, three for direct attacks and two for flanking manoeuvres or troops that hit hard against enemy weak spots.

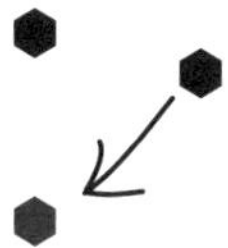

If you have double the enemy number, divide your force so that you can attack the enemy on two or more fronts. They will have to respond to your move and this will weaken their formations. Have harassing or flanking troops to help put the enemy at a disadvantage.

The Chinese commentator Chen Hao states that these guidelines are only for when attacking a fortified city. Almost all other translations and commentaries see this as a set of rules for open battle. However, there are certain variations. For example, Clements translates it as:

- Ten to one – surround the enemy
- Five to one – invade the enemy
- Two to one – attack the enemy

Trapp and Ames say that in the case of dividing, the text actually means "to divide the enemy forces" not your own. So there are various, equally valid ways to understand this lesson.

**WAR TIP: If you outnumber the enemy by ten to one, surround them. If you outnumber them by five to one, attack on many fronts. If you are double their number, make flanking attacks.**

# LESSON 50

## TEACHINGS FOR WHEN YOU ARE EQUAL TO OR OUTNUMBERED BY THE ENEMY

Attack

If you are equal to the enemy in number you can engage them in battle. The victor will be whoever has done more pre-war preparation and who is in the better position with the better plan.

Defend

If the enemy is of a larger number but they do not have enough troops to destroy you completely, focus on defence, mobility, location, exit and strategy. A smaller military force can defeat a larger one, but it is a difficult task. Therefore, focus on defending the centre and on manoeuvrability. Be prepared to outwait the enemy, use deception, move into full defence or exit the situation quickly.

Retreat

If you are so outnumbered that there is no possibility of victory, move out and do not engage the enemy force. Move with swift lightness, using terrain to your advantage to stay out of the enemy's range. Sun Tzu warns that the worst thing you can do is stand your ground. A smaller army that waits for a larger army will be crushed. Never make a death stand or a last-ditch attack when vastly outnumbered. Instead, focus all your thoughts on how to escape.

**WAR TIP: If you are equal in number with the enemy, engage them with tactics. If you are somewhat fewer in number, take a defensive position. If you are totally outnumbered, move away.**

## SUN TZU SAYS

*Now the general is the bulwark of the state; if the bulwark is complete at all points, the state will be strong; if the bulwark is defective, the state will be weak.*

*There are three ways in which a ruler can bring misfortune upon his army:*

1. *By commanding the army to advance or to retreat, being ignorant of the fact that it cannot obey. This is called hobbling the army.*
2. *By attempting to govern an army in the same way as he administers a kingdom, being ignorant of the conditions which obtain in an army. This causes restlessness in the soldiers' minds.*
3. *By employing the officers of his army without discrimination, through ignorance of the military principle of adaptation to circumstances. This shakes the confidence of the soldiers.*

*But when the army is restless and distrustful, trouble is sure to come from the other feudal princes. This is simply bringing anarchy into the army, and flinging victory away.*

*Thus we may know that there are five essentials for victory:*

1. *He will win who knows when to fight and when not to fight.*
2. *He will win who knows how to handle both superior and inferior forces.*
3. *He will win whose army is animated by the same spirit throughout all its ranks.*
4. *He will win who, prepared himself, waits to take the enemy unprepared.*
5. *He will win who has military capacity and is not interfered with by the sovereign.*

*Hence the saying: if you know the enemy and know yourself, you need not fear the result of a hundred battles. If you know yourself but not the enemy, for every victory gained you will also suffer a defeat. If you know neither the enemy nor yourself, you will succumb in every battle.*

# LESSON 51

## THE MILITARY LEADER IS THE FOUNDATION OF THE NATION

A military leader has to be both an expert and an innovator. You need to be well versed in the ancient principles, but build on them so that you do not become predictable. Otherwise you will be caught in the past. Military leaders must earn the right to command by understanding the complex subject of warfare, not simply be handed their position based on family connections or privilege. One author interprets the ideogram used here as a pole that supports a chariot's frame, the implication being that, like this vehicle strut, if a good general is missing from the state, the state will fall over and collapse. Only those of the highest calibre should be considered for this position and Sun Tzu warns that there are three ways in which an unsuitable person can bring down a country if mistakenly given command of the army. These are explored in the next lesson.

**WAR TIP: Never put incompetent people in command of an army.**

# LESSON 52

## THE THREE FAULTS OF AN INCOMPETENT LEADER

### 1 MISTIMING ADVANCES AND RETREATS

If a military leader does not know when to advance and when to retreat, then defeat is inevitable. Armies of all sizes will face certain situations where retreat is the best option. Being outnumbered is not the only reason to retreat; other factors, including terrain, weather, political change and espionage, can also come into play. A good military leader can assimilate all information and use it to identify the right time to advance and the right time to retreat. If they do not know how to do this they will restrict the capability of their army.

Many translations use the term "hobbling" here because Sun Tzu uses an ideogram that refers to "tying up an ox's legs" to stop it from wandering. The sense is that if the commander does not know when to advance or retreat then the army will become immobile just like a great ox tied to a stake.

### 2 GOVERNING AN ARMY AS IF IT WERE A STATE

Military victories give rise to royal dynasties, royal dynasties give rise to professional armies, and professional armies give rise to professional military commanders. This division between state and military is fixed by edict. If a civilian or royal leader is appointed military commander and leads with a civilian mind, or if civilian leaders interfere with military matters, the army will become confused. Therefore, a military commander must be a professional soldier and this position must never be given to a civilian.

### 3 PUTTING CIVILIAN OFFICERS IN CHARGE OF MILITARY MATTERS

If officers are appointed from civilian ranks to enter the army and if they are unaware of military protocol they will confuse all matters, and when involved in any task within the force they will cause disruption.

Any of these three faults can lead to the failure of the allied army.

**WAR TIP: Appoint only military personnel to leadership positions. Make sure all officers are military-trained professionals and do not allow civilian leaders to interfere with the day-to-day running of the military.**

# LESSON 53

## USE STRENGTH AS A DETERRENT

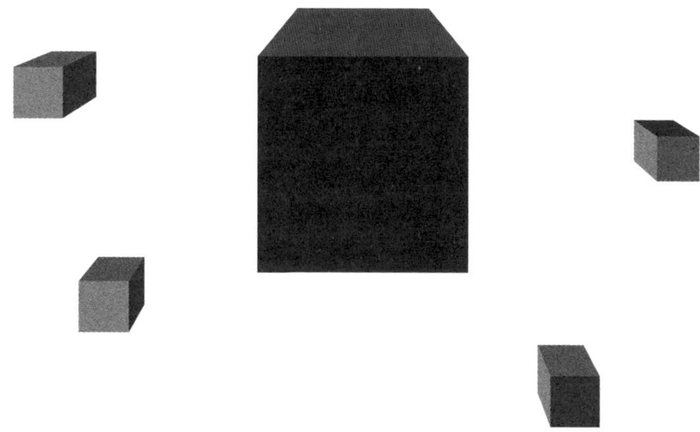

It is just as important to have a strong army during peacetime as during wartime. If the army is in disarray because of one or more of the three faults discussed in the previous lesson, rival states will move in to take advantage of the weakness. A strong army is a powerful deterrent, without which a country risks invasion.

**WAR TIP: In times of peace make sure to maintain a robust military so that other nations do not find opportunity to attack and conquer your lands.**

# LESSON 54

## THE FIVE PRINCIPLES OF VICTORY

The following points are the foundations on which victory is built:

- Timing

- Size
- Harmony
- Preparation
- Leadership

### 1 KNOW WHEN TO FIGHT AND WHEN NOT TO FIGHT

If you enter into direct combat every time you are provoked, you are sure to lose in certain situations. Therefore, know that there will be times when to wait, withdraw or outmanoeuvre are better options.

### 2 RECOGNIZE WHEN IT IS BETTER TO USE A SMALL FORCE

The basic rule of thumb is that a bigger force will defeat a smaller force. However, there are certain situations in which this rule does not apply. For example, in difficult terrain, an urban setting or adverse weather a large force may become trapped and vulnerable to a smaller, cannier, more mobile opponent. Assess the conditions and use the correct number of troops for the situation.

### 3 ESTABLISH AN ESPRIT DE CORPS

There must be harmony between officers and lower ranks, all must have the same hunger for victory and believe in the objectives set forth. Make sure you explain clearly to the troops the purpose of the war they are entering so that they all strive for the same result. If all people know they will profit from victory, the force will be united.

### 4 ALWAYS BE PREPARED AND ATTACK THOSE WHO ARE UNPREPARED

Translations of this point differ slightly, but all versions stress the importance of preparation and acknowledge that those who are prepared will defeat those who are unprepared. However, some versions lean more toward the idea of constant preparedness, whereas others focus on being prepared during a campaign. The core teaching holds true across all versions: always be ready to move into action so that you can attack others when they are not ready.

### 5 BE IN TOTAL COMMAND AND ACCEPT NO INTERFERENCE

The decision to go to war is made by political leaders, but once that decision has been made the politicians should step back and leave the army to get the job done without interference. It is now time for you as the military commander to use all your vast training to deliver the victory.

**WAR TIP: Know when to fight and how many troops to use, make sure all ranks are focused and in harmony, be prepared, and when ready, move out and leave the world of politics behind. Simply go to war and bring home victory.**

# LESSON 55

## ACHIEVE THE HIGHEST LEVEL AS A MILITARY LEADER

Sun Tzu says that the highest level of leader will gain victory in all confrontations; a middle-level leader will win half of the time; and a low-level leader will never taste success. He defines these levels in terms of knowledge of one's own forces and knowledge of the enemy. High-level leaders have deep knowledge of both sides; middle-level leaders know their own side, but not the enemy; and low-level leaders show little or no understanding of either side.

Knowledge of your own side includes the following factors:

- Knowing the capabilities of your troops, so that you do not waste their talents
- Judging how much they can endure, so that you push them to the limit but not beyond
- Understanding and addressing the problems facing all ranks, from the lowest to the highest

Knowledge of the enemy and enemy territory is gained through scouting and espionage. The objective is to be able to read the mind of the enemy leader. Without such insight, you will be leading your troops blind into a hostile situation. Do not make the mistakes of the lowest-level commanders, who rely solely on what they can see with their own eyes.

**WAR TIP: To achieve the highest level of leadership, ensure that a constant stream of information flows through your headquarters, even in times of peace. Discard and update old data so that a form of "living knowledge" pulses through the command team. Then you will be ready for any conflict at any time.**

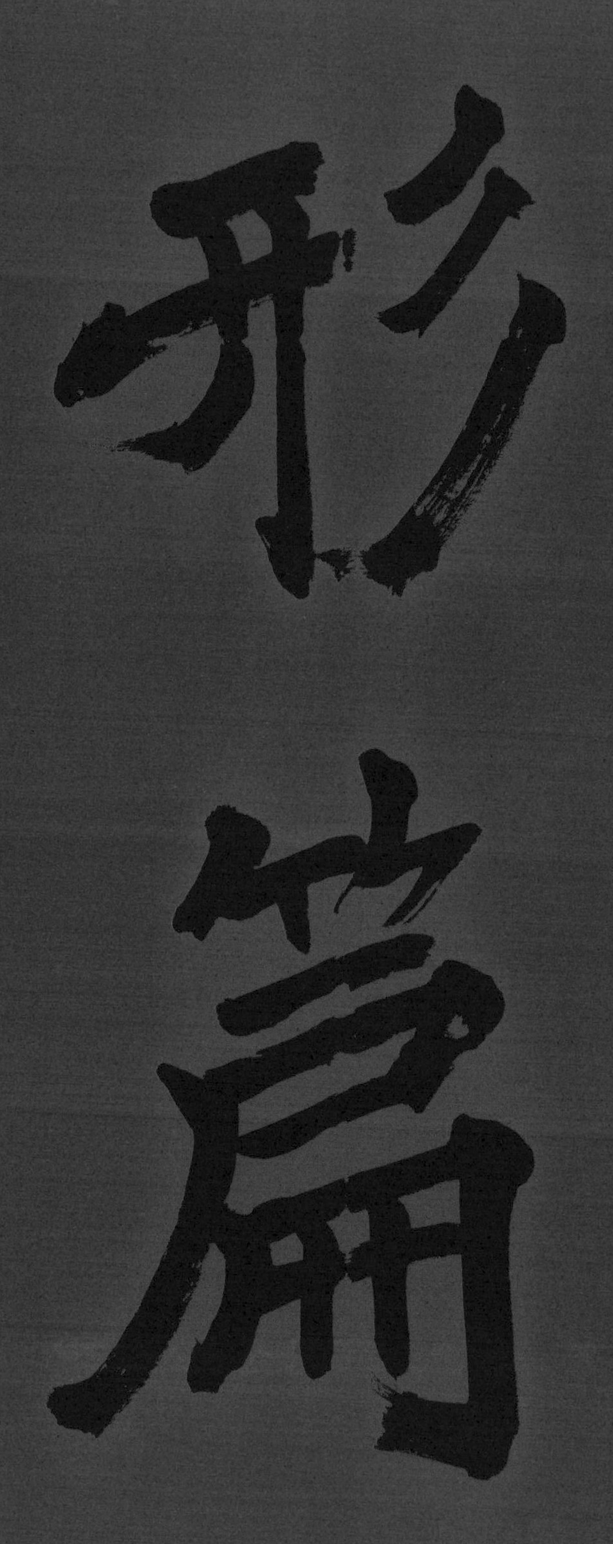
形篇

# CHAPTER 4

# THE SCROLL OF OBSERVING PATTERNS

# THE SCROLL OF OBSERVING PATTERNS

The title of Sun Tzu's fourth chapter uses the ideogram 形, meaning "shapes" or "patterns", in the sense of observing a situation as it takes shape in order to predict the outcome. The chapter looks at three main areas:

1 The essence and foundation of defence
2 The moral alignment of a leader
3 The positioning of the army and unleashing of its power

First Sun Tzu talks about how great military leaders of old could see beyond the basic situation and spot the initial signs of enemy hostility. He goes on to underline the need for a leader to follow a moral code and strictly enforce military discipline. Finally, he explains how all your hidden pre-conflict political moves and military manoeuvrings are the precursor to a single powerful stroke to defeat the enemy.

Overall this chapter is about pre-empting events by seeing how small elements come together. In this way, a war can be won even before it starts.

## SUN TZU SAYS

*The good fighters of old first put themselves beyond the possibility of defeat, and then waited for an opportunity of defeating the enemy. To secure ourselves against defeat lies in our own hands, but the opportunity of defeating the enemy is provided by the enemy himself. Thus the good fighter is able to secure himself against defeat, but cannot make certain of defeating the enemy. Hence the saying: One may know how to conquer without being able to do it.*

*Security against defeat implies defensive tactics; ability to defeat the enemy means taking the offensive. Standing on the defensive indicates insufficient strength; attacking, a superabundance of strength. The general who is skilled in defence hides in the most secret recesses of the earth; he who is skilled in attack flashes forth from the topmost heights of heaven. Thus on the one hand we have ability to protect ourselves; on the other, a victory that is complete.*

> *To see victory only when it is within the ken of the common herd is not the acme of excellence. Neither is it the acme of excellence if you fight and conquer and the whole empire says, "Well done!" To lift an autumn hair is no sign of great strength; to see the sun and moon is no sign of sharp sight; to hear the noise of thunder is no sign of a quick ear.*
>
> *What the ancients called a clever fighter is one who not only wins, but excels in winning with ease. Hence his victories bring him neither reputation for wisdom nor credit for courage. He wins his battles by making no mistakes. Making no mistakes is what establishes the certainty of victory, for it means conquering an enemy that is already defeated. Hence the skilful fighter puts himself into a position which makes defeat impossible, and does not miss the moment for defeating the enemy. Thus it is that in war the victorious strategist only seeks battle after the victory has been won, whereas he who is destined to defeat first fights and afterwards looks for victory.*

# LESSON 56

## THE ESSENCE OF BEING A CONQUEROR

An enemy army is never invincible. It goes through phases of solidity and weakness, with any movement creating gaps that can be closed only through high levels of discipline. When cracks start appearing within the enemy formation, you will know that you can gain victory.

A good commander can create a solid and harmonious fighting force that gives no clues to the enemy of its internal workings and offers no gaps in its defensive formation. Such a strongly knit unit will become unconquerable because the enemy will find no weakness to exploit. However, if the force moves or is slack for any reason, then gaps in your defence will appear and opportunities to attack will present themselves.

Therefore, good military leaders first secure their own forces, then use all their arts to provoke reaction and movement in the enemy and then they take advantage of any opening. This is what Sun Tzu means by: "To secure ourselves against defeat lies in our own hands, but the opportunity of defeating the enemy is provided by the enemy himself."

A good commander can keep an enemy at bay and remain in total defence, but is always relying on the enemy to make a decision that produces a gap, as gaps are weaknesses and weaknesses bring opportunity. Having a perfect plan will not work unless the enemy makes the wrong move.

**WAR TIP: Secure your defences, then use all of your strategies to bring about change in the enemy and when suitable gaps appear, move on them. If you create the right conditions, the enemy will make a mistake that hands you victory.**

# LESSON 57

## KNOW THE CORRECT RATIO OF ATTACK AND DEFENCE

A military leader should attack if there is a significant chance of success but defend when there is a limited chance. This follows on from the previous lesson of knowing to wait for enemy gaps. However, simply seeing a gap is not enough; a leader must know which openings give a strong chance of victory.

This point is one of the more contested in the *Art of War*, with commentators interpreting it in two main ways.

According to the first version, advocated by the Chinese commentator Zhang Yu among others, you should start in a fully defensive mode. After each side has made its opening feints and you have your strategy in place, wait for the enemy to move in a way that creates a gap. When this happens, assess whether it is a true gap or a feint in itself. If you judge the gap to be genuine, strike the enemy and take victory.

Much criticized by Zhang Yu, the second version holds that when an allied army is weaker than the enemy and does not have the military might to take a victory, it should stay on the defensive even when gaps appear in the enemy line. The allied army should move on the offensive when gaps appear only if it has the power to take victory.

**WAR TIP: If the enemy opens up a gap, check that it is a real gap and not a trick and move to take victory only if you have the resources to mount a telling attack.**

# LESSON 58

## HIDE LOW AND STRIKE FROM HIGH

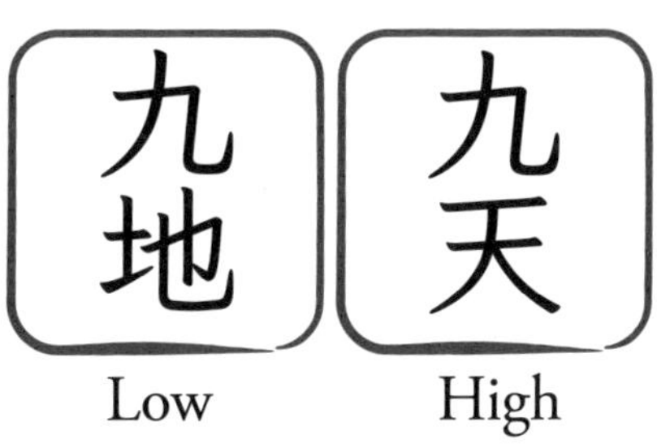


**ABOVE:** These are the original ideograms for the "nine earths" and "nine heavens", which represent the deepest parts of the earth and the highest heights respectively.

Here Sun Tzu teaches ways of expertise in the two sides of warfare: defence and attack. The literal translation of the ideograms in the original text is "hiding in the nine worlds" (九地), which Giles renders as "the most secret recesses of the earth", and "striking from the nine heavens" (九天), which Giles translates as "flashing forth from the topmost heights of heaven". All translators agree on the basic idea that you should be able to hide in the terrain and strike from high places. However, the ancient Chinese commentators add three further layers of interpretation:

- Using the advantages of landscape and weather. In defence this entails hiding in the mountains, crossing rivers and using natural features as fortifications. In attack it means taking advantage of sudden changes in the weather to strike with speed.
- Conducting guerrilla warfare. In defence be "ghostlike" and silent, move without the enemy knowing where you are. Be unseen and unheard. In attack stay visible to the enemy, but make fast, unpredictable movements so that the enemy cannot keep up with the changes.
- Taking on an attitude of defence or attack. When in defensive mode make your army fully visible to the enemy but take on an attitude of full defence. The text becomes a poetic teaching about remaining in position and immoveable instead of hiding out of sight. When in attacking mode, make your army fully visible but take on an attitude of attack and forward movement to take advantage of any gap the enemy exposes.

**WAR TIP: Use the land and weather to your advantage, move your force into hiding if needs be and strike from hidden places, but also know the difference between full defence and full attack when in open battle.**

# LESSON 59

## THINK AND PLAN MANY MOVES AHEAD

The greatest tacticians, strategists and thinkers do not see events as single entities, but as an accumulation of fragments. To identify separate issues from apparently unrelated areas and predict the outcome they will combine to produce is the mark of the highest military leader. Those whose achievements come from seeing what is obvious do not show true excellence. The real standard of excellence is set by those who see the separate parts of a problem developing and who are able to avert the problem before others realize it even exists. Therefore, it is folly to praise a general who has just returned victorious from a hard campaign, as the general should have found a way to avoid the campaign becoming so difficult in the first place.

Sun Tzu gives five analogies to underline the point that basic achievements should not be mistaken for excellence:

- Seeing a clear victory in the present is not considered as correctly predicting future events.
- Being victorious in a one-sided battle is not a demonstration of excellent strategy.
- Lifting something that is very light (an "autumn hair", the exact meaning of which is unknown) is not a show of strength.

- Seeing the sun and moon is not a demonstration of good observation.
- Hearing thunder is not a demonstration of good hearing.

The greatest leaders win little fame, because they do not become embroiled in major battles. They make faultless plans that avert dangerous situations before they arise. Sun Tzu said that this type of expert military leader could be found in the ancient days.

**WAR TIP: Look at the separate parts that build a situation as it arises so that you can deal with the situation before it becomes problematic.**

# LESSON 60

## ESTABLISH A POSITION OF TOTAL DEFENCE, THEN STRIKE

Following on from the idea of seeing the problems in a conflict well in advance, good military leaders need to position themselves in the correct place and time just before the problem emerges. If the situation cannot be resolved before all the pieces are in position then find the best place to work from, be it physical, tactical or political. Strike hard and defeat the enemy before it has time to create a real threat.

**WAR TIP: Identify the signs of hostile movement within the enemy, position yourself in the best place and strike the weakest point as it forms.**

SUN TZU SAYS

*The consummate leader cultivates the moral law, and strictly adheres to method and discipline; thus it is in his power to control success.*

*In respect of military method, we have, firstly, measurement; secondly, estimation of quantity; thirdly, calculation; fourthly, balancing of chances; fifthly, victory. Measurement owes its existence to earth; estimation of quantity to measurement; calculation to estimation of quantity; balancing of chances to calculation; and victory to balancing of chances.*

# LESSON 61

## FOLLOW THE WAY AND MAINTAIN DISCIPLINE

Sun Tzu reminds us here about two of the five constant factors: the way and military organization (*see* lessons 3 and 7). His point is that a military leader's ability to pre-empt a situation will count for little without the ability also to maintain harmony among the troops by establishing proper codes of conduct and a punishment and reward system that is fair to all.

**ABOVE:** The original ideograms for "way" and "organization", two of the five constant factors.

The Chinese commentator Li Quan says that the way means to attack only real enemies and to leave alone those who live in peace and are of no threat. Furthermore, he notes that victorious troops should behave correctly and not destroy the population and belongings of a conquered land. Sun Tzu finishes this section by stating that military leaders who follow these ways are able to control how their troops conduct themselves in victory.

**WAR TIP: Both before and after victory, maintain positive morality, harmony between the people and fair discipline for all.**

# LESSON 62

## USE THE FIVE FOUNDATIONS TO PLAN A MILITARY CAMPAIGN

The planning of a military campaign can be summarized as a five-step process (note that these steps are not the same as the five constant factors):

1. Measurement of the land
2. Estimation of types of forces that need to be used on the land
3. Calculation of troop numbers available
4. Comparison between the two armies
5. Assessment of likelihood of victory, based on the previous four stages

If you measure the terrain you will know the size and formation of the landscape. By understanding the landscape you will know what types of troops the enemy will use. Knowing what type of force the enemy will use means that you can calculate how many troops they will have or need. Knowing this will allow you to compare them to your own forces and such a comparison will tell you whether you can gain victory.

Because the original text is lacking in detail and simply lists the steps, some translations differ in the second point. Rather than it being a case of estimating what types of troops the enemy will use on the terrain in question, some versions give this step as an estimation of the amount of produce that can be supplied by this area and type of land. This still leads in to the same third step: calculating how many troops the enemy will have at its disposal.

**WAR TIP: Measure the land, use that knowledge to estimate the enemy forces, their type and their numbers, compare both armies and then determine if you can win.**

SUN TZU SAYS

*A victorious army opposed to a routed one, is as a pound's weight placed in the scale against a single grain. The onrush of a conquering force is like the bursting of pent-up waters into a chasm a thousand fathoms deep.*

# LESSON 63

## UNLEASH THE FORCE

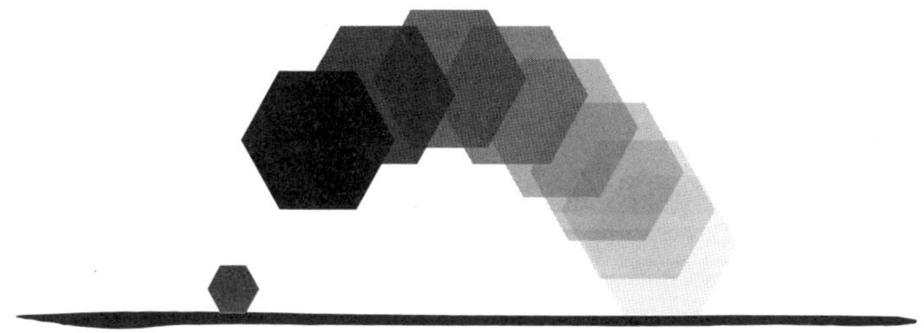

By following the previous lessons, you will have identified all eventualities, planned the correct course of action, moved your forces into position and pinpointed enemy weaknesses.

Now it is time to unleash the onslaught you have prepared.

Sun Tzu describes this collision of mismatched forces in metaphorical terms. Depending on the translation, he says it is like a pound's weight balanced against that of a single grain, or a feather being struck on an anvil, or a torrent of water crashing down from a great height. When the enemy makes its move it will be overwhelmed by a counterattack made so ferocious and so unexpected by your strategic power that the enemy will be unable to comprehend what is happening.

**WAR TIP: Start at the beginning and go through all analysis and calculations. Stack everything to your advantage until you have eradicated all possibility of defeat and then crush the enemy forces before they realize what has hit them.**

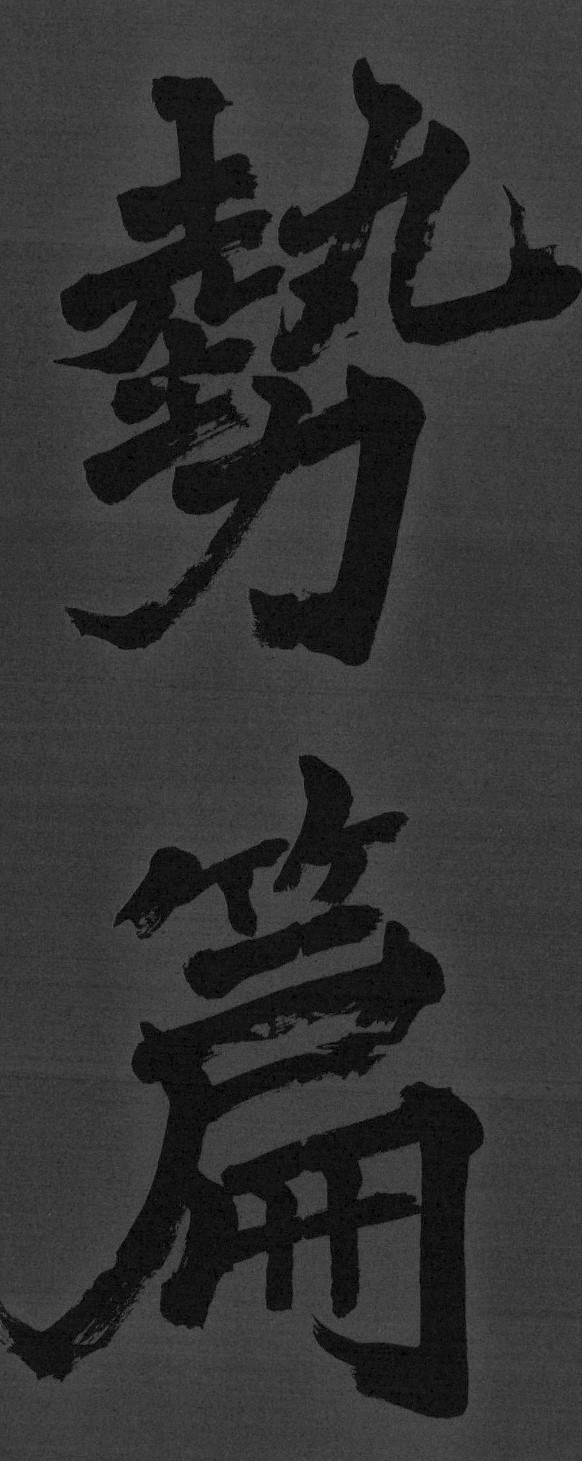
勢篇

# CHAPTER 5

# THE SCROLL OF POWER

# THE SCROLL OF POWER

The title of Sun Tzu's fifth chapter uses the ideogram 勢, meaning "power" or "energy", in this case referring to "military strength". The chapter is divided into four main areas:

1 The size of the army not affecting the way it is managed
2 The difference between direct and indirect
3 The ability to hide disorder
4 The energy of the troops

The first part of the chapter explains that no matter how big or small an army is, the systems in place to govern it remain the same. The second part presents the concept of direct and indirect, according to which a force must have solid direct troops and methods but also indirect troops and methods. The third part shows how a military leader can hide order inside of feigned disorder to confuse the enemy. The chapter concludes with a section on how to use specific types of people to build different forms of energy and power.

Overall this chapter deals with the "feel" and energy of the force.

### SUN TZU SAYS

*The control of a large force is the same principle as the control of a few men: it is merely a question of dividing up their numbers. Fighting with a large army under your command is nowise different from fighting with a small one: it is merely a question of instituting signs and signals.*

# LESSON 64

## COMMAND A LARGE FORCE JUST AS YOU WOULD A SMALL ONE

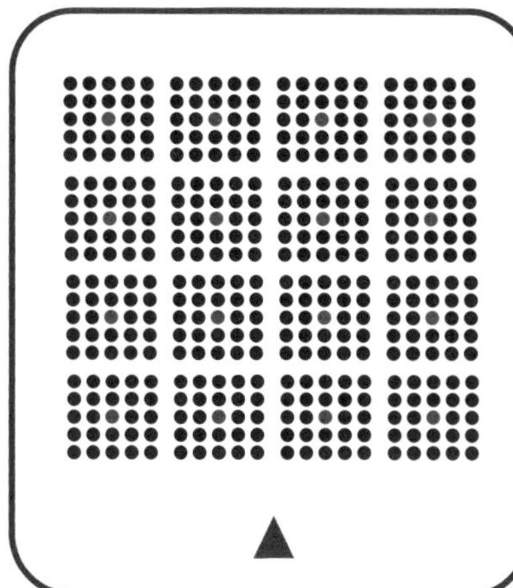

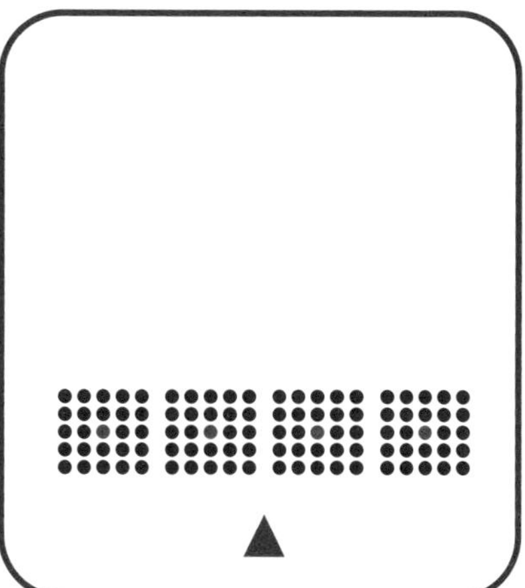

Whether you are commanding a small troop or a vast army, the same principle applies. All forces are divided up into units divisible by five, with units of five used to construct the whole army. Each unit will have its own name, identifying markers and flags, and will be commanded with horns, gongs and drums. All units will be aware of the overall military structure and their place within it and will know how to adjust for a change in numbers if troops are added or lost. It does not matter if it is 50 troops or 50,000 troops, the principle of five as a building block remains the same. Communication and division are of primary importance.

**WAR TIP: Set up an army in sets of five troops so that no matter how many troops are added or taken away, everyone understands how to adjust for the change in numbers.**

## SUN TZU SAYS

*To ensure that your whole host may withstand the brunt of the enemy's attack and remain unshaken, this is effected by manoeuvres direct and indirect. That the impact of your army may be like a grindstone dashed against an egg, this is effected by the science of weak points and strong. In all fighting, the direct method may be used for joining battle, but indirect methods will be needed in order to secure victory. Indirect tactics, efficiently applied, are inexhaustible as heaven and earth, unending as the flow of rivers and streams; like the sun and moon, they end but to begin anew; like the four seasons, they pass away to return once more.*

*There are not more than five musical notes, yet the combinations of these five give rise to more melodies than can ever be heard. There are not more than five primary colours (blue, yellow, red, white and black), yet in combination they produce more hues than can ever be seen. There are not more than five cardinal tastes (sour, acrid, salt, sweet, bitter), yet combinations of them yield more flavours than can ever be tasted. In battle, there are not more than two methods of attack, the direct and the indirect; yet these two in combination give rise to an endless series of manoeuvres. The direct and the indirect lead on to each other in turn. It is like moving in a circle, you never come to an end. Who can exhaust the possibilities of their combination?*

*The onset of troops is like the rush of a torrent which will even roll stones along in its course. The quality of decision is like the well-timed swoop of a falcon which enables it to strike and destroy its victim. Therefore the good fighter will be terrible in his onset, and prompt in his decision. Energy may be likened to the bending of a crossbow; decision, to the releasing of a trigger.*

# LESSON 65

## GAIN VICTORY BY MIXING THE SUBSTANTIAL AND INSUBSTANTIAL

This teaching takes up the bulk of this chapter and the following lessons are linked to this fundamental theme. Sun Tzu uses sets of opposite pairs to show a military concept that is often translated in different ways (more on this in chapter 6). Understand that there is a movement between: direct and indirect, substantial and insubstantial, orthodox and unorthodox, and truth and illusion. This includes presenting the substantial as insubstantial to the enemy and vice versa. A good military commander should be able to move between two modes of warfare, or even operate them simultaneously.

**ABOVE:** The yin-yang symbol represents two opposites in movement and balance, an idea found in Sun Tzu's teaching of the relationship between orthodox and unorthodox tactics.

**WAR TIP: Move between standard ways of war and special tactics, using the orthodox and unorthodox in accord with each other.**

# LESSON 66

## START WITH THE DIRECT BUT GAIN VICTORY WITH THE INDIRECT

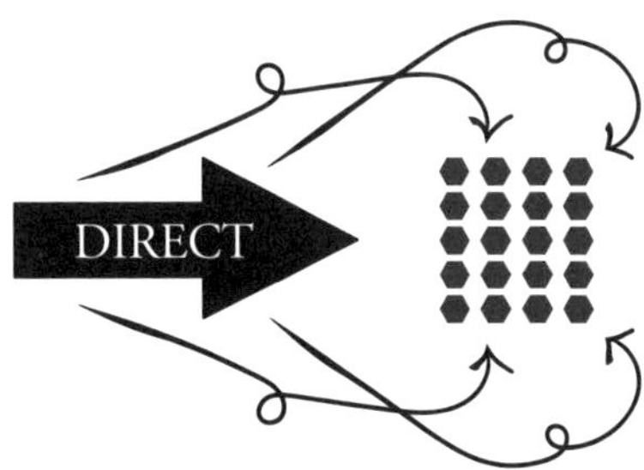


Sun Tzu here says that you should start a battle with the substantial – i.e. direct, conventional tactics – but that you will secure victory by turning to surprise, deception or unorthodox tactics. However, that does not mean you should do everything in plain sight up until the point that you switch. Deception, tactics, the presentation of the substantial as insubstantial, espionage, scouting, etc., are all measures that you will have used before the battle. When battle is joined, your first move may be a direct thrust with a substantial force, but ultimate victory is brought about by the indirect tactics you put into play at the start of the conflict, which come to fruition at the end.

**WAR TIP: Have a plan for the whole battle: use direct forces to start combat, then finish the enemy off with tricks, traps and surprise attacks.**

# LESSON 67

## UNDERSTAND THE SCOPE OF WARFARE

Sun Tzu now starts to build on the concept he introduced in the previous lessons in preparation for chapter 6. He reinforces the idea of using the two opposites of orthodox and unorthodox or direct and indirect in a fluid movement, but also highlights the vast scope of their applications. He says that the scope of warfare is limitless and never-ending, just like the heavens, the earth, the flow of rivers and tides of seas, the changing seasons and the rising and setting of the sun and moon.

**WAR TIP: The only limit to your tactics is the limit of your mind. Mix the direct with the indirect to form countless plans that can be changed to suit any situation.**

# LESSON 68

## THINK IN FIVES

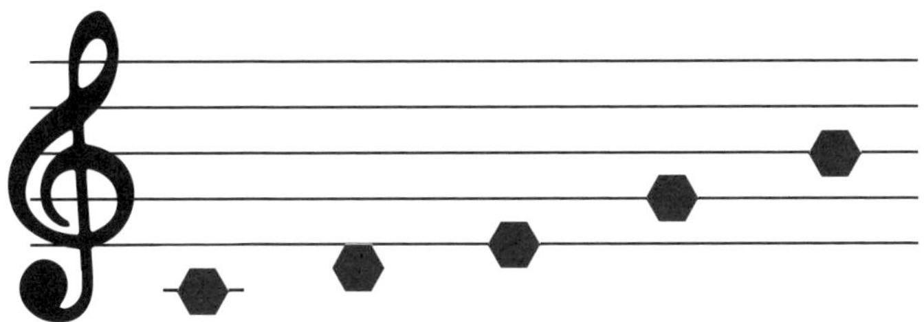

The Chinese often use the number five as a base, including a musical scale of five notes. Sun Tzu builds on the idea of combining a limited number of elements to make an infinite number of variations. Just as there are only five musical notes but endless songs, five flavours but endless dishes, so the tactics of warfare can be put together in endless permutations.

| The five musical notes | The five flavours | The five punishments | The five colours |
|---|---|---|---|
| 宫 Gong | 酸 sour | 墨 tattooing | 黑 black |
| 商 Shang | 辛 spicy | 劓 nose removal | 青 blue |
| 角 Jue | 鹹 salty | 剕 hobbling | 赤 red |
| 徵 Zhi | 甘 sweet | 宫 castration | 白 white |
| 羽 Yu | 苦 bitter | 大辟 death/ banishment | 黄 yellow |

**WAR TIP: Understand that there is a finite number of elements of warfare, but an infinite number of ways to combine them.**

# LESSON 69

## UNLEASH YOUR ARMY'S ENERGY TO MAXIMUM EFFECT

There are two main points here:

- An army that is properly constructed has an enormous amount of energy held in check, like an undischarged dam, a fully drawn crossbow or a primed catapult.
- Make the most of this energy by aiming it at the right target and releasing it at the right time.

Build up power within the army through positioning, discipline and advantage of the landscape, then release it like a weight. Target your enemy's weakest point with the precision of an expert archer or hawk.

**WAR TIP: It is no good striking with power if you miss the mark or the moment.**

**SUN TZU SAYS**

*Amid the turmoil and tumult of battle, there may be seeming disorder and yet no real disorder at all; amid confusion and chaos, your array may be without head or tail, yet it will be proof against defeat. Simulated disorder postulates perfect discipline; simulated fear postulates courage; simulated weakness postulates strength.*

*Hiding order beneath the cloak of disorder is simply a question of subdivision; concealing courage under a show of timidity presupposes a fund of latent energy; masking strength with weakness is to be effected by tactical dispositions.*

*Thus one who is skilful at keeping the enemy on the move maintains deceitful appearances, according to which the enemy will act. He sacrifices something, so that the enemy may snatch at it. By holding out baits, he keeps him on the march; then with a body of picked men he lies in wait for him.*

# LESSON 70

## THE CYCLE OF THE ORTHODOX AND UNORTHODOX

Most of the translators see this as a discussion of the cycle of orthodoxy (正) and unorthodoxy (奇), as mentioned in many other lessons within the text. Sun Tzu tells us to build both elements into our plans, to produce endless tactical variations.

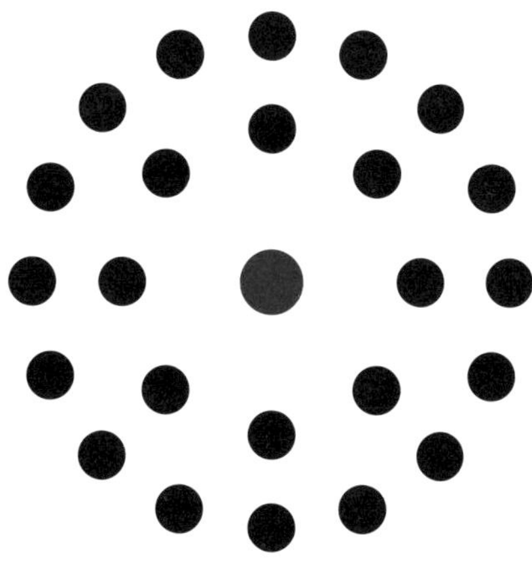

**ABOVE:** A circular formation makes a fluid shape without head or tail.

However, Sawyer and Giles differ from most of the other translators by seeing not an abstract cycle but a physical circle, i.e. a circular formation. Drilling your army in the art of the formless formation means that even in the chaos of battle you will quickly be able to form your troops into any shape so that they can be pointed and focused in any direction. The circular formation is also defensive, giving you a base on which to build an offensive.

**WAR TIP: Switch between orthodox and unorthodox tactics or use them at the same time. Also, train your troops to move in a formless manner and then they will be able to take any shape or formation you wish in any direction you choose.**

# LESSON 71

## BRING ORDER FROM DISORDER

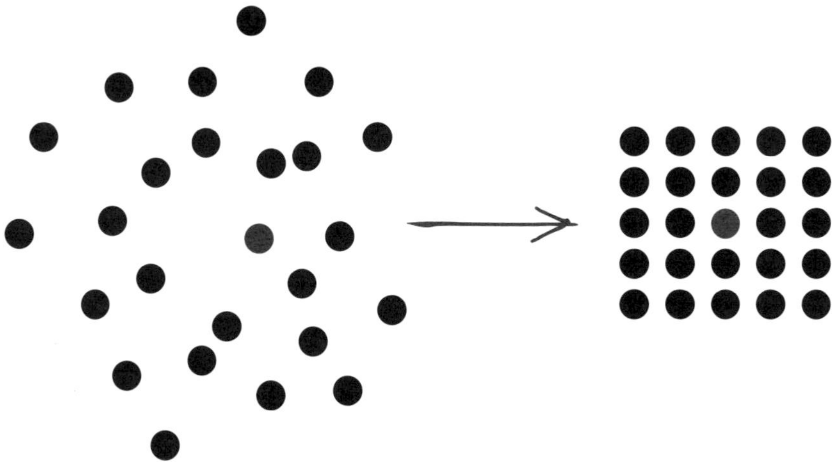

This section is one of the more enigmatic in the *Art of War* and the translations on this point differ quite markedly, although all focus on the concept of order and disorder in battle. The following list represents the full range of interpretations:

- Disorder comes out of order.
- If you expect order from undisciplined troops you will get disorder.
- If you assume people will be strong and courageous, they will be weak.

- If you are well organized you will have order; if not then you will have disorder.
- Tricking the enemy into thinking that you are disordered requires extremely good organization – feigned disorder is based on perfect order.
- Move in a sluggish way to make the enemy think you have lost courage. Or hide your forces to make you appear weak in number. Or lay your troops out in a wrong-headed way that looks like it must be a mistake. Use tactics like these to draw the enemy into a trap, then turn to speed and force upon a given signal.
- Order and disorder are based on regulations.
- Momentum builds courage. If your army is in a phase of power, even the weak will join in and be powerful.
- In governing a state or an army, if you do not lead with authority the people will fall into disorder.

From these various interpretations three main points emerge:

1 To feign disorder your forces must be extremely well disciplined.
2 To feign cowardice your forces must be extremely brave.
3 If you do not have order you will have disorder.

The secret lies in the deception – to make the deception realistic the troops must actually be the opposite of what they are pretending to be.

**WAR TIP: Make the enemy think you are in disorder, but have signals at the ready to put the force back in order at the correct time. This is the way of order from disorder, courage from fear and strength from weakness.**

# LESSON 72

## PRESENT THE BAIT TO THE ENEMY

Be it across a theatre of war or on a single battlefield, a good military leader dangles morsels before the enemy. You might deliberately form your troops in a way that looks incorrect, appear to be limited in number, or give the impression of being trapped. Find something in your situation to tempt the enemy so that they will move in order to take the bait. Then exploit the weakness that their movement opens up.

**WAR TIP: Present a false weakness so that the enemy will try to snatch the upper hand but end up falling into your trap.**

# LESSON 73

## LURE THE ENEMY INTO AN ADVANTAGEOUS POSITION OR SITUATION

When the enemy is static, they are well defended; it is only movement that opens up opportunity. Remember that a good military leader can plan a perfect attack, but if the enemy leader does not move there is no way to make your plan work. Use the kind of bait described in the previous lesson – something tempting enough to make the enemy forget caution – then move the bait to an area where you are in full advantage of the situation, the terrain and the momentum. The idea is to manoeuvre the enemy to a place where you can unleash a massive force upon them.

**WAR TIP: Lead the enemy into the location you want, then smash them with a powerful force.**

## SUN TZU SAYS

*The clever combatant looks to the effect of combined energy, and does not require too much from individuals. Hence his ability to pick out the right men and utilize combined energy. When he utilizes combined energy, his fighting men become as it were like unto rolling logs or stones. For it is the nature of a log or stone to remain motionless on level ground, and to move when on a slope; if four-cornered, to come to a standstill, but if round-shaped, to go rolling down.*

*Thus the energy developed by good fighting men is as the momentum of a round stone rolled down a mountain thousands of feet in height. So much on the subject of energy.*

# LESSON 74

## KNOW WHEN TO MIX YOUR TROOPS AND WHEN TO MATCH THEM

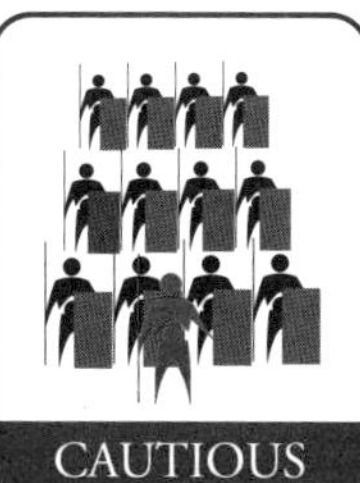

There are two opposing principles at work here. In standard units you should combine troops of different talents and levels of ability. However, when putting together specialist units select troops who have a similar temperament and skill set. For example, rapid assault squads should comprise your quickest, bravest people. Then they will feed off the "vibe" between them and their combined energy will build to a greater power. The words "power" and "momentum" here refer to the unified energy of troops with similar abilities. Conversely, if you mix the brave with the cautious, or the hasty with the contemplative, you will cause discord.

**WAR TIP: Pick troops with the same attitude for specialist units, but use a mixture of troop types to build your core military units.**

# LESSON 75

## BUILD UNSTOPPABLE MOMENTUM

A good military leader will unite the troops into the correct units, which will be led by qualified officers, and the entire army will pulse with energy and enthusiasm. Rewards and punishments are clearly defined and the campaign objective is a dream shared by all. With all these elements in place, the army takes on a feeling of invulnerability and its momentum becomes unstoppable, like a round boulder rolling down a steep mountainside.

**WAR TIP: Construct your army so that it vibrates with unstoppable energy, then unleash it on the enemy with full force.**

虛實篇

# CHAPTER 6

# THE SCROLL OF DECEPTION

# THE SCROLL OF DECEPTION

The title of Sun Tzu's sixth chapter uses the ideograms 虚, meaning "insubstantial", and 実, meaning "substantial". Together they convey a dualistic idea of falsehood and truth. The chapter covers two main areas:

1 Setting up a better position than the enemy
2 Being formless and unpredictable to the enemy

The whole chapter is dedicated to the art of deception; to presenting the truth as false and the false as truth; showing the enemy you are strong where you are weak and weak where you are strong. The enemy will be watching you, so give them a false impression that will make them act incorrectly for the situation. Once they are at a disadvantage, make it worse by using other forms of deception to confuse even more.

## SUN TZU SAYS

*Whoever is first in the field and awaits the coming of the enemy, will be fresh for the fight; whoever is second in the field and has to hasten to battle will arrive exhausted. Therefore the clever combatant imposes his will on the enemy, but does not allow the enemy's will to be imposed on him. By holding out advantages to him, he can cause the enemy to approach of his own accord; or, by inflicting damage, he can make it impossible for the enemy to draw near. If the enemy is taking his ease, he can harass him; if well supplied with food, he can starve him out; if quietly encamped, he can force him to move.*

*Appear at points which the enemy must hasten to defend; march swiftly to places where you are not expected. An army may march great distances without distress, if it marches through country where the enemy is not. You can be sure of succeeding in your attacks if you only attack places which are undefended. You can ensure the safety of your defence if you only hold positions that cannot be attacked. Hence that general is skilful in attack whose opponent does not know what to defend; and he is skilful in defence whose opponent does not know what to attack.*

*O divine art of subtlety and secrecy! Through you we learn to be invisible, through you inaudible; and hence we can hold the enemy's fate in our hands. You may advance and be absolutely irresistible, if you make for the enemy's weak points; you may retire and be safe from pursuit if your movements are more rapid than those of the enemy.*

*If we wish to fight, the enemy can be forced to an engagement even though he be sheltered behind a high rampart and a deep ditch. All we need do is attack some other place that he will be obliged to relieve. If we do not wish to fight, we can prevent the enemy from engaging us even though the lines of our encampment be merely traced out on the ground. All we need do is to throw something odd and unaccountable in his way.*

*By discovering the enemy's dispositions and remaining invisible ourselves, we can keep our forces concentrated, while the enemy's must be divided. We can form a single united body, while the enemy must split up into fractions. Hence there will be a whole pitted against separate parts of a whole, which means that we shall be many to the enemy's few. And if we are able thus to attack an inferior force with a superior one, our opponents will be in dire straits.*

*The spot where we intend to fight must not be made known; for then the enemy will have to prepare against a possible attack at several different points; and his forces being thus distributed in many directions, the numbers we shall have to face at any given point will be proportionately few. For should the enemy strengthen his van, he will weaken his rear; should he strengthen his rear, he will weaken his van; should he strengthen his left, he will weaken his right; should he strengthen his right, he will weaken his left. If he sends reinforcements everywhere, he will everywhere be weak. Numerical weakness comes from having to prepare against possible attacks; numerical strength, from compelling our adversary to make these preparations against us.*

*Knowing the place and the time of the coming battle, we may concentrate from the greatest distances in order to fight. But if neither time nor place be known, then the left wing will be impotent to succour the right, the right equally impotent to succour the left, the van unable to relieve the rear, or the rear to support the van. How much more so if the furthest portions of the army are anything under a hundred li apart, and even the nearest are separated by several li!*

> *Though according to my estimate the soldiers of Yue exceed our own in number, that shall advantage them nothing in the matter of victory. I say then that victory can be achieved. Though the enemy be stronger in numbers, we may prevent him from fighting. Scheme so as to discover his plans and the likelihood of their success.*

# LESSON 76

## DICTATE THE BATTLEGROUND

The army that reaches the battleground first will have various advantages over the enemy army:

- Time to rest and get into position at ease
- Advantage of location
- Advantage over the landscape
- Advantage over the exit route
- Time to lay ambushes
- Time to install mechanical devices or tricks of war
- Opportunity to harass the enemy before they are ready

If the enemy arrives before you, retreat so that the enemy is forced to come to you.

**WAR TIP: Always be the one to decide the battlefield and be the first to set up when entering open battle.**

# LESSON 77

## DANGLE THE CARROT AND WIELD THE STICK

One way to manipulate the enemy is through reward and punishment. There is no actual reward here, only the illusion of a possible victory, which is used to lure the enemy into a trap. The punishment aspect involves swiftly attacking any forward troops or scouts who venture into no man's land. Do this to keep the enemy in check. Other ways to "punish" the enemy include holding strategic roads or access points to restrict movement, or sending strike forces to important locations so that the enemy has to defend them.

On one hand entice the enemy to move; on the other hand strike at the enemy to bring them to a halt.

**WAR TIP: Move the enemy by offering advantages and halt the enemy by attacking them.**

# LESSON 78

## MAKE THE ENEMY UNCOMFORTABLE

This section consists of a series of couplets that talk about disrupting the status of the enemy.

### IF THEY ARE AT REST, MAKE THEM TIRED

If the enemy is well rested, they have good watch systems and all their troops are having a steady amount of sleep, find a way to rouse them into action. False night raids, false attacks, incorrect intelligence, anything that will disrupt the enemy routine and cause them stress. The key is to set their troops on edge and make them work more and sleep less.

### IF THEY ARE WELL FED, STARVE THEM

If the enemy has stockpiles of food, destroy them, burn the landscape around them, poison the water and wells. Most armies would have been stocked on the way out and then would feed from the land or the local towns. Therefore destroy everything in their path so that there is nothing for them to eat or drink.

The Chinese commentator Du Mu gives an elaborate example of this strategy. When one general negotiated a peace treaty with his intended enemy, the enemy leaders were relieved that war had been averted and so allowed the city stores to be opened to feed the population. The general waited for the enemy stocks to be lowered, then broke the treaty and waged war on a soon-to-be-starving population that had no back-up supply of grain.

### IF THEY ARE STATIONARY, MOVE THEM

If the enemy is settled in a single place, bring about a situation where they have to go on the move. This disrupts them and also opens up gaps in their defence.

### GO TO PLACES WHERE THEY MUST FOLLOW YOU OR DO NOT EXPECT YOU TO GO

This final section creates problems because different translations of the text show different interpretations. Some, like the Giles version, say you should go to places where the enemy has to follow you; others say you should go to places where the enemy cannot follow you. Not all translations mention going to places the enemy does not expect you to go, although this point has become one of the most famous of Sun Tzu's maxims: "Attack where the enemy does not expect you."

The general idea is that you should force the enemy to follow you to locations it does not want to go but knows it must, either because it is a location that needs defending or because not going there would hand you a great advantage.

**WAR TIP: Whenever the enemy is in a positive state, do all you can to change that to a negative. Tire them out, starve them, keep them on the move, force them to follow you, be in places they have difficulty getting to, appear where they do not expect you.**

# LESSON 79

## TRAVEL THROUGH UNOCCUPIED TERRITORY

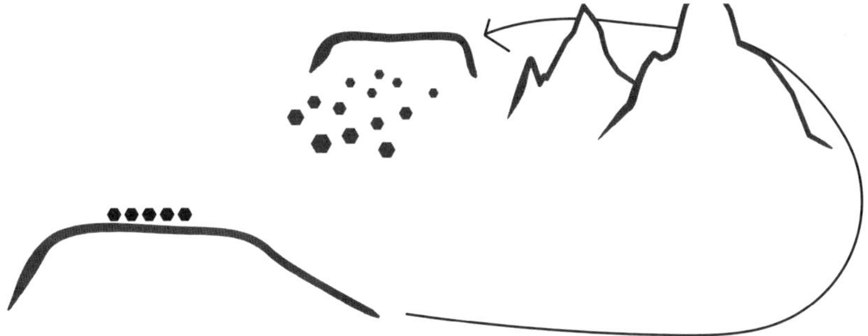

It is better to take an indirect route through an area offering little or no resistance than to take a more direct path through a well-defended area. Even if the hostile area is closer to your target, the journey may be much harder; therefore, find a longer but easier way to the target.

**WAR TIP: Taking a longer road through undefended territory is better than fighting through a shorter, more heavily guarded route.**

# LESSON 80

## ATTACK THE GAPS

The primary message of this teaching is that you should attack the enemy's least defended point. Whether sizing up an enemy castle or deciding which enemy town to target, the principle is the same: identify where they have positioned the fewest troops and pick that as a focus for your attack.

People often assume you have to attack the enemy where they have set up, that a battle has to involve two sides coming together head to head, like stags in rutting season. However, a good military leader will be steps ahead and attack where the enemy has fewer or less able forces. That way, you can deal them a blow and capture stores and equipment without incurring any great losses yourself, before moving on to the next situation. This strategy will create a chain of events that the enemy has to react to and that gradually saps their strength.

**WAR TIP: Rather than attacking where the enemy has prepared for you to attack, target a position where they have put less effort into defence.**

# LESSON 81

## MAKE YOUR FORTRESS IMPREGNABLE

Position your fortress deep in your own territory, somewhere that it would be treacherous for the enemy to march to and extremely difficult for them to retreat from after their attack. It is better for your own troops to have to travel further to reach the enemy but have a higher level of security. If the risk is not worth the reward, the enemy will ignore your base of operations and try to lure you out instead.

**WAR TIP: Establish your base in a remote and difficult location to deter the enemy from attacking it.**

# LESSON 82

## BE A MASTER OF ATTACK AND A MASTER OF DEFENCE

Trying to defend against a true master of warfare is like looking for an arrow coming out of heavy fog. And trying to attack them is like looking for a needle in a haystack. Therefore, never choose the obvious target and never let the enemy know where to find you. To truly excel in warfare know that you have to be "invisible" in all you do so that your moves are always unpredictable.

**WAR TIP: Avoid predictability at all costs, keep the enemy on its toes.**

# LESSON 83

## BE SUBTLE! BE SUBTLE!

微哉微哉

To dictate the outcome of an encounter with the enemy, be so subtle that the enemy cannot begin to perceive what you are doing. This means eradicating any patterns in your strategy that the enemy can read to predict your next move.

This lesson is an oft quoted section of Sun Tzu, but translated in different ways:

- Be subtle! Be subtle!
- Be without form.
- Be spiritual! Be spiritual!

**ABOVE:** The ideograms for this lesson are made up of 微, "subtle", and 乎, which is a form of exclamation mark. They are repeated to emphasize the importance of this teaching.

- Be without sound.
- Subtle beyond subtle.
- Spiritual beyond the spiritual.
- Depths of subtlety.
- Mystery of mysteries.

All of them convey a similar idea: be a mystery to the enemy so that they cannot see your intentions. A variation of this teaching appears in chapter 13 (lesson 228).

**WAR TIP: Present the enemy with so much falsehood and misdirection that they can see none of your plans.**

# LESSON 84

## MOUNT THE PERFECT ATTACK AND RETREAT

This lesson revisits some of the previous ones concerning attacking where the enemy is vulnerable and retreating at speed. Make sure even your slowest troops are faster than the enemy's, target the enemy's weak points and attack only when you are in a position of strength.

**WAR TIP: Target the enemy's weakest position and make sure your troops are faster than the enemy's so that you can retreat in safety.**

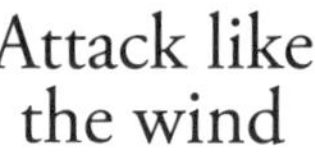

Retreat like lightening

**ABOVE:** Chinese commentators use the saying "Attack like the wind and retreat like lightning."

# LESSON 85

## FORCE THE ENEMY TO LEAVE THEIR FORTRESS

If the enemy is in an impregnable fortress or any other kind of strong defensive position, nullify their advantage by forcing them to come out. Attack a position elsewhere that they cannot allow you to capture. This might mean destroying populations under their protection or attacking a sacred site – anything that will compel them to leave their fortress.

**WAR TIP: If the enemy is in an unassailable position, attack a new target to bring them out of defence.**

# LESSON 86

## STEER THE ENEMY AWAY FROM YOUR DEFENCES

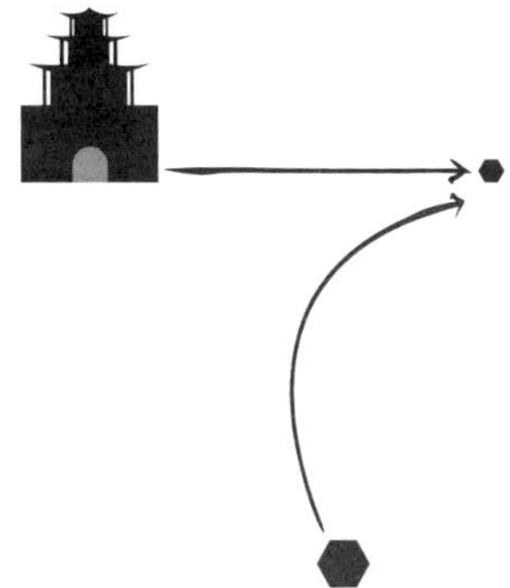

If it becomes obvious that your defences will not hold, lure the enemy away from your position to a new target so you do not have to make a stand that you will lose. Lead them on a "wild goose chase", exhaust them by taking them all over the landscape.

Different Chinese commentators have variations on this lesson, including using a double bluff strategy to make the enemy suspect a trap where there is none so that they change their plans out of fear. The point is to take the enemy's attention away from your base or some other vital position. Sun Tzu says that if you can do this then all you need to defend your position is a line drawn in the ground – there is no need for a physical defence because the enemy will not attack you there.

**WAR TIP: If you know you cannot hold your position, redirect the enemy's attention somewhere else.**

# LESSON 87

## DIVIDE AND CONQUER

The legendary rule of divide and conquer. Be invisible, or at least make your intentions invisible, forcing the enemy to cover all their bases, or use trickery to make them go where you want them to be. Having control of the whole situation, you can pick off the divided enemy one by one.

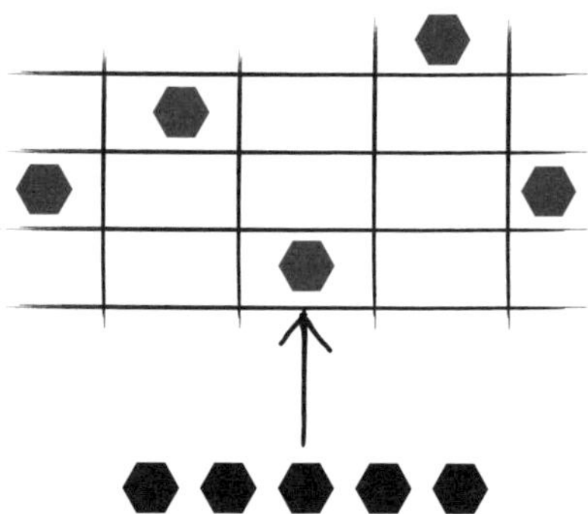

**ABOVE:** Sun Tzu cites a ratio of ten to one, but most likely this is a generic term for "massively outnumbering".

The Chinese commentator Chang Yu returns to the idea of "insubstantial and substantial" – which is the theme of the whole chapter. He reminds us to make the enemy believe that you are insubstantial where you are substantial and substantial where you are insubstantial. Use all forms of deception and intelligence to make the enemy attack where you are powerful and attack the enemy where they are weak.

**WAR TIP: Bamboozle the enemy into attacking you where you are strongest, divide their force and destroy them section by section.**

# LESSON 88

## HIDE YOUR FORM

The original text reinforces the last few lessons by restating the point that the enemy must never know where you are. Chinese commentators teach that you must hide your form so that the enemy has to divide its forces because it does not know where you will attack from. This does not just mean literally hiding; it can also be done by spreading misinformation through converted spies and propaganda agents, laying false leads, or redirecting your plans to look like you will attack one place when you are, in fact, preparing to attack another.

**WAR TIP: Present the enemy with an "alternative truth", create a story that causes the enemy to make the wrong moves.**

# LESSON 89

## THREATEN ONE SIDE TO WEAKEN THE OTHER

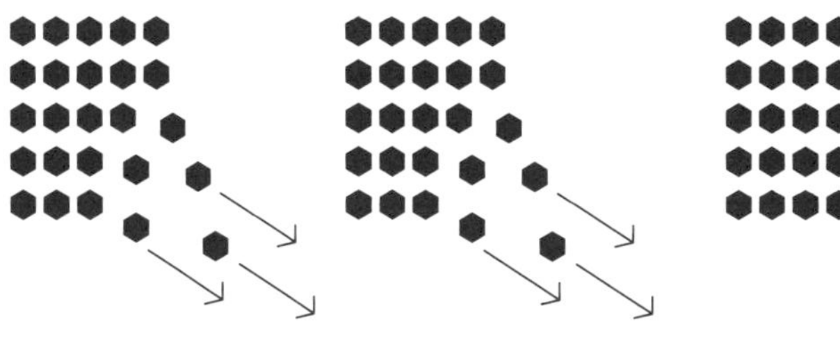

If the enemy is in position, attack one side with some of your troops to draw reinforcements to that side. This will weaken the rest of the enemy force and then you can attack from another direction with the rest of your troops. The trick is to fool the enemy into thinking that the initial attack is a substantial one when it is, in fact, insubstantial. Ways to do this include:

- Ordering your embedded spies to spread false information or passing on false reports to enemy spies
- Raising extra flags
- Lighting extra fires
- Making dust
- Moving troops from place to place

Having been fooled, the enemy will feel compelled to make a move to protect the position that you are targeting.

**WAR TIP: Harass the enemy from one direction, but have troops ready to attack from another.**

# LESSON 90

## BE THE PUPPET MASTER, NOT THE PUPPET

All the while that you are trying to divide the enemy's forces, the enemy will be trying to do the same to you. No matter how aggressive their attempts, do not be manipulated. Dividing your troops in response to an enemy move is a sign of poor command and strategy.

**WAR TIP: Never let the enemy manipulate you into dividing your forces. Always do this on your own terms.**

# LESSON 91

## KNOW WHERE THE BATTLE WILL TAKE PLACE

An army does not always march as a single unit. The Chinese traditionally split their armies into three divisions, each of which would have further subdivisions within them. These divisions might be separated from each other by many miles and take different routes over the landscape but still be in close communication via flags, signals and messengers.

Being in command of such a vast and complex system, often involving tens of thousands of troops, you must be able to read the enemy's intentions to judge where the battle is to take place. Then you can send signals to all sections of the army to ensure that your full force will appear at the correct location, at the correct time and in the correct manner. Also, if one section of the army is to join battle then they can call for reinforcements from another section who can travel with direct speed.

Sun Tzu says that it is better to restrict the distance between divisions to a few miles if possible. This will ensure that reinforcements can be dispatched in time. It is not a question of responding to enemy moves, which would go against the previous lesson about being manipulated. Rather, the point is that being able to move your divisions quickly will enable you to roll out your own plan of attack and keep the advantage in your favour.

**WAR TIP: With professionalism, good communication and speed of movement, the divisions of your army can swiftly join together in readiness for battle.**

# LESSON 92

## KNOW THAT EVEN THE SUPERIOR CAN FALL

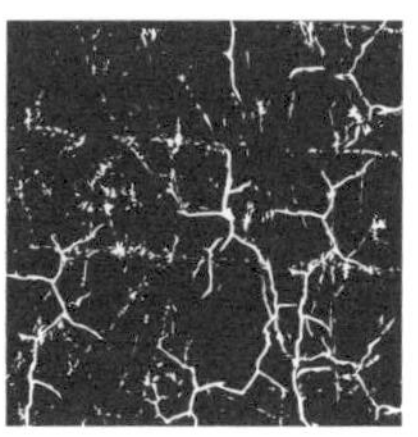

This is one of the few occasions that Sun Tzu talks about the politics and military history of his time. He uses the conflict that his home state, Wu, fought against its neighbour Yue to illustrate his point. The Yue army was superior in size to the Wu army, but it was still defeated. The larger, better trained and better armed force usually wins, but an outstanding military commander can scheme to overturn the odds by fracturing the enemy from within.

**WAR TIP: When facing a larger enemy, use cunning to break up their force into smaller, beatable sections.**

# LESSON 93

## COMPARE AND COMPARE AGAIN

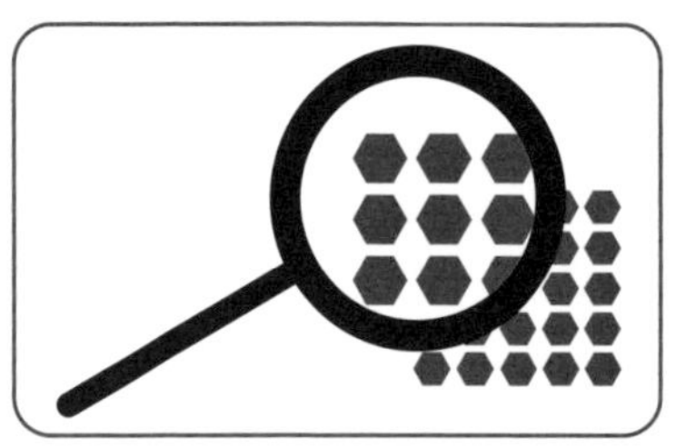

The five constant factors (lessons 2–7) and the seven considerations (lesson 8) are not only for use when preparing for war. Even when you have set your troops in position and are about to engage the enemy, use these essential tools to re-evaluate the pros and cons of the situation and the balance of power between the two forces.

**WAR TIP: Before you launch an attack, revisit your comparison of the two armies to make sure your side still holds the advantage.**

### SUN TZU SAYS

*Rouse [the enemy], and learn the principle of his activity or inactivity. Force him to reveal himself, so as to find out his vulnerable spots. Carefully compare the opposing army with your own, so that you may know where strength is superabundant and where it is deficient.*

*In making tactical dispositions, the highest pitch you can attain is to conceal them; conceal your dispositions, and you will be safe from the prying of the subtlest spies, from the machinations of the wisest brains. How victory may be produced for them out of the enemy's own tactics – that is what the multitude cannot comprehend. All men can see the tactics whereby I conquer, but what none can see is the strategy out of which victory is evolved. Do not repeat the tactics which have gained you one victory, but let your methods be regulated by the infinite variety of circumstances.*

*Military tactics are like unto water; for water in its natural course runs away from high places and hastens downwards. So in war, the way is to avoid what is strong and to strike at what is weak. Water shapes its course according to the nature of the ground over which it flows; the soldier works out his victory in relation to the foe whom he is facing. Therefore, just as water retains no constant shape, so in warfare there are no constant conditions.*

*He who can modify his tactics in relation to his opponent and thereby succeed in winning, may be called a heaven-born captain. The five elements (water, fire, wood, metal, earth) are not always equally predominant; the four seasons make way for each other in turn. There are short days and long; the moon has its periods of waning and waxing.*

# LESSON 94

## USE A FALSE ATTACK TO SEE HOW THE ENEMY REACTS

Take a troop and simulate an attack upon the enemy, but have observers in place to assess how the enemy reacts. From this you will understand their protocols and response training. After this withdraw and reassess your knowledge of the enemy. The troops used in this action should not enter into combat but should only pose enough threat to provoke a reaction. This way you will know if the enemy will go on the defensive or move to an assault.

Interestingly, the Chinese commentator Du Mu talks about how such troops are allowed to withdraw without fear of punishment, which would not normally be the case. This makes it clear that these are specialist strike-and-run troops. If the enemy does not advance, you can assume that the enemy commander is skilled and will not be baited; if they do respond, then it shows a rashness in their leadership.

**WAR TIP: Stage a bogus strike on enemy space so that you can observe their response.**

# LESSON 95

## FORCE THE ENEMY TO ADOPT A FORMATION

Having tested the enemy for their reactions and protocols and to gauge the commander's ability and temperament, it is now time to push them further. Your aim is to discover the formations they will take, and the tactics they will use, in actual combat. Therefore, use various ruses to make the enemy think that you are about to enter the battlefield and make a proper attack. The Chinese commentator Li Quan suggests doing the opposite, that you should stage a false retreat and light bogus campfires to indicate a change in position.

Whichever tricks you use to make the enemy form up on the offensive, be sure to have observers in place to watch them. This is where you can check your strengths versus their strengths and your weaknesses versus their weaknesses and adjust your battle plan according to the types of movements they make.

**WAR TIP: Trick the enemy into thinking the battle is about to start and then observe how they prepare for combat. From this you can know how to defeat them.**

# LESSON 96

## DO NOT ENGAGE WITH ENEMY PROBING

The enemy commander will try to play the same tricks on you. Therefore, Sun Tzu says that you must remain formless – you must not show your "hand" when the enemy makes small moves to provoke you. Hide your intentions so that even the best of spies cannot discern what you are thinking. The greatest trick of all is to remain formless to enemy eyes but manipulate the enemy into showing you everything about themselves.

**WAR TIP: Never react to an enemy that is just trying to provoke you. Only react if you actually have to.**

# LESSON 97

## SEE THE STRANDS OF VICTORY

People can see, smell and hear what is obvious, but here Sun Tzu revisits the skill of gaining victory by identifying abstract and minute parts before they form together. These hidden, constantly evolving parts are discernible to very few people. Those who have this skill will always be at an advantage because they can tell that war is coming before anyone else. Absorbing the lessons in this book will help you to join this select group.

**WAR TIP: Use the smallest signals from the enemy to calculate a plan long before they actually move into action.**

# LESSON 98

## NEVER REPEAT YOURSELF

Just because a strategy worked once before does not mean it will work again. In fact, it will be less likely to succeed, because the enemy will see it coming. Use the principles of war to understand what will be best to defeat the enemy in the current situation, which will inevitably be different from any previous situation.

**WAR TIP: Do not fall back on a previously successful strategy. Observe enemy changes and build a new plan.**

# LESSON 99

## FLOW LIKE WATER

Water follows the easiest path down a mountain, avoiding the difficult areas, but it will destroy that mountain in the end.

Sun Tzu tells us to be like water, to "flow" with the enemy. That does not mean you should get caught in the enemy's flow, responding to their every move and handing control of the battle to them. Quite the opposite. You should be the flow.

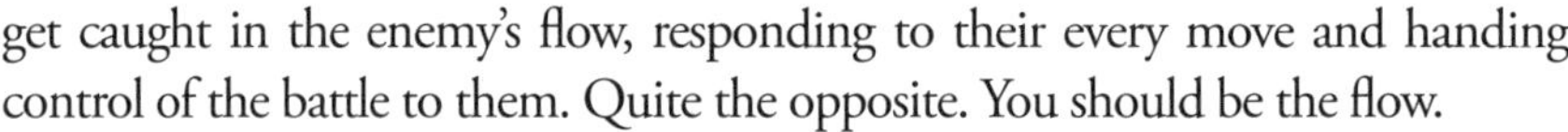

Like water, do not smash yourself against a difficult place or try to flow uphill. Observe the weakest points of the enemy and target them, just as water always finds the easiest way down a mountain in streams before it becomes a gushing force. And when the enemy changes in any way, observe the new vulnerabilities that open up and attack those. Be proactive, not responsive.

**WAR TIP: Be like water: flow into the enemy's weak points and when the enemy changes, discover where their new weaknesses are.**

# LESSON 100

## THE FIVE ELEMENTS

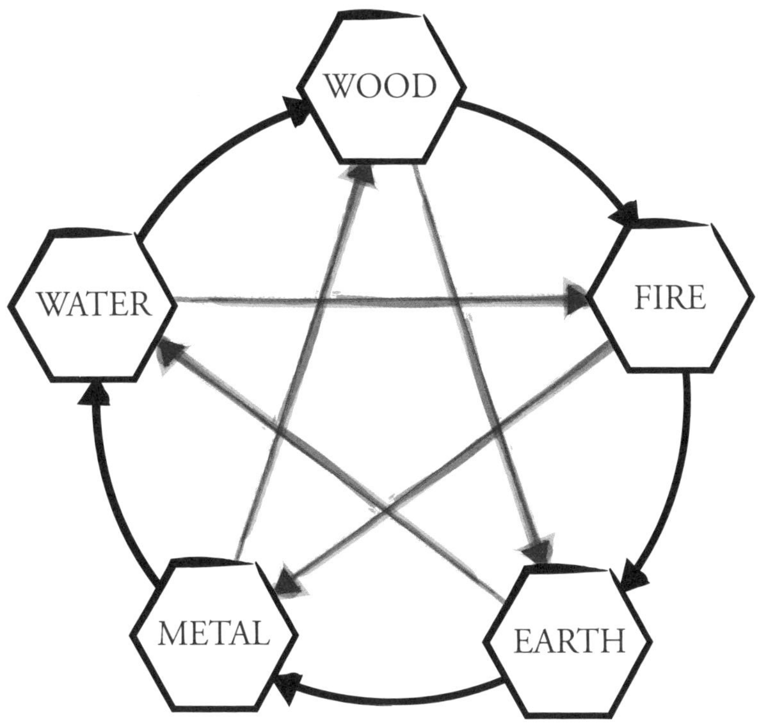


**ABOVE:** The Chinese Five Elements, in cycles of creation and of destruction.

Sun Tzu's writing is notable for its pragmatism. At very few points in the text does he venture into the spiritual, esoteric underpinnings of Chinese warfare. However, here he touches upon the Taoist theory of Five Elements, which describes the movement of energy between five natural states: Water, Fire, Wood, Metal and Earth. Five Element theory includes multiple cycles of interaction between the energies in relation to time, direction and landscape. Sun Tzu mentions the Five Elements at this point to highlight the fluidity of change.

The Five Elements are in a constant state of flux as the season changes from spring to summer to autumn to winter, the days grow longer and shorter,

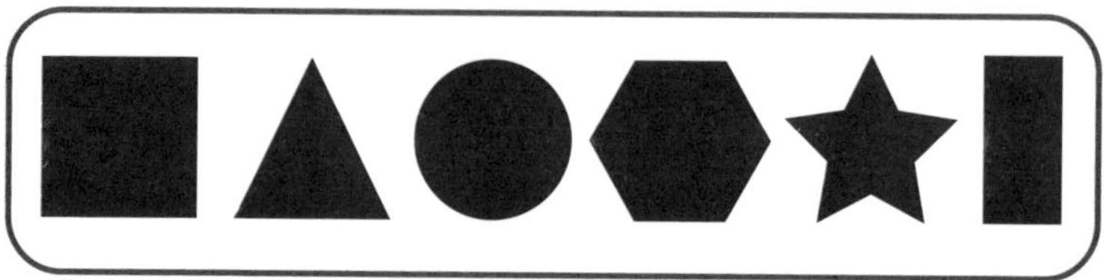

**ABOVE:** Flow with change – change "shape" and adapt yourself to all situations.

and the moon waxes and wanes. The key is to be aware of changes, follow their patterns, and predict them, so that you are always at least one step ahead of the enemy. The Chinese commentator Li Quan talks about many forms of change as they relate to the military sphere. These include size, morale, tension, relaxation, greed and suspicion. In short, look for the changes in all things and use them to your advantage.

**WAR TIP: Five Element theory tells us that the situation will change from hour to hour and day to day. Follow these changes and adapt your thinking and plans accordingly.**

軍爭篇

# CHAPTER 7

# THE SCROLL OF MILITARY COMBAT

# THE SCROLL OF MILITARY COMBAT

The title of Sun Tzu's seventh chapter uses the ideograms 軍, meaning "military", and 争, meaning "combat" or "conflict". The chapter is divided into four main areas:

1 The beginning, middle and end of all things
2 Direct and indirect
3 Movement
4 Phases of power

The first part consists of a short warning that a commander must see things through from the beginnings all the way to the very end. The second section explains that a leader should make sure all of their own movements and plans have focus and are direct; each move should be measured and precise. This does not mean you should always take the easiest option; it means that your plans should be clear and well laid out, whereas the enemy should be led on a wild goose chase, tiring them out and sending them in all directions. The third section looks at actual movement during combat, such as the signals used in war and the flags that give commands. The final section deals with phases of power and explains when to move against the enemy and when to wait for them to move.

### SUN TZU SAYS

*In war, the general receives his commands from the sovereign. Having collected an army and concentrated his forces, he must blend and harmonize the different elements thereof before pitching his camp. After that, comes tactical manoeuvring, than which there is nothing more difficult.*

# LESSON 101

## PLAN EVERY PHASE OF WAR

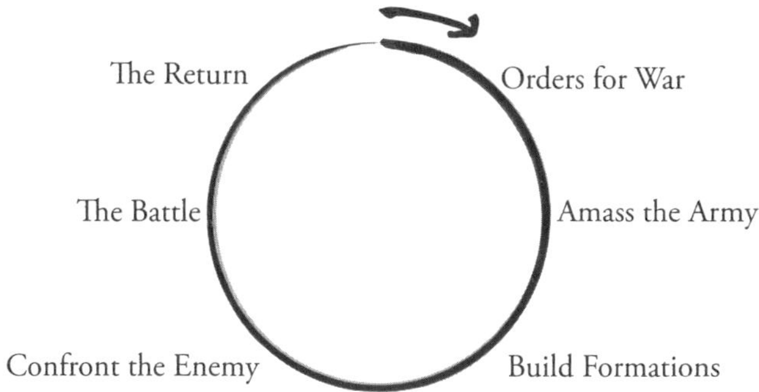


Make sure to identify all the phases of war. Be aware of the beginning, the middle and the end and know who should be where and when they should be there throughout the whole conflict. War is not just a series of actions, but a fully planned set of stages with adaptive measures in place.

**WAR TIP: Consider war from its beginning to its very end and assess all the stages in between before you do anything else.**

# LESSON 102

## THE CURVED AND THE STRAIGHT

When two armies are moving toward each other, a good military commander will delay the enemy so that the allied forces reach the battlefield first. Use bait teams and other strategies to trick the enemy into taking a longer route or send them to the wrong place – anything that means they waste energy on a wild goose chase.

The Chinese commentator Cao Cao suggests varying the pace of your march to disrupt the enemy's rhythm, while Du Mu says that you should fool the enemy into thinking you are being lackadaisical, then suddenly accelerate to beat them to the goal.

These commentators view the point purely in terms of the physical journey to the battlefield, whereas others see it as a journey across the political landscape – meaning that you should put political obstacles in the enemy's way to distract them in their preparations. An example might be to use an embedded spy to sow discord in the enemy ranks. In either case, the point is to make your own route straight (and straightforward) but twist or complicate the enemy path.

**WAR TIP: Whenever you and the enemy are racing to a position, delay the enemy with distractions and diversions so that you get there first.**

## SUN TZU SAYS

*The difficulty of tactical manoeuvring consists in turning the devious into the direct, and misfortune into gain. Thus, to take a long and circuitous route, after enticing the enemy out of the way, and though starting after him, to contrive to reach the goal before him, shows knowledge of the artifice of deviation.*

*Manoeuvring with an army is advantageous; with an undisciplined multitude, most dangerous. If you set a fully equipped army in march in order to snatch an advantage, the chances are that you will be too late. On the other hand, to detach a flying column for the purpose involves the sacrifice of its baggage and stores. Thus, if you order your men to roll up their buff-coats, and make forced marches without halting day or night, covering double the usual distance at a stretch, doing a hundred li in order to wrest an advantage, the leaders of all your three divisions will fall into the hands of the enemy. The stronger men will be in front, the jaded ones will fall behind, and on this plan only one tenth of your army will reach its destination. If you march fifty li in order to outmanoeuvre the enemy, you will lose the leader of your first division, and only half your force will reach the goal. If you march thirty li with the same object, two thirds of your army will arrive. We may take it then that an army without its baggage train is lost; without provisions it is lost; without bases of supply it is lost.*

> *We cannot enter into alliances until we are acquainted with the designs of our neighbours. We are not fit to lead an army on the march unless we are familiar with the face of the country – its mountains and forests, its pitfalls and precipices, its marshes and swamps. We shall be unable to turn natural advantage to account unless we make use of local guides.*

# LESSON 103

## KEEP INTERNAL RIVALRY IN CHECK

Ancient Chinese armies were divided into three main divisions. Often the divisional leaders competed against each other for the honour of being the first to arrive at the battlefield and the practical benefits of gaining enemy loot or the most advantageous position. However, Sun Tzu warns that this is a terrible error.

If divisions force march their troops over great distances to get to the battlefield before the other divisions, they will give the enemy an advantage. The strongest troops will naturally move to the front, but when they duly reach the battlefield first they will not only be exhausted but also outnumbered, and so you will end up losing your best soldiers.

Therefore, the main commander must make it clear to all divisions that no one should be allowed to race for an advantage apart from specialized troops working outside of the main force. It is much better to follow the previous lesson and delay the enemy instead of rushing your own army with forced overnight marches.

The Chinese commentator Tu Mu says that in certain circumstances, if there is no other option, sending the best 10 per cent of your soldiers ahead is acceptable. They will arrive to hold the enemy at bay until the rest of the army catches up. Because they have not had to rush, the weaker, slower soldiers will arrive at the battle relatively fresh and so will be able to fight effectively.

**WAR TIP: Do not let divisional leaders break off and follow their own aims, and do not rush to meet the enemy because your forces will naturally become stretched out and exhausted.**

# LESSON 104

## ALWAYS KEEP YOUR STORES AND EQUIPMENT WITH YOU

It may be tempting for some commanders to drop their stores and equipment to lighten the load so that they can travel at greater speed across country, but this is folly. The army may initially go quicker by doing this, but will soon regret not having their stores when they run out of energy and need to refuel. Also, without the correct equipment they will be ill equipped to face the enemy. Therefore, never leave stores behind. If you are "playing catch-up" you have made a mistake in your plans, so change direction and reassess.

**WAR TIP: Without food and stores the army will starve and not be able to fight. Therefore, leaving stores behind in exchange for greater speed is the worst trade you can make.**

# LESSON 105

## KNOW THE MIND OF YOUR ENEMY

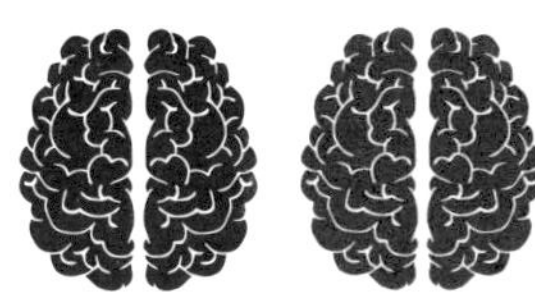

In every conflict there are more than just two leaders. A good commander should know the plans and aspirations of all people of influence – on the allied side as well as among the enemy. Remember that there are important people beyond the armies themselves – you also need to understand the standpoint of different political leaders and opinion-formers. And there may be other states waiting to exploit any weakness shown by the warring parties. Be aware of what their leaders are thinking, too. Use all means at your disposal to discover information on all key figures.

**WAR TIP: Know the hearts and minds of all people of influence – both on your side and on the enemy side – before you go to war.**

# LESSON 106

## USE SCOUTS AND GUIDES

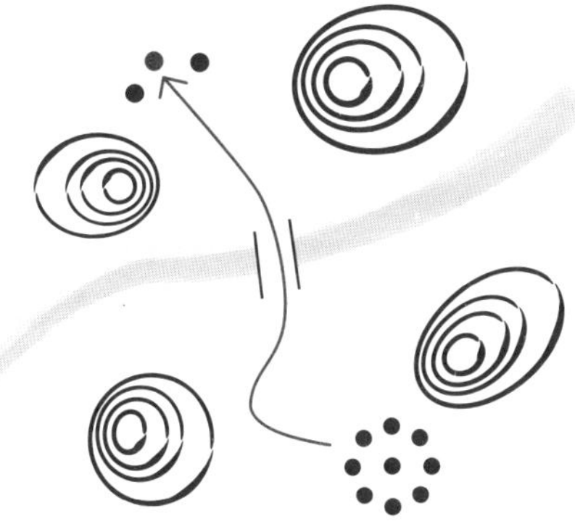

You will find it impossible to move through enemy lands without scouts and guides. Scouts are your own troops sent ahead to find out about the land you are going to march through, whereas guides are local people who will know the land of their birth in great detail. They will help you avoid ambushes, traps, difficult areas and dead ends if you pay them well enough or coerce them with enough force. However, remember that the enemy may have placed spies to lead you into difficult places.

The Chinese commentator Mei Yaochen says that it is better to use your own trained scouts rather than local guides. Li Ching agrees, saying that a leader should develop brave soldiers who will venture deep into enemy territory unseen. He recommends they use devices such as fake animal feet to disguise their tracks and also hats with decoy birds on them so that they can sit in the undergrowth and observe the enemy without being discovered.

**WAR TIP: Send scouts ahead of the main army or pay or force local people to guide you through their lands, but make sure they are not enemy spies.**

### SUN TZU SAYS

*In war, practise dissimulation, and you will succeed. Whether to concentrate or to divide your troops, must be decided by circumstances. Let your rapidity be that of the wind, your compactness that of the forest. In raiding and plundering be like fire, in immovability like a mountain. Let your plans be dark and impenetrable as night, and when you move, fall like a thunderbolt.*

*When you plunder a countryside, let the spoil be divided amongst your men; when you capture new territory, cut it up into allotments for the benefit of the soldiery.*

*Ponder and deliberate before you make a move. He will conquer who has learned the artifice of deviation. Such is the art of manoeuvring.*

*The Book of Army Management says, "On the field of battle, the spoken word does not carry far enough: hence the institution of gongs and drums. Nor can ordinary objects be seen clearly enough: hence the institution of banners and flags." Gongs and drums, banners and flags, are means whereby the ears and eyes of the host may be focused on one particular point. The host thus forming a single united body, is it impossible either for the brave to advance alone, or for the cowardly to retreat alone. This is the art of handling large masses of men. In night-fighting, then, make much use of signal-fires and drums, and in fighting by day, of flags and banners, as a means of influencing the ears and eyes of your army.*

# LESSON 107

## DIVIDE AND REUNIFY THE ARMY

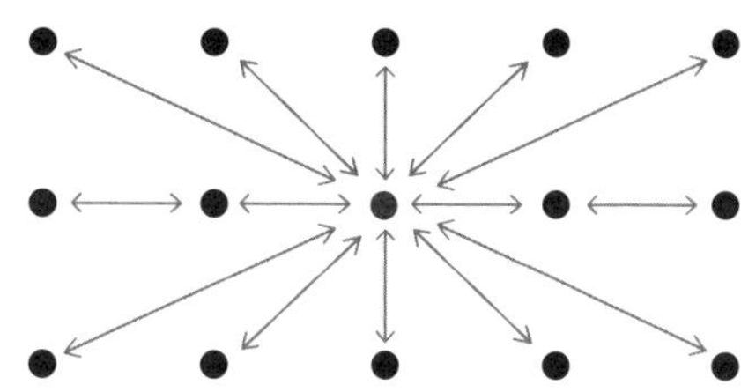

A Chinese army is broken up into subdivisions. This structure enables divisions to split off and move separately and then reunite with each other and move as one. There should be clear signals for this so that it can be done perfectly smoothly even across vast swathes of land or on difficult terrain.

Use this dividing and reuniting manoeuvre as a deception to fool the enemy into making the changes that you want them to make.

**WAR TIP: Drill your force so that it can split up and reunite effortlessly no matter what the distance.**

# LESSON 108

## BE LIKE NATURE IN YOUR WAYS

This is one of the most famous passages of Sun Tzu and has been quoted by many other strategists through the ages. He uses powerful images from nature to convey the way an army should approach certain situations:

- Be as swift as the wind – an army must march as one at great speed.
- Be as ordered as a forest – the army must be ordered like rows of trees and silent when standing in uniform.

- Be as secure as a mountain – if there is no advantage to be taken from a situation the army must remain solid and closed, impenetrable like a mountain.
- Be as devastating as fire.
- Be as impenetrable as darkness – the commander's plans must be cloaked in darkness (or clouds in Griffith's version).
- Strike like thunder and lightning.

**WAR TIP: Move over the land at speed and in strict order, have a firm defence, be destructive when unleashed, do not display your intentions and face the enemy with unstoppable force.**

# LESSON 109

## PLUNDER AND PILLAGE RESPONSIBLY

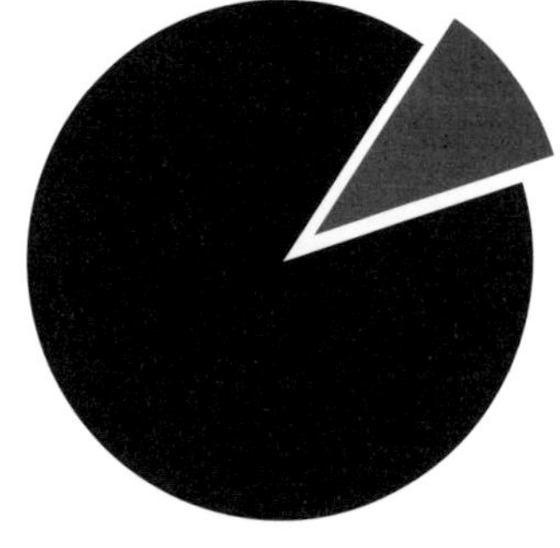

Translators interpret this lesson in two markedly different ways. Some, including Giles, see it as meaning that when you have defeated an enemy, you should divide the spoils of war fairly among your troops.

Others, including the ancient Chinese commentator Zhang Yu, think that Sun Tzu is saying that you should divide your troops into smaller bands and send them out to take what they need from the whole territory. This is a more sustainable way of living off the enemy land than ravaging a single area, which would devastate that community.

**WAR TIP: After an area has been defeated, take only what you need to supply your own troops. Do not plunder recklessly or you will ruin the local population.**

# LESSON 110

## ALLOCATE ENEMY LAND AMONG YOUR TROOPS

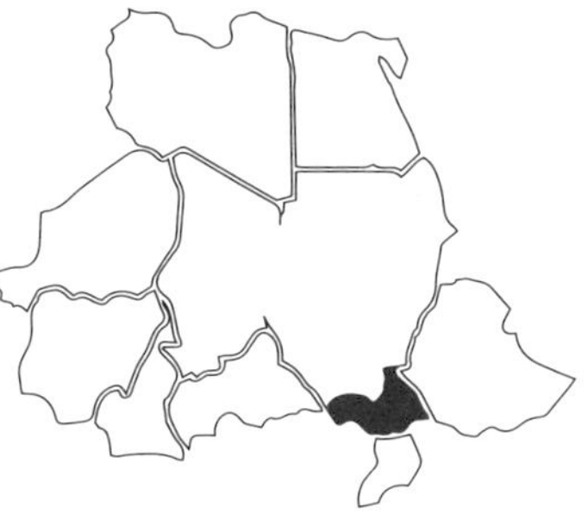

When new territory is conquered, divide it among your troops to expand the allied holdings. Again Zhang Yu has a different view: he says that this means to divide up the spoils of war and have separate groups guard it so that the enemy cannot take it back.

After this, Sun Tzu returns to the theme of the curved (indirect) and the straight (direct). This is one of the foundations of military prowess.

**WAR TIP: Redistribute captured land among your troops and guard that which you have acquired.**

# LESSON 111

## ESTABLISH CLEAR COMMUNICATIONS

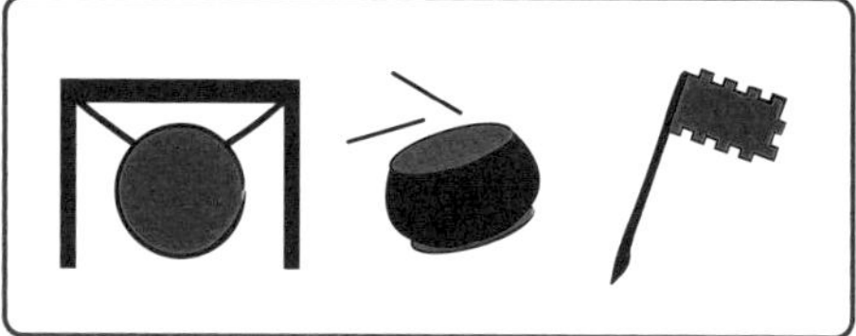

Communications are key. During battle spoken instructions cannot be heard, so you must establish another way to make your orders clear to everyone (but not the enemy). In ancient China this was done by banging gongs or drums, raising flags and lighting fire signals (for night combat). Each army would have its own system. Different instructions would be conveyed by a particular number of beats on a drum or gong or by different flags moved in certain ways.

**WAR TIP: Set up direct communication systems that cannot be misinterpreted by your troops or intercepted by the enemy.**

# LESSON 112

## KEEP THE STRONG AND THE WEAK TOGETHER

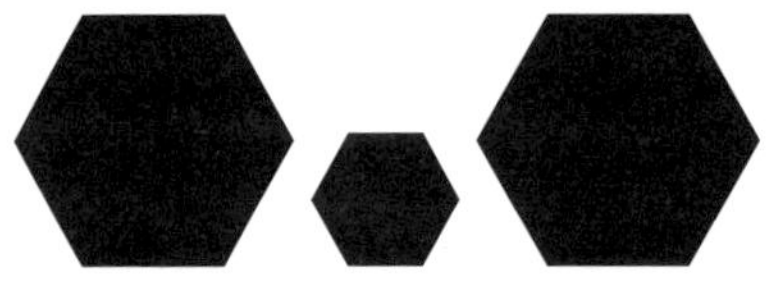

Use clear signals to bind the army together. If not, the stronger soldiers will tend to rush ahead and the weaker ones drop back. Keeping soldiers of all abilities marching together will make your force stronger overall. This does not apply, of course, to specialist advance troops.

**WAR TIP: Distribute strong and weak soldiers evenly and then use signals and orders to hold them together as a bonded army.**

# LESSON 113

## NIGHT SIGNALS

At night sound signals like gong or drum strikes can still be heard, but there may be times when visual signals are also required. Clearly, flags will not be effective in the darkness, so use fire or light signals instead. The arts of fire come in many forms and Chinese military manuals have extensive descriptions of the various tools and weapons.

**WAR TIP: Use light signals to communicate with the troops at night.**

# LESSON 114

## USE SIGNALS TO INSPIRE

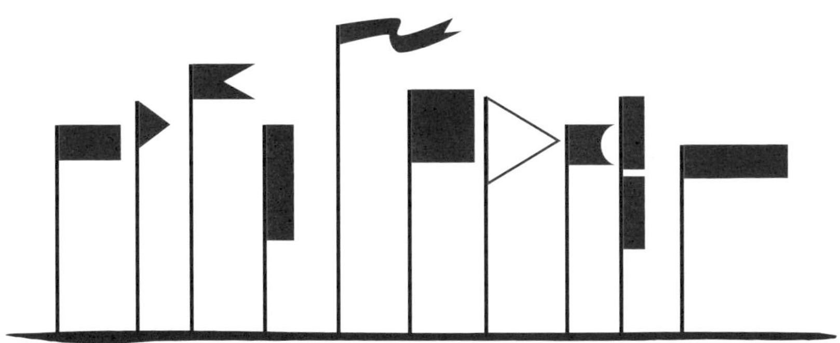

The primary purpose of signals is to communicate orders, but they can also be used en masse to boost the morale of the troops, just as sports fans wave a host of banners and shout as loudly as they can to urge their team on – and to intimidate the opposition. It is not clear whether Sun Tzu had this idea in mind here – he just says to have "numerous" signals – but some commentators have given this secondary point.

**WAR TIP: Signals can be used not only for communication but also for encouragement.**

### SUN TZU SAYS

*A whole army may be robbed of its spirit; a commander-in-chief may be robbed of his presence of mind. Now a soldier's spirit is keenest in the morning; by noonday it has begun to flag; and in the evening, his mind is bent only on returning to camp. A clever general, therefore, avoids an army when its spirit is keen, but attacks it when it is sluggish and inclined to return. This is the art of studying moods.*

*Disciplined and calm, to await the appearance of disorder and hubbub amongst the enemy – this is the art of retaining self-possession. To be near the goal while the enemy is still far from it, to wait at ease while the enemy is toiling and struggling, to be well-fed while the enemy is famished – this is the art of husbanding one's strength.*

> *To refrain from intercepting an enemy whose banners are in perfect order, to refrain from attacking an army drawn up in calm and confident array – this is the art of studying circumstances.*
>
> *It is a military axiom not to advance uphill against the enemy, nor to oppose him when he comes downhill. Do not pursue an enemy who simulates flight; do not attack soldiers whose temper is keen. Do not swallow bait offered by the enemy. Do not interfere with an army that is returning home. When you surround an army, leave an outlet free. Do not press a desperate foe too hard. Such is the art of warfare.*

# LESSON 115

## CONTROL THE WILL

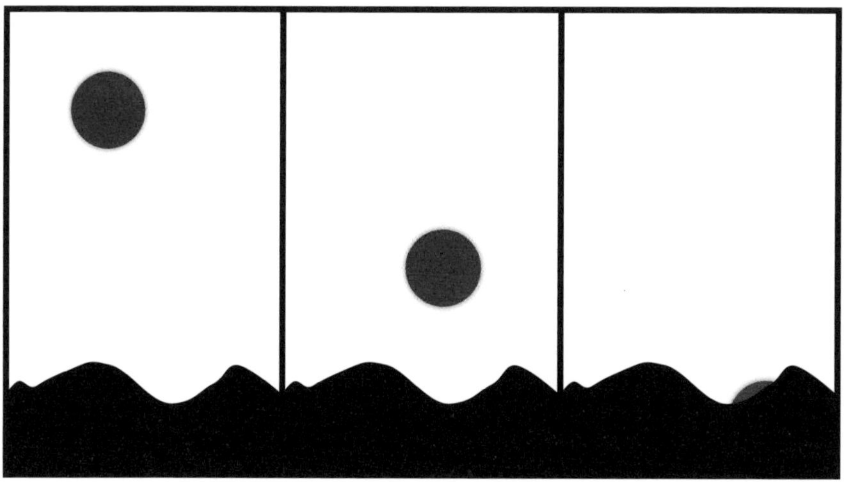

*This is the first of four lessons on control.*

Remember that war is fought just as much in the mind as it is on the battlefield. An entire army can have its morale taken from it and a commander can lose heart. By breaking the enemy's spirit, you will break them physically, too.

Sun Tzu divides the power and morale of a force into three stages, symbolized by times of the day:

1 The morning or beginning – fresh and alert, ready for action
2 The afternoon or middle – flagging and starting to lose heart
3 The evening or end – exhausted and ready to surrender

Never attack an enemy who is in a phase of power. Wait until they are in a lull. Sun Tzu says this is the way to manipulate the chi or energy of the army.

The Chinese commentator Zhang Yu points out that this principle also applies to your own forces. There is little point waiting for the enemy's energy to drop if your troops' energy is also declining. So before you engage the enemy, rally your own troops into positive action.

**WAR TIP: Wait until the enemy's spirit and energy are sagging before you attack and make sure your own troops' morale is buoyant – this is the way to control the will.**

# LESSON 116

## CONTROL THE MIND

*This is the second of four lessons on control.*

An ill-disciplined, disordered, "noisy" mind will be distracted and useless in battle. Therefore, train your troops to still their thoughts through the discipline of repetition, preparation and meditation so that when they fight their minds will be clear and focused only on victory. At the same time, disrupt the enemy with tricks in order to unsettle their minds.

**WAR TIP: Maintain proper order and tranquillity among your troops, but introduce chaos and doubt into the enemy's thoughts – this is the way to control the mind.**

# LESSON 117

## CONTROL STRENGTH

Distance ⬢ Recovery ⬢ Vitality

*This is the third of four lessons on control.*

Conserve your strength while sapping the strength of the enemy. A good military commander will follow these three strategies:

1 Do not travel far to meet the enemy, but make them travel to you.
2 Give your troops time to rest, but do not let the enemy recover.
3 Feed your troops well, but do not give the enemy time to eat.

Do this and the enemy will always be at a disadvantage.

**WAR TIP: Make the enemy travel while your troops stay in one place; exhaust the enemy while your troops rest; starve the enemy while your troops eat – this is the way to control strength.**

# LESSON 118

## CONTROL CHANGE

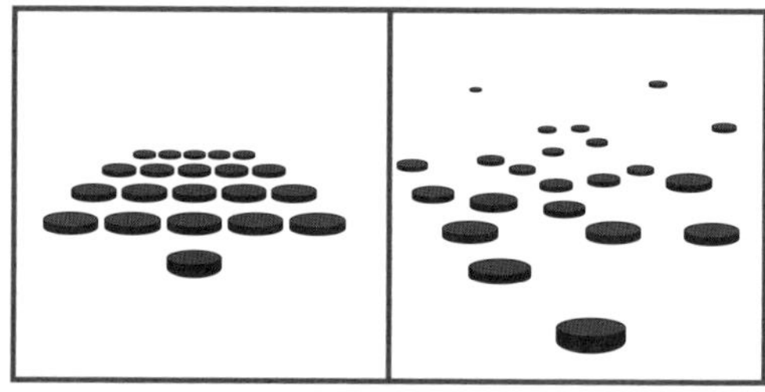

*This is the last of four lessons on control.*

The basic lesson here is that you should never attack when the enemy's banners are in good order and its troops are set up in a strong formation. Be a master of change. Make things happen that create gaps within the enemy.

**WAR TIP: Do not attack a strong enemy. Bring about change before you strike – this is the way to control change.**

# LESSON 119

## NEVER MARCH UP A STEEP HILL

*This is the first of Sun Tzu's eight military ways.*

If a mountain is steep on one side, do not climb from that side. Instead go the long way around or find an easier gradient. Mountains can be classified by the side on which their slopes are least steep. Scouts will report back and establish the best route for an army. The movement of an army must be planned in advance.

**WAR TIP: Always find the easiest way to cross over a mountain. Ascend on the shallowest gradient and descend on the steepest.**

# LESSON 120

## DO NOT ATTACK AN ARMY THAT HAS A HEIGHT BEHIND IT

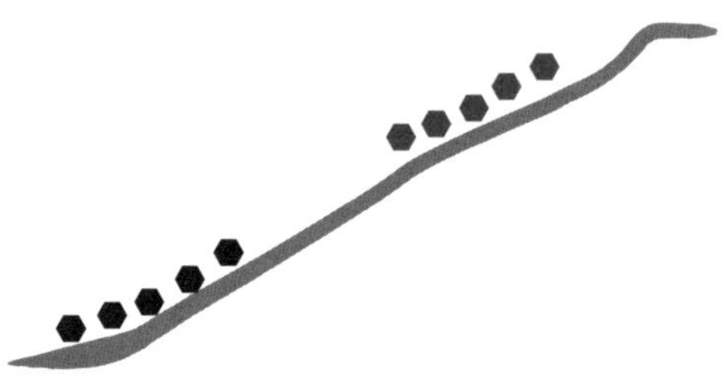

*This is the second of Sun Tzu's eight military ways.*

An army that has high ground to its rear can retreat to a position of strength, leaving its opponent a hazardous pursuit uphill. Avoid marching against an army that has an easy slope and a high vantage point behind it.

**WAR TIP: Do not attack from a lower to a higher position.**

# LESSON 121

## NEVER CHASE A FAKE RETREAT

*This is the third of Sun Tzu's eight military ways.*

The enemy might stage a fake retreat to lure you into giving chase. However, if you fall for this you will be sending your troops to their deaths. An army that chases recklessly after the enemy will inevitably break into smaller groups and will be ambushed by a waiting solid force.

Use your scouts and spies to help spot a trick. Also, if you know that the enemy force consists of a certain number, but only half that number is on the field, you should be suspicious.

**WAR TIP: Do not be fooled by a fake retreat. If you give chase, your destruction awaits.**

# LESSON 122

## DO NOT ATTACK TROOPS IN A STATE OF POWER

*This is the fourth of Sun Tzu's eight military ways.*

Energy is important. If your troops are in a constant state of heightened energy they will burn out, so identify when they need rest and when they need stimulation. A troop in a phase of excitement and power should be used to attack, but never attack an enemy in the same state. Attack when your energy is on the rise and the enemy's is in decline. When the enemy is in a state of high power, defend until you can bring about change.

**WAR TIP: Observe the enemy's rising and falling levels of energy. Only attack when their energy is in decline.**

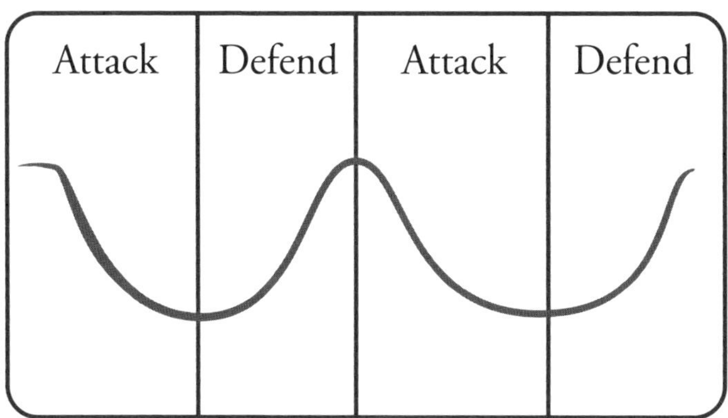

# LESSON 123

## DO NOT FALL FOR THE BAIT

*This is the fifth of Sun Tzu's eight military ways.*

Both sides will bait each other using tactics such as bait teams, fake retreats, false information and false attacks in order to glean information or inflict casualties. Cleary and Du Mu mention armies leaving poisoned food for their enemy to eat. Never react to these tricks. Always suspect a trap until you know otherwise.

**WAR TIP: Look carefully at enemy movements to tell whether they are trying to tempt you. Never succumb.**

# LESSON 124

## LET THE ENEMY RETREAT

*This is the sixth of Sun Tzu's eight military ways.*

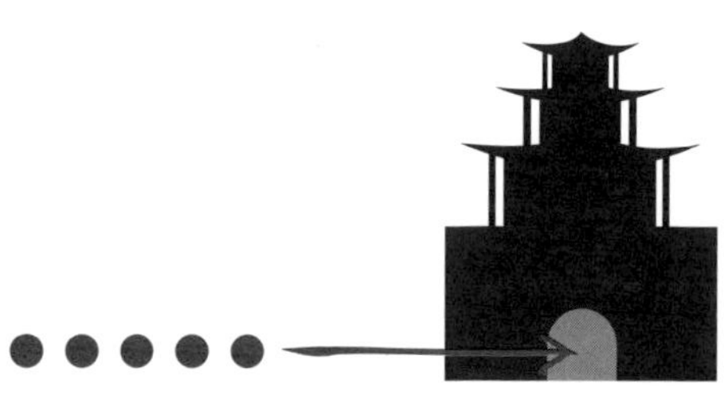

If the enemy decides to retreat, it may be because it has run out of food, or lost its will or concluded that the fight will be too hard. However, if you get in their way they will rally and fight hard because troops always want to go home and they will resent your trying to stop them. Let them go – it will take a long time and a lot of money for them to reform in the future and meanwhile you will have freedom to move about as you wish.

**WAR TIP: If the enemy is genuinely retreating to go home, just let them go. It will give you time to make more moves. Trying to stop them will only make them rally in strength.**

# LESSON 125

## GIVE THE ENEMY A WAY OUT

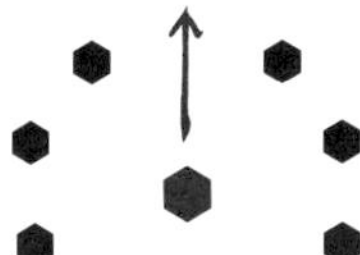

*This is the seventh of Sun Tzu's eight military ways.*

It may seem counter-intuitive to allow the enemy to have a safe retreat, but think about it: an army completely surrounded has no option but to fight to the death, which will make the fight much harder for your side, too. If you give them a way out, you can take their position or fortress with little effort. Once the enemy realizes that defeat is inevitable, they will gladly seize the opportunity to escape.

**WAR TIP: Leave an exit for the enemy when you surround them so that they can flee.**

# LESSON 126

## DO NOT PRESS A DESPERATE ENEMY

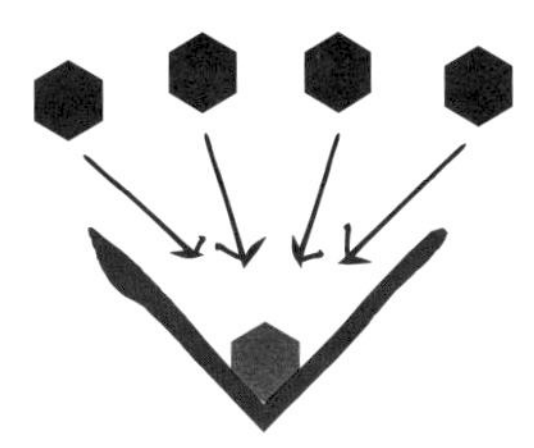

*This is the last of Sun Tzu's eight military ways.*

While it is correct to attack the enemy when it is at a low point of power, you should ease off when they have reached a state of complete desperation. The lowest point is only one step away from the highest; like animals, they will fight to the death with furious energy if they see no way out. Therefore, always attack an enemy in a state of weakness but allow them to escape defeated and broken.

**WAR TIP: Cornered soldiers who have lost all hope will fight to the death with renewed vigour, so recognize when you have won and let the remnants of the enemy army escape.**

# 九變文篇

# CHAPTER 8

# THE SCROLL OF CHANGING SITUATIONS

# THE SCROLL OF CHANGING SITUATIONS

The title of Sun Tzu's eighth chapter uses the ideograms 九, which means "nine" (but which in old Chinese can also represent "the highest number", meaning "all things"), and 変, which means "changes" or "various situations". When combined, they mean "all changing situations". The chapter is divided into three main areas:

1 The nine situations and five dangers
2 Advantages and disadvantages and harm and gain
3 The five types of bad leader

The "nine situations" referred to in the first section is slightly misleading as Sun Tzu actually lays down ten situations. However, as discussed above, the number nine can be used to represent "the highest number" in certain Chinese thought systems, so it can mean "all situations" or "many situations". The "five dangers" are not itemized but we can infer what they are.

The second section focuses on how to weigh up the advantages and disadvantages of a situation, and how to find the advantages. It also looks at harm and gain – how to not focus only on getting gain from the enemy or aiming only to do them harm. The final section examines the five types of bad leader, or more specifically the five types of personality traits that should be avoided, concluding that a leader should be balanced and not prone to a single emotion.

### SUN TZU SAYS

*In war, the general receives his commands from the sovereign, collects his army and concentrates his forces.*

*When in difficult country, do not encamp. In country where high roads intersect, join hands with your allies. Do not linger in dangerously isolated positions. In hemmed-in situations, you must resort to stratagem. In desperate*

> *position, you must fight. There are roads which must not be followed, armies which must not be attacked, towns which must be besieged, positions which must not be contested, commands of the sovereign which must not be obeyed.*
>
> *The general who thoroughly understands the advantages that accompany variation of tactics knows how to handle his troops. The general who does not understand these, may be well acquainted with the configuration of the country, yet he will not be able to turn his knowledge to practical account. So, the student of war who is unversed in the art of war of varying his plans, even though he be acquainted with the five advantages, will fail to make the best use of his men.*

# LESSON 127

## DO NOT CAMP IN A TRAP

The army must set up camp each night after it has finished its daily march. However, armies do not march blindly, and positions for camping are secured beforehand by scouts that go ahead. Avoid encamping overnight where it is easy for the enemy to trap your forces, where your forces are open to assault and the enemy can retreat with ease. Pick a defendable position.

**WAR TIP: Do not camp in a position where the enemy has easy access and easy retreat. Find somewhere that can be defended easily.**

# LESSON 128

## REGROUP AT JUNCTION POINTS

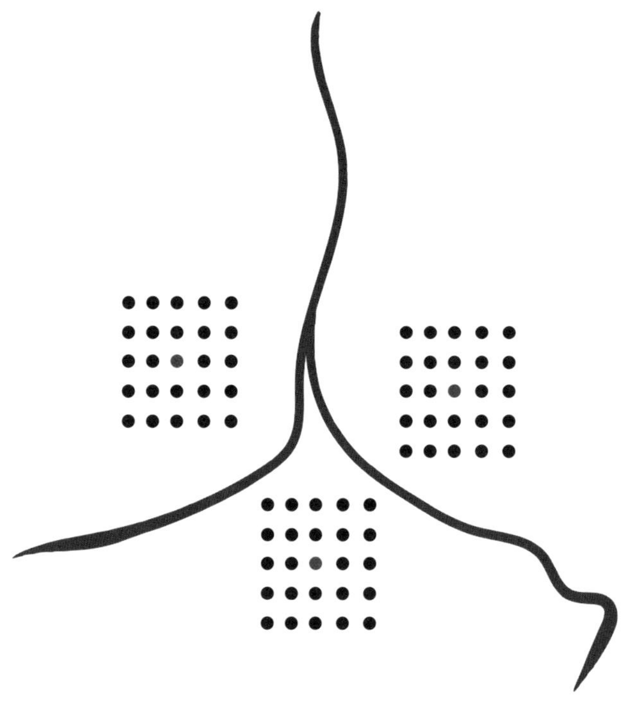

There are very few comments by ancient Chinese commentators on this point and the meaning is up for debate. The term in the original means "intersection", which could refer to a boundary between states, and therefore a place where alliances are made between the forces of different states. However, it is perhaps more likely to refer to a junction where the three divisions of the same army can reunite with ease, having travelled separately through enemy land.

Trapp interprets this point to mean that if the roads in the area are well maintained then use them to keep good communications between the various divisions of your forces.

**WAR TIP: Forces that have taken separate ways should regroup at a junction point that is easily accessible for each division.**

# LESSON 129

## CROSS DANGEROUS TERRITORY WITH HASTE

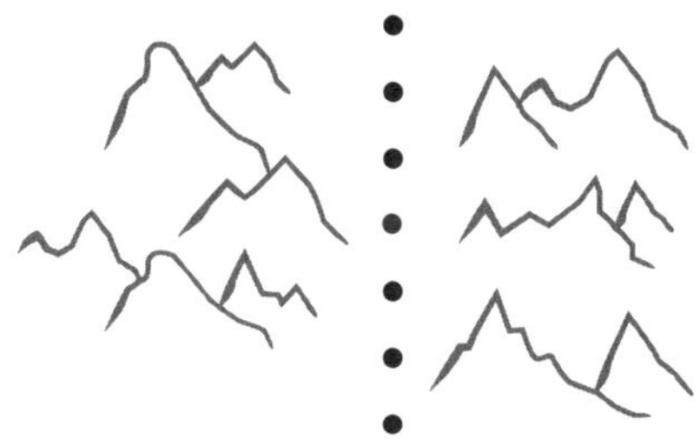

Do not linger when crossing territory in which you are vulnerable to attack. The danger could be anything from an open flank on one side or a steep drop, or a choke point or possible ambush positions. If it is obvious that your forces will be at risk then have extra scouts move around those areas on full alert and then get all forces through quickly.

**WAR TIP: If you have to cross an area where you are open to attack, move with speed to get to safer ground.**

# LESSON 130

## MAKE A PLAN BEFORE CROSSING DIFFICULT LANDSCAPE

When the land encloses your forces and any passage through it is bound to be complex, do not just march forward in hope. A good military commander will use all available information to plan how to get through such territory. Each situation is unique and factors such as ground, types of troops and visibility will all come into play.

**WAR TIP: If the land around you does not offer direct access then make careful plans to get your troops through it in safety.**

# LESSON 131

## IF NEEDS MUST THEN GO TO BATTLE

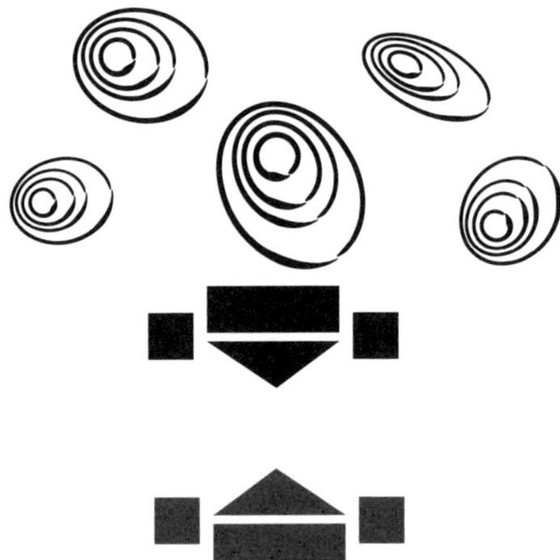

If the route ahead is difficult and will require you to break up your army and become vulnerable, then set up in formation and make war upon the enemy right where you are. Do not let your focus on making progress hand the advantage to the enemy. Sometimes staying where you are to fight is the best way to move ahead.

**WAR TIP: At times it may be better to enter into combat with the enemy instead of marching into dangerous territory. Be prepared to change your focus from movement to battle if the situation requires.**

# LESSON 132

## RECOGNIZE WHAT YOU DO NOT HAVE TO DO

There are times when it is correct not to do things that you might think should be done. It is easy to become trapped in conventional ways of thinking, but instead you should step back and look at the bigger picture. Then you may realize that the thing you thought you had to do is not actually the right thing to do. The examples in the text are:

- Roads that need not be travelled
- Armies that need not be attacked.
- Fortresses that need not be besieged

- Land that need not be captured
- Orders that need not be obeyed

The Chinese commentator Du Mu also lists examples from other parts of the text:

- Do not attack elite troops (lesson 178).
- Do not stop an army that is returning home (lesson 124).
- Do not attack "death ground" (lesson 177).

**WAR TIP: Always take a fresh look at a situation and ask yourself whether something you thought needed to be done does actually need to be done.**

# LESSON 133

## THE NINE CHANGES AND THE FIVE DANGERS

Sun Tzu warns us that a leader who does not understand the concept of the nine changes will not understand the advantages or disadvantages of each type of situation and will not be able to use the landscape to their benefit. If you understand the concept of the five dangers but do not understand the nine changes, you will not get the best out of your troops.

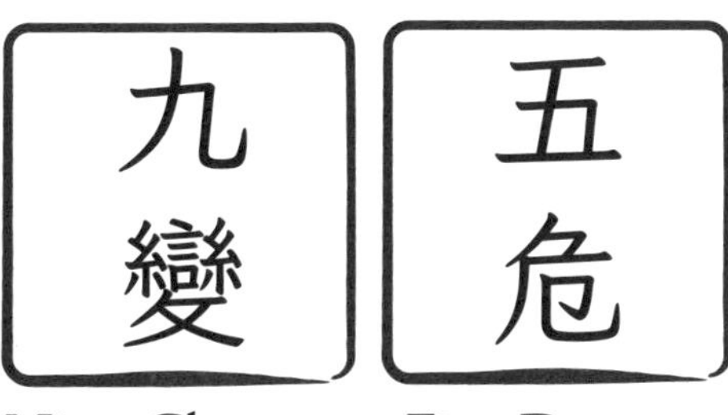


**ABOVE:** The original ideograms for "nine changes" and "five dangers".

The nine changes (where "nine" is the highest number in Chinese thought and so means "all" or "many") can be taken to comprise the following ten situations:

1. Do not make camp where you will be trapped.
2. Meet allies where roads come together.
3. Do not stay in isolated places.
4. In complex places use plans and tactics.
5. In a place where there is no way out go to battle.
6. There are some roads you should not use.
7. There are some armies you should not attack.
8. There are some fortifications and cities you should not attack.
9. There are some locations you should not fight over.
10. There are some orders from civil leaders you should ignore.

The five dangers are not made completely clear, but they are probably the five landscape situations within the nine changes (numbers 1–5 in the list above). However, the Chinese commentator Chia Lin states the five dangers to be:

1. Travelling on dangerous roads
2. Engaging an enemy who will fight to the death
3. Besieging a fortress that is well stocked with experienced men
4. Capturing ground that you cannot defend
5. Following orders that are politically motivated

Griffith's translation of the point about government orders states that you should ignore orders if you know they contain "the danger of harmful superintendence of affairs from the capital". However this point is translated, it is clear that Sun Tzu expected military leaders to question the wisdom of political authority.

**WAR TIP: Just knowing the landscape is not enough to gain benefit; knowing what to do in that landscape is the mark of a good leader. And another sign of strong leadership is not being bound by conventional wisdom or blindly following political orders.**

SUN TZU SAYS

*Hence in the wise leader's plans, considerations of advantage and of disadvantage will be blended together. If our expectation of advantage be tempered in this way, we may succeed in accomplishing the essential part of our schemes. If, on the other hand, in the midst of difficulties we are always ready to seize an advantage, we may extricate ourselves from misfortune.*

*Reduce the hostile chiefs by inflicting damage on them; and make trouble for them, and keep them constantly engaged; hold out specious allurements, and make them rush to any given point.*

*The art of war teaches us to rely not on the likelihood of the enemy's not coming, but on our own readiness to receive him; not on the chance of his not attacking, but rather on the fact that we have made our position unassailable.*

# LESSON 134

## CONSIDER BOTH GAIN AND HARM

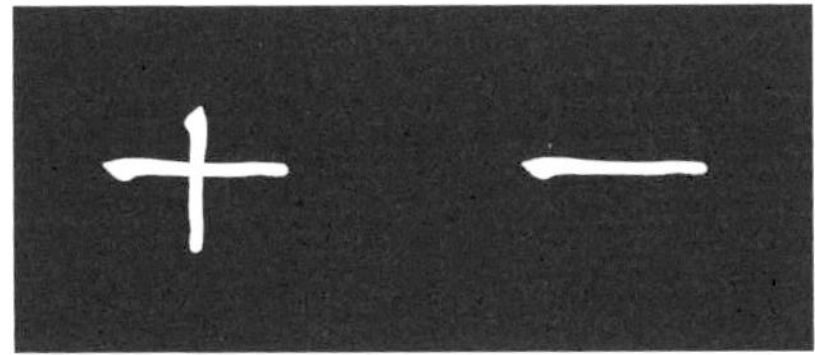

Every situation offers potential gain while also threatening harm. Therefore, a good military leader will deliberate on the opportunities and threats of the situation when preparing for an upcoming conflict.

**WAR TIP: Always weigh up the gain versus the loss in all situations and re-evaluate at different stages.**

# LESSON 135

## STAY FOCUSED ON THE TRUE GOAL

To become a better, more balanced commander, overcome your hunger for gain and your wish to harm the enemy. Remove emotions from the equation. Greed and vindictiveness can cause you to lose sight of the overall goal and lead your force into a difficult situation. Have patience in all matters and benefits will come to you.

**WAR TIP: Do not be distracted by a desire to capture the enemy's wealth or pursue their destruction. Stay focused on the one true goal of achieving a successful outcome.**

# LESSON 136

## USING HARM AND GAIN TO YOUR ADVANTAGE

There are various ways to use the concepts of harm and gain to your advantage.

### HARM

If the enemy believes itself to be in harm's way or about to be attacked it keeps them busy. A pointed sword is always a threat. Choose the best times to keep the enemy busy and do this to make them feel threatened. Exhaust their troops with task upon task to perform to ward off the perceived threat, while your forces rest or move into a favourable position.

### GAIN

As well as offering a threat, present a false weakness to the enemy. The enemy leader will see a chance to make a gain and waste time and attention trying to reach for it. Manipulate them into doing what you want them to do and then have a follow-up plan ready for when they fall into your trap.

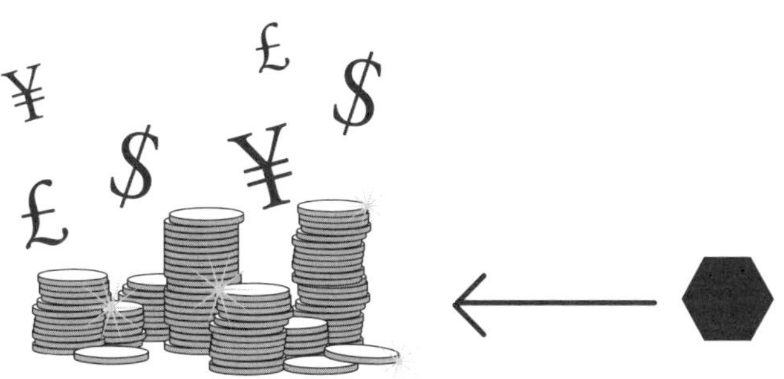


**WAR TIP: Threaten the enemy to keep them in a state of anxiety, at the same time as offering them gains to get them to move to the place you want them to go.**

# LESSON 137

## BANISH WISHFUL THINKING

Prayer is not a valid form of defence. Any part of your strategy that relies on hope should be considered a fatal weakness.

So if your plans include "let us hope that they do not attack us here," know that this is something you will need to address. It is an important part of planning to identify your weak points, but the process does not stop there – you then have to change your vulnerabilities, by moving to a different position, or work out how you are going to defend them.

**WAR TIP: Never leave anything to chance. Plan for the worst case.**

### SUN TZU SAYS

*There are five dangerous faults which may affect a general:*

1 *Recklessness, which leads to destruction*
2 *Cowardice, which leads to capture*
3 *A hasty temper, which can be provoked by insults*
4 *A delicacy of honour, which is sensitive to shame*
5 *Over-solicitude for his men, which exposes him to worry and trouble*

*These are the five besetting sins of a general, ruinous to the conduct of war. When an army is overthrown and its leader slain, the cause will surely be found among these five dangerous faults. Let them be a subject of meditation.*

# LESSON 138

## THE FIVE TYPES OF BAD LEADER

- Reckless
- Over-cautious
- Hot-headed
- Vain
- Too compassionate

Sun Tzu lists the following five characteristics that, if found to dominate a leader's personality, will bring the downfall of that leader's army:

1 RECKLESSNESS. Leaders who move forward to fight at every opportunity and see all situations as reason for a battle will get their army killed in the end.

2 OVER-CAUTIOUSNESS. Leaders who always avoid fights, look for the way out and are preoccupied by a wish to return home

safely will end up being cornered and captured, because the enemy will find a way to chase them into a trap.

3 HOT-HEADEDNESS. Leaders who are easily angered can be provoked into declaring war without a plan in place.

4 VANITY. Leaders who have a high self-esteem and a desire to preserve their noble reputation at all costs can be manipulated through character assassination and slander.

5 EXCESSIVE COMPASSION. Leaders who care too much about the welfare of their people can lose sight of their objectives. Hard as it may sound, you have to be prepared to accept a certain amount of collateral damage in a campaign. If the enemy suspects that you are trying to avoid incurring any casualties whatsoever, they may try to manipulate you by targeting civilians knowing that this will throw you into confusion.

The above five characteristics exist in all humans, but none of them should be dominant. Do not let your personality become an obvious target for the enemy.

**WAR TIP: Do not be too quick to battle or too quick to retreat. Do not anger in haste or place too much importance on your personal honour. Learn to accept that there will be casualties in war.**

行軍篇

# CHAPTER 9

# THE SCROLL OF MILITARY MOVEMENT

# THE SCROLL OF MILITARY MOVEMENT

The title of Sun Tzu's ninth chapter uses the ideograms 行, meaning "movement", and 軍, meaning "military". The chapter is one of the longest of the original text and is divided into seven main sections:

1 Mountains
2 Rivers and wet and dry lands
3 Troops within the landscape
4 Enemy movement within the landscape
5 Observing signs of enemy discontent
6 Facing the enemy
7 Bonding with your troops

The first section is short; after a brief introduction, it discusses where to position a military camp in the mountains. The second section focuses on rivers – particularly how to cross them – as well as wetlands and bogs alongside dry land. The third section looks at how troops can move within different types of landscape, while the fourth part is about how to glean information about the enemy by observing their movement within the landscape. The fifth section explains how to identify any dissatisfaction or low morale in the enemy camp. The sixth section looks at the point where the two forces meet and how to tell what the other side is thinking by observing speech and action. The final section describes the process of bonding with your own troops when on a military campaign.

### SUN TZU SAYS

*We come now to the question of encamping the army, and observing signs of the enemy. Pass quickly over mountains, and keep in the neighbourhood of valleys. Camp in high places, facing the sun. Do not climb heights in order to fight. So much for mountain warfare.*

# LESSON 139

## HOW TO MOVE IN THE MOUNTAINS

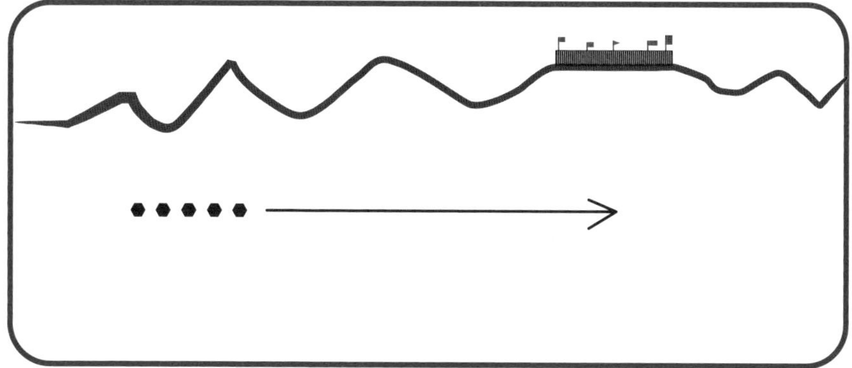

Sun Tzu gives the following teachings on traversing mountainous areas:

### STICK TO THE VALLEYS

Move along the valleys instead of trying to climb over the heights of the mountains. The army, of course, needs to be preceded by scouts to make sure the route is clear. The Chinese commentator Li Quan suggests that an advantage of following the valleys is that you stay close to water and are able to gather fodder growing at the banks to feed animals.

### KEEP TO "LIFE GROUND"

This section is problematic and more open to interpretation than others. The actual ideograms used are 視生處高, but their meaning is not altogether clear. Sawyer uses the term "tenable ground", and identifies this with the term yang, which literally means "the side of the mountain with sunlight upon it". Minford says that this is to "face the open" and the Denma Group uses "life ground". This point has been translated in multiple ways as:

- Stick to open, light places.
- Find ground that is easy to defend.
- Face the sun.
- Face south.

However, all translators and commentators agree that it is a positive location to position your forces.

### CAMP ON HIGH

Make camp higher up the mountainside and not in the lower places where you should travel.

### DO NOT FIGHT UPHILL

If you have to fight in the mountains, do not engage the enemy uphill. Always manoeuvre so that your forces come down on the enemy from above, or withdraw if that is not possible.

**WAR TIP: When in mountains use the valleys, stick to safe, open ground, camp your troops in high vantage places and never fight by moving uphill.**

### SUN TZU SAYS

*After crossing a river, you should get far away from it. When an invading force crosses a river in its onward march, do not advance to meet it in mid-stream. It will be best to let half the army get across, and then deliver your attack. If you are anxious to fight, you should not go to meet the invader near a river which he has to cross. Moor your craft higher up than the enemy, and facing the sun. Do not move upstream to meet the enemy. So much for river warfare.*

*In crossing salt-marshes, your sole concern should be to get over them quickly, without any delay. If forced to fight in a salt-marsh, you should have water and grass near you, and get your back to a clump of trees. So much for operations in salt-marshes.*

*In dry, level country, take up an easily accessible position with rising ground to your right and on your rear, so that the danger may be in front, and safety lie behind. So much for campaigning in flat country.*

*These are the four useful branches of military knowledge which enabled the Yellow Emperor to vanquish four several sovereigns.*

# LESSON 140

## CREATE SPACE AFTER CROSSING A RIVER

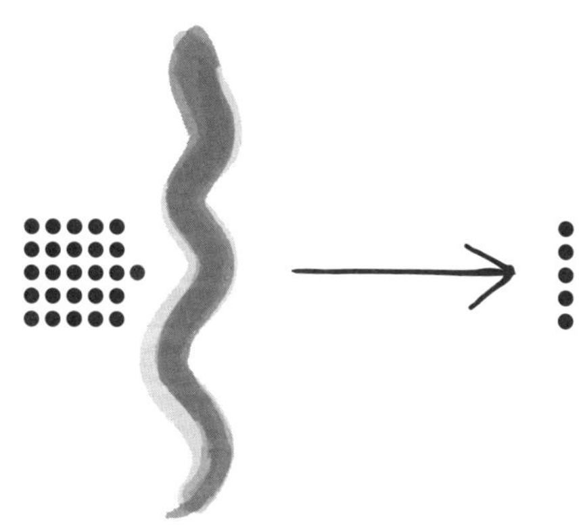

When your forward force has crossed over, it must not linger near the edge of the water. The enemy will wait for most of your troops to cross before attacking, so the forward force should immediately move further out into open land to create a defence. Otherwise, they may end up being trapped near the river. When the whole army is across they should reform in open land with space behind them.

**WAR TIP: After crossing a river, make sure your forward force leaves space for the rest of the army to form up.**

# LESSON 141

## ATTACK THE ENEMY WHILE IT IS CROSSING A RIVER

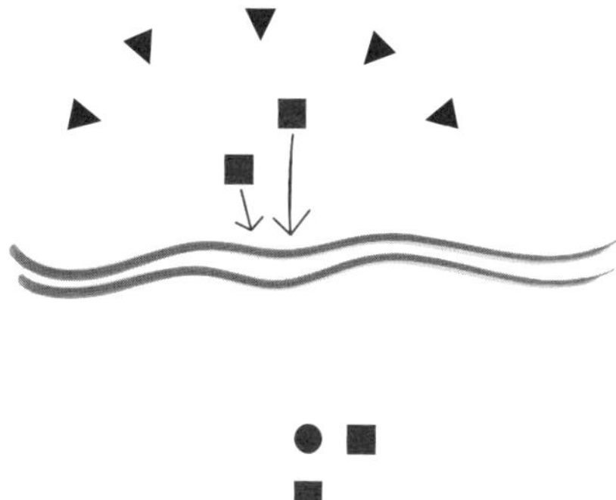

Do not rush to attack the enemy as soon as it starts to cross a river, otherwise the two armies will be on opposite sides of the river and the enemy will be able to escape. Wait for half of their force to cross over, then attack. This will force the troops who have crossed to turn back on the people crossing behind them, trapping the first half and making the second half redundant. This is the very reason why you should create space when your own troops cross.

**WAR TIP: Wait until the enemy has got half its troops across a river, then dash in and strike hard.**

# LESSON 142

## MOVE AWAY FROM A RIVER TO DO BATTLE

If you wish to engage the enemy near water, move away from the river or body of water and take up position on open ground. This will make sure that you will not be trapped in boggy areas or have your backs against the river. Take an uphill position.

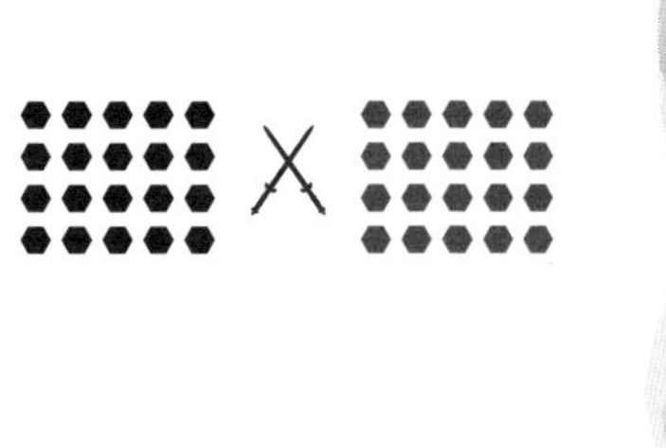

**WAR TIP: Never do open battle near a river.**

# LESSON 143

## DO NOT MOVE FROM DOWNSTREAM TO UPSTREAM

The text states that you should not go against the current, but this can be taken to mean do not be downstream. It is difficult to walk upstream against the flow and easier to move with the flow downstream. The Chinese commentator Jia Lin states that this is to stop you from being flooded or poisoned, and Du Mu says that this is to stop the enemy using the river's power to destroy any water craft you have. However, as it would be impossible to only travel downstream while on military campaign, this point is most likely concerned with the positioning of troops in relation to the enemy when battle is imminent.

**WAR TIP: Always be upstream of the enemy.**

# LESSON 144

## CROSS MARSHES WITH HASTE

Sun Tzu gives the following teachings on how to cross marshes and deal with the enemy when near them.

If you have to cross marshland, get over it as quickly as possible. Being in marshland is dangerous. While you are crossing, your forces will be an easy target.

When confronted by an enemy in marshland, face them with dense foliage and trees to the rear of your forces. In wetlands, trees and larger plants mean firmer, slightly higher ground. It is still difficult to fight on, but not as hard-going as the lowest ground, which is always the wettest and full of bogs and sludge.

To support his ideas, Sun Tzu refers to the Yellow Emperor who defeated four other emperors by understanding these different types of warfare situations.

**WAR TIP: Cross wetlands with speed and put firmer, higher ground to your rear if you have to fight there.**

### SUN TZU SAYS

*All armies prefer high ground to low and sunny places to dark. If you are careful of your men, and camp on hard ground, the army will be free from disease of every kind, and this will spell victory. When you come to a hill or a bank, occupy the sunny side, with the slope on your right rear. Thus you will at once act for the benefit of your soldiers and utilize the natural advantages of the ground.*

*When, in consequence of heavy rains up-country, a river which you wish to ford is swollen and flecked with foam, you must wait until it subsides. Country in which there are precipitous cliffs with torrents running between, deep natural hollows, confined places, tangled thickets, quagmires and crevasses, should be left with all possible speed and not approached. While we keep away from such places, we should get the enemy to approach them; while we face them, we should let the enemy have them on his rear.*

*If in the neighbourhood of your camp there should be any hilly country, ponds surrounded by aquatic grass, hollow basins filled with reeds, or woods with thick undergrowth, they must be carefully rooted out and searched; for these are places where men in ambush or insidious spies are likely to be lurking.*

# LESSON 145

## POSITION YOURSELF ON EASY GROUND

Position the army on ground that is easy to move along so that there is access between the troops and you can establish lines of movement and communication. To the rear have space and freedom, with elevated land to the rear right, which you can retreat to if necessary to give you a height advantage over the enemy.

Taigong says that rivers and wetland should be on the left, while hills should be on the right, and Mei Yaochen says that having hills to the rear right gives an army momentum when attacking. Logically, right-handed fighters are better having a rise to their right so that they can attack downward and to the left. This is because they hold their shield in their left hand and they want to advance to the left with the shield in front of them for protection. For the same reason there is a natural tendency for a troop to retreat to the right. Therefore, having a hill on this side offers protection, because it forces the enemy to attack uphill.

**WAR TIP: Get to flat, easy land and put the enemy to the front, but have a rise to the rear right to allow for retreat.**

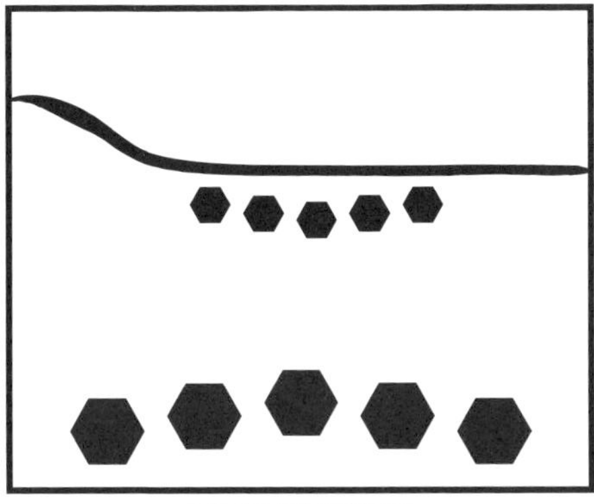

FRONT VIEW

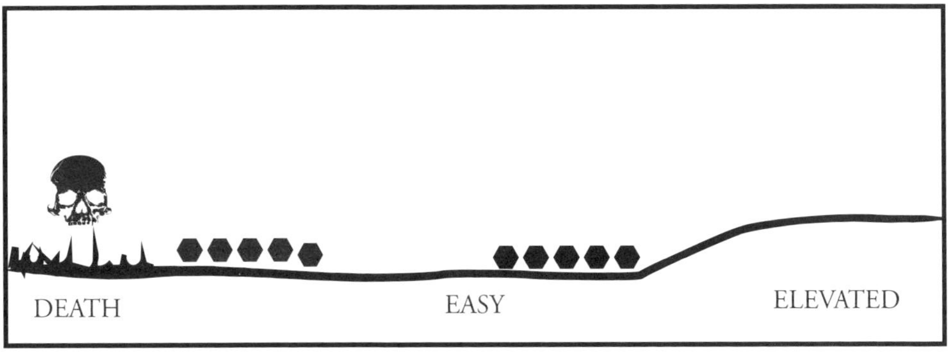

DEATH EASY ELEVATED

SIDE VIEW

# LESSON 146

## AIM FOR THE HIGH GROUND

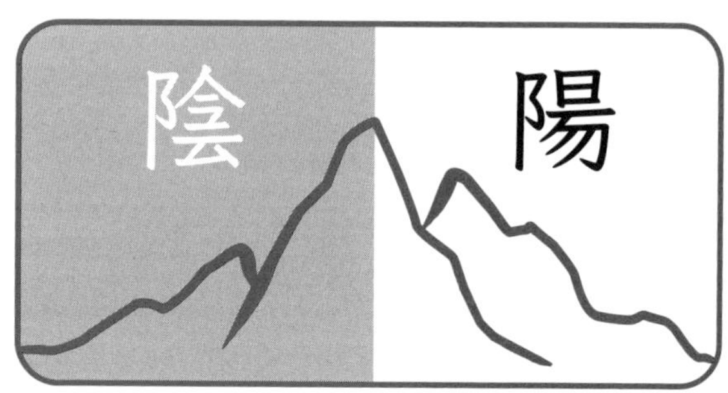


High areas are airy and have good drainage. This makes them good places for large masses of troops to camp or march, because in these conditions diseases do not take root. In contrast, infections spread easily in low, boggy areas. The terms used here are yin and yang, darkness and light, which can refer, for example, to the dark and light sides of a mountain or to low and high areas. Sun Tzu says to avoid the yin (dark/low) areas and stick to the yang (light/high) areas.

**WAR TIP: Keep troops out of dark, dank places. Position them on high ground, where it is easier to move and keep a lookout and where illness will not breed.**

# LESSON 147

## DIRECT THE ENEMY TO THE LOW GROUND

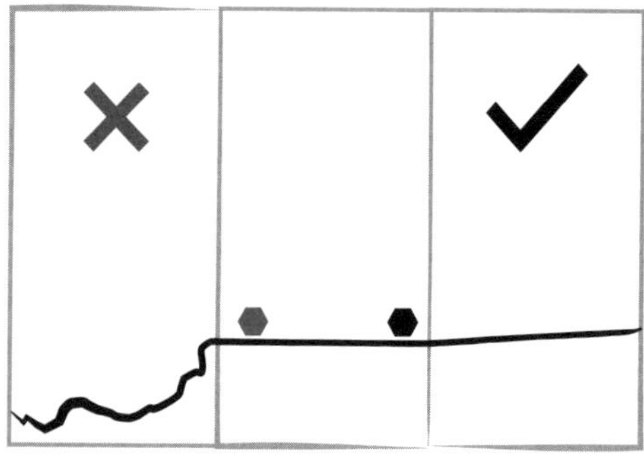

As well as keeping your own troops on the solid, light, higher yang land, you should force the enemy to occupy the boggy, shady, lower yin places, or manoeuvre the enemy so that these disadvantages are at their rear.

**WAR TIP: Use the landscape to your advantage: position your troops so that they have easy land behind them, and ensure there is difficult land behind enemy troops.**

# LESSON 148

## BEWARE OF FLASH FLOODS

Rain falls evenly across the whole area, and so the water level in rivers rises only a small amount to begin with. However, be aware that there is often a delayed effect, as rain cascades down mountains, gathering momentum. When this water surges into a river, it can cause the banks to break and anything that stands in its path will be swept away. Observe the rainfall and do not cross rivers that are in flood or that are susceptible to flash floods. Give the water time to pass.

The Denma Group interprets the word "surge" figuratively here, to mean a "surge in enemy forces" instead of rainfall.

**WAR TIP: If there has been heavy rainfall, wait before crossing a river to allow the water to pass.**

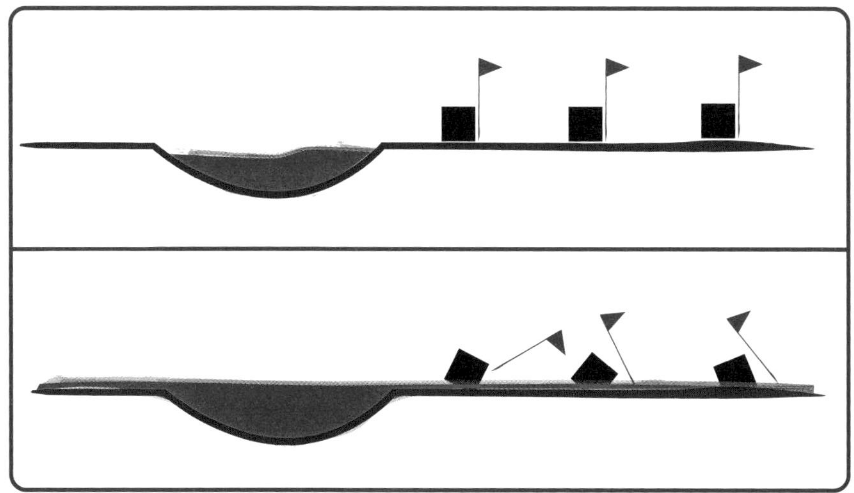

# LESSON 149

## AVOID WATERY DEATH TRAPS

Always stay away from any gorges and dangerous areas with your main force; go the long way around if you must. Sun Tzu advises to stay away from six types of land that will trap an army. The table below gives the literal, poetic translation of the ideograms for each of these death traps, alongside the geographical descriptions provided by Sawyer and the Chinese commentator Cao Cao (translated by Clements):

| IDEOGRAM | Literal translation | Sawyer's translation | Cao Cao's description |
|---|---|---|---|
| 絶澗 | Watery end | Ravines and steep torrents | Rapids in high mountains |
| 天井 | Heaven's well | Valley surrounded on three sides | Low ground surrounded by mountains |
| 天牢 | Heaven's prison | Valley surrounded on four sides | Areas at the bottom of a gorge |
| 天羅 | Heaven's net | Dense growth and woodland | Gorge where troops can be trapped |
| 天陥 | Heaven's trap | Wetlands and marsh | Sunken gorge |
| 天隙 | Heaven's cracks | Fissures and narrow passages | Road at bottom of gorge |

Avoid these areas at all costs and make sure to keep them behind the enemy if you can. Being in these areas will make it easy for the enemy to kill you.

**WAR TIP: If possible, avoid ravines, deep and surrounded valleys, overgrown areas, marshlands and narrow places.**

# LESSON 150

## SEARCH FOR AMBUSHES AND SPIES

Be wary of places where enemy ambushes and observation scouts are likely to be hiding. These include mountains with streams, hilly grass-covered areas, swamps, marshlands, forests and overgrown patches. As your forces move toward these areas, send scouts ahead to search for traps.

**WAR TIP: Always search areas where ambushes and spies may be hiding.**

### SUN TZU SAYS

*When the enemy is close at hand and remains quiet, he is relying on the natural strength of his position. When he keeps aloof and tries to provoke a battle, he is anxious for the other side to advance. If his place of encampment is easy of access, he is tendering a bait.*

*Movement amongst the trees of a forest shows that the enemy is advancing. The appearance of a number of screens in the midst of thick grass means that the enemy wants to make us suspicious. The rising of birds in their flight is the sign of an ambuscade. Startled beasts indicate that a sudden attack is coming. When there is dust rising in a high column, it is the sign of chariots advancing; when the dust is low, but spread over a wide area, it betokens the approach of infantry. When it branches out in different directions, it shows that parties have been sent to collect firewood. A few clouds of dust moving to and fro signify that the army is encamping.*

> *Humble words and increased preparations are signs that the enemy is about to advance. Violent language and driving forward as if to the attack are signs that he will retreat. When the light chariots come out first and take up a position on the wings, it is a sign that the enemy is forming for battle. Peace proposals unaccompanied by a sworn covenant indicate a plot. When there is much running about and the soldiers fall into rank, it means that the critical moment has come. When some are seen advancing and some retreating, it is a lure.*

# LESSON 151

## KNOW WHEN THE ENEMY IS STRONG

If the enemy is close by and makes no noise and is just waiting, they have the advantage of terrain, and are waiting for you to attack. If they are at a distance and try to provoke your troops into moving toward them, know that they are luring you onto difficult terrain while they hold the strong ground.

**WAR TIP: If the enemy is quiet, that means it is in a strong position. If they try to lure you to a new position, do not go because you will be at a disadvantage.**

# LESSON 152

## LOOK FOR MOVEMENT IN THE TREES

There is very little commentary on this point. You should observe the tops of smaller trees, large bushes and tall grasses, because any troops advancing through them will cause a ripple of movement. The ideograms used here are 樹, "trees", and 草, "grasses".

Although troops will not make large trees sway, it is possible that enemy activity within a forest or across a tree line will show up as dark, shadowy movement.

**WAR TIP: Look for ripples across areas of vegetation or shadows in wooded areas, which may be caused by covert enemy movement.**

# LESSON 153

## BEWARE OF FAKE ENEMY POSITIONS

When you observe shields, screens or sections of fences in a field, be aware that the enemy may be trying to trick you into thinking that they are waiting behind them. (Calthrop gives the alternative translation of broken branches and clear disturbance of the ground, but the intention is the same.) They might do this to stop you from moving into that area and so to force you to take a different route that better suits their strategic interests. Do not let the enemy dictate your movements. Have scouts check what, if anything, is behind the large objects and observe the birds (*see* next lesson).

**WAR TIP: The enemy may place defences to make it look as if their troops are in that area, but it may in fact be a ruse to stop you moving in that direction.**

# LESSON 154

## WATCH THE BIRDS AND THE BEASTS

Most birds will avoid humans, so they will fly away from an area if people approach it or keep away from the area if people are already there. Watch the landscape, if birds fly up startled in a wave across the landscape then people are on the move. If birds avoid a certain place then troops have been positioned there in ambush. However, some birds, such as pigeons, are attracted to human populations for food, so be aware of the bird types.

If animals run out of a wooded area and look like they are fleeing from danger, prepare your troops. This is a clear sign that enemy shock troops are about to emerge from this place. Because the animals run faster than the people behind them, they give you a valuable advance warning that you must not ignore. Prepare yourself for an attack.

**WAR TIP: Watch the birds and the beasts; their behaviour can give you clues to enemy activity.**

# LESSON 155

## LEARN THE LANGUAGE OF DUST CLOUDS

As troops move, particularly in the arid expanses of central China, they cannot avoid stirring up clouds of dust that give away their position. Other types of enemy activity create their own signature in the air. Sun Tzu lists four main types of dust cloud and what they tell us about the enemy.

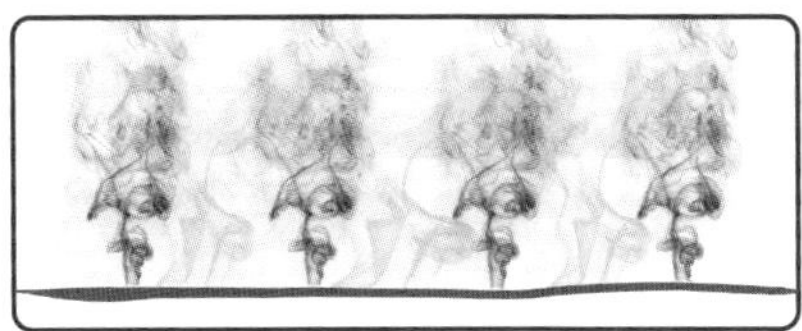

### HIGH COLUMNS

High columns of dust indicate chariots or troops on horseback – vehicles or horses travelling at speed kick dust high up in the air.

### LOW-HANGING

A lingering cloud of low-hanging dust tells you that a large body of troops is marching slowly across the ground. Troops on foot will displace dirt and dust lower than horses and vehicles travelling at speed.

### THIN SHAFTS, SAME TIME, DIFFERENT PLACES

Thin shafts of dust here and there may come from small groups of troops radiating out from a camp to collect firewood. You will see that the troops are not moving in a single direction but foraging in many different places across the landscape.

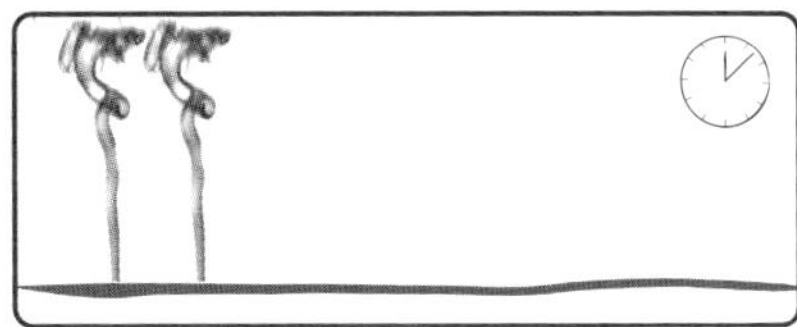

### THIN SHAFTS, DIFFERENT TIMES, SAME PLACE

Dust rising up at random times and in slightly different places but clustered around a single location may tell you that the enemy is making camp. Each phase and area of construction will throw up its own dust cloud. The clouds look similar to the ones created during firewood collection, but the big difference is that those clouds occur at the same time across a wide area, whereas clouds from camp construction occur at different times across a limited area. Therefore, watch for the location and regularity of the shafts of dust.

The Chinese commentator Mei Yaochen says that because only a small number of advance troops are involved in setting up the camp, only small amounts of dust are thrown up in the air as they work on each area in turn.

**WAR TIP: Observe different types of dust cloud and know what each one tells you about the enemy.**

# LESSON 156

## MISTRUST ENEMY WORDS

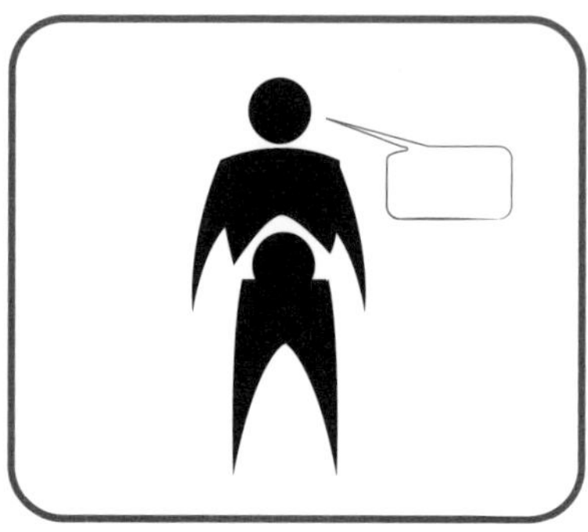

Certain types of speech may be used as a ruse in war. They often tell you the opposite of what the enemy wants you to believe.

For example, if the enemy is taking a soft, conciliatory tone in its communication with you but there is no obvious reason for them to be so amicable, check what they are doing with their troops. If they are moving in a way that indicates an advance or movement of strength, know that their friendly words are just to distract you from the attack they are preparing. In such a situation, continue the dialogue without revealing your suspicions but go on full alert.

On the other hand, if the enemy demeanour is aggressive and hostile, including threats of war and provocative actions, this may mean that they are preparing to flee. They may be trying to get you to move to a full defensive position, in which your troops are embedded in a static formation. This will give them time to escape because it takes longer to move your troops out of such a set-up. Look for signs of enemy troops readying themselves for a retreat and keep your own troops poised to attack.

**WAR TIP: Do not be fooled by enemy conduct. Aggressive behaviour may be a sign that they are about to retreat, while friendly words may precede an attack.**

# LESSON 157

## OBSERVE FLANKING VEHICLES

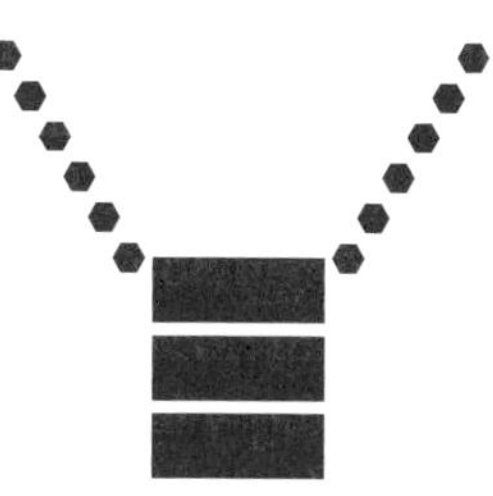

The main part of the army is made up of the infantry, which will march up the centre line. Light vehicles are often positioned on the flanks to defend the main force as it advances. Therefore, if you see enemy vehicles moving to the sides, know that the enemy commander is setting up the parameters of the battlefield and is preparing to move the main force up. You will then be able to work out the area in which the enemy is intending to operate, because they are trying to stop you moving on the outside of their flanking troops.

**WAR TIP: Use the positioning of the enemy's flanking vehicles to tell you the area in which the enemy intends to fight.**

# LESSON 158

## DO NOT FALL FOR A FALSE PEACE OFFER

A sudden offer of peace after a period of hostility should be treated with extreme suspicion. Unless the enemy backs up the offer with genuine de-escalation and a signed legal treaty, know that they are almost certainly plotting something. The Chinese commentator Chen Hao says that this kind of move by the enemy indicates that their situation has changed in some way. They may be preparing for action against you, or they may have trouble in their home territory and need to stall you. Either way, this is a trick to put you off your guard. Do not be fooled – raise your alert level.

**WAR TIP: If the enemy offers peace but does not follow through with it, know that this is a ruse to make you complacent. Prepare for action.**

# LESSON 159

## OBSERVE THE ENEMY WHEN THEY FORM UP

This section is one that translators and commentators have interpreted in a variety of ways. The different versions include:

- When they form up, they are dictating the time of battle. (Ames)
- The movement of troops and messengers means battle is to start. (Calthrop)
- Those who form up are expecting reinforcements. (Cleary)
- When they form up it is time for battle. (Clements, Giles and Trapp)
- When they rush out and form up, it means they are seizing the moment. (Denma Group)
- When the troops form up they will rendezvous with others. (Griffith)
- When the soldiers are forming up they are expecting something. (Minford)
- Troops that race off and form up have a predetermined schedule. (Sawyer)

As can be seen the various translations do differ but stick to a similar theme. They break down into two main groups – the enemy forming up means either that battle will start shortly or that the enemy is expecting to join up with other forces and attack.

**WAR TIP: When the enemy starts to form up, prepare for battle and send scouts to check whether enemy reinforcements are on their way.**

# LESSON 160

## HALF THE FORCE, TWICE THE DANGER

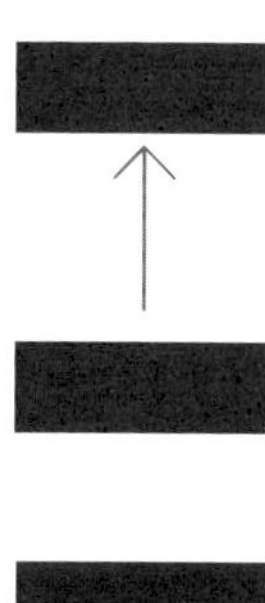

When the enemy divides its force in half and the rear retreats, they are offering you bait. They want you to attack the weakened force at the front, but they will have a plan in place. They might have hidden extra troops nearby, or they might be trying to lead you into a trap in the landscape or they might be preparing to outflank you. Do not attack a seemingly abandoned troop – the enemy is trying to lure you into danger.

**WAR TIP: If the enemy leaves half its force behind for you to attack, know that this a trap. Do not take the bait.**

### SUN TZU SAYS

*When the soldiers stand leaning on their spears, they are faint from want of food. If those who are sent to draw water begin by drinking themselves, the army is suffering from thirst. If the enemy sees an advantage to be gained and makes no effort to secure it, the soldiers are exhausted.*

*If birds gather on any spot, it is unoccupied. Clamour by night betokens nervousness. If there is disturbance in the camp, the general's authority is weak. If the banners and flags are shifted about, sedition is afoot. If the officers are angry, it means that the men are weary.*

*When an army feeds its horses with grain and kills its cattle for food, and when the men do not hang their cooking-pots over the camp-fires, showing that they will not return to their tents, you may know that they are determined to fight to the death.*

*The sight of men whispering together in small knots or speaking in subdued tones points to disaffection amongst the rank and file. Too frequent rewards signify that the enemy is at the end of his resources; too many punishments betray a condition of dire distress.*

# LESSON 161

## IDENTIFY WHEN THE ENEMY IS IN A STATE OF EXHAUSTION

⬢ Starvation ⬢ Thirst ⬢ Exhaustion

Observe the enemy for tell-tale signs of physical weakness:

- Troops who need to lean on their weapons for support are undernourished.
- Troops sent to collect water who take a drink immediately rather than waiting until they are back at camp are suffering from thirst.
- An enemy that cannot be bothered to take advantage of an obvious benefit is exhausted.

**WAR TIP: Use scouts and spies to observe the enemy for signs of starvation, thirst and exhaustion.**

# LESSON 162

## IF BIRDS ARE PRESENT THE ENEMY IS ABSENT

As we saw in lesson 154, most birds will keep clear of humans in the wilds. Therefore, if a fortification, camp or position has birds coming and going from it, then no one is actually there. You will know that this is a false position that has been put there to deter you from moving in that direction.

**WAR TIP: If birds and wildlife are nesting in an enemy position without any sign of disturbance, know that there are no humans there.**

# LESSON 163

## LOOK FOR SIGNS OF FEAR AND DISORDER IN THE ENEMY

Even from a distance, it is possible to observe signs of anxiety or disarray within the enemy ranks. Sun Tzu gives the following examples:

- Enemy troops shouting words of encouragement or reassurance to each other at night are afraid. Troops who have no fear do not need to do this.
- Troops who are milling about in the wrong place and ignoring protocols have no respect for their leaders. Otherwise they would jump to attention and move with haste and purpose.
- Chaotic use of flags tells you that the enemy has lost control of its systems of communication and identification. A disciplined army will have flags that move at the correct time, in unison and in set positions. Observe the enemy's normal use of flags. If this breaks down, you will know that the enemy force is in disarray.
- Displays of impatience, such as harsh orders and angry outbursts, by officers toward the troops indicate that there is tiredness within the enemy ranks. Such signs of aggravated behaviour show that the enemy needs rest.

**WAR TIP: Carefully observe the way enemy troops and officers treat each other for signs of fear, disorder and fatigue. Anxious shouts of reassurance, poor discipline, chaotic use of flags and short-tempered behaviour are all indications that something is not right.**

# LESSON 164

## RECOGNIZE PREPARATIONS FOR A FINAL ASSAULT

If the enemy is preparing to launch a final, all-or-nothing assault their routine will change in certain ways. Look for the following signs:

- Feeding patterns will change. Translations on this differ – some versions say that the enemy will butcher the horses for meat to give the troops strength; others say that they will feed the horses more than usual to give the horses strength.
- They do not tend to their cooking pots. Mealtimes for an army are a massive event, and follow a clearly identifiable routine. If the enemy breaks with what it has done before and does not wash and put away cooking utensils after use, then you can tell that this is a final meal before the climactic assault. Some generals even smash the pots to show that there is no going back.
- Troops do not return to their quarters as normal after eating. Particularly if accompanied by the other signs discussed above. This tells you that they are about to form up and mount a last-ditch attack.

**WAR TIP: If the enemy gives the troops the last of the food, and breaks or discards pots and pans, it can mean they intend to make a final, do-or-die assault.**

SUN TZU SAYS

*To begin by bluster, but afterwards to take fright at the enemy's numbers, shows a supreme lack of intelligence. When envoys are sent with compliments in their mouths, it is a sign that the enemy wishes for a truce. If the enemy's troops march up angrily and remain facing ours for a long time without either joining battle or taking themselves off again, the situation is one that demands great vigilance and circumspection.*

*If our troops are no more in number than the enemy, that is amply sufficient; it only means that no direct attack can be made. What we can do is simply to concentrate all our available strength, keep a close watch on the enemy, and obtain reinforcements. He who exercises no forethought but makes light of his opponents is sure to be captured by them.*

# LESSON 165

## RECOGNIZE DISCORD AMONG THE ENEMY

Use spies and scouts to observe the enemy at close hand. If they report back with any of the following signs, you will have reason to suspect that all is not well within the enemy ranks:

- Troops gathering in small groups and talking in hushed whispers may be planning either to revolt or to desert.
- Leaders who hand out rewards and honours too freely are trying to get dissatisfied troops back on side or inspire exhausted troops to perform.
- Frequent, excessive punishments indicate that the leadership has lost its natural authority over the troops. No longer able to count on the troops' loyalty, the leaders have to resort to control by fear. However, such harshness will only work for so long. At a certain point troops will turn on their masters, who will then be the ones to have fear of retribution for their brutality.

Also be aware that if the enemy sends envoys to offer peace despite not having been defeated in battle, this may be a false offer designed to buy time to sort out internal strife (*see* lesson 158).

**WAR TIP: Observe the enemy closely. If the troops conspire together, if rewards are given out too easily or if punishment is too harsh, your foe is breaking up from within.**

# LESSON 166

## BEWARE OF AN ENEMY THAT ADVANCES BUT DOES NOT ENGAGE

Be particularly suspicious of an enemy force that takes up an aggressive formation, appears to be in high spirits and advances toward your position with obvious intent to attack, but does not actually engage. Although there is nothing extra on this lesson from the commentators, one can assume that this is an enemy tactic to read your reactions and adjust their plans accordingly.

**WAR TIP: If the enemy looks like it wants to fight but pulls away at the last minute, this is a trap. Do not fall into it.**

# LESSON 167

## STRENGTH VERSUS TACTICS

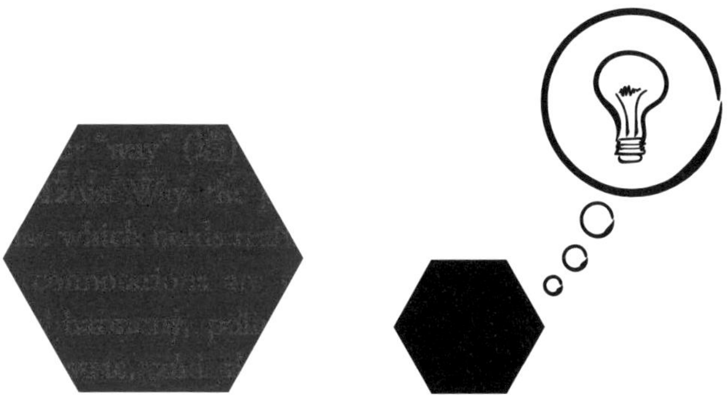

A smaller force can defeat a larger one by using skills of observation, prediction and manipulation to set the terms of the battle. Indeed, this is the essence of tactical warfare. However, there comes a point where the mismatch in numbers between two sides is too great and the larger force will always win no matter how much ingenuity the leader of the underdogs brings to the fight. Then, as some versions observe, all you can do if you are massively outnumbered is consolidate your forces and wait for reinforcements.

Having large numbers means that you can aggressively attack with little thought to complex tactics because you know you will win the day. However, if you ignore tactics completely and rely on force alone, at some point you will lose. It becomes a game of odds that you simply cannot always win.

**WAR TIP: Even the shrewdest tactics will fail if you are massively outnumbered. However, if your side is more powerful, do not rely solely on strength of numbers.**

## SUN TZU SAYS

*If soldiers are punished before they have grown attached to you, they will not prove submissive; and, unless submissive, they will be practically useless. If, when the soldiers have become attached to you, punishments are not enforced, they will still be useless. Therefore soldiers must be treated in the first instance with humanity, but kept under control by means of iron discipline. This is a certain road to victory.*

*If in training soldiers' commands are habitually enforced, the army will be well-disciplined; if not, its discipline will be bad. If a general shows confidence in his men but always insists on his orders being obeyed, the gain will be mutual.*

# LESSON 168

## GAIN THE LOYALTY OF YOUR TROOPS

Sun Tzu recognizes the importance of a positive relationship between leader and followers and gives the following ways to build and maintain these bonds:

- Never punish before bonds have been established. When you first take command, communicate your expectations through a clear set of rules. However, give your troops time to get used to your regime – do not immediately hand out punishments. You do not want to start off with a negatively aggressive approach. Be strong and confident and create a happy, positive climate.
- Form bonds through shared experience. Work and live close to your troops, share in their activities, form goals together and encourage each other, while maintaining a clear line between leader and follower.
- Place importance on loyalty above military prowess or anything else. While other qualities have their place, nothing is as important as loyalty to a military leader.

- Start to enforce your rules more strictly once bonds have been formed and loyalty has been established. Now that they have bought into your system, the troops will feel shame and dishonour if they do not fulfil their duties and will accept the resulting punishment that comes their way.
- Always treat your troops with respect. Even when handing out the most severe punishments and reprimands, be calm, civil and polite.
- Create a framework of military protocol. Make sure that the troops have set routines and systems to structure their days and keep them busy. Living in a military style binds the troops together and establishes a collective mindset.
- Be consistent. Apply your systems of punishment and reward equally to everyone. It is important that your troops know exactly what will please you and what will anger you, and that each person has a clear idea of where they fit in your structure. Save your unpredictability for the enemy.
- Foster mutual trust. If your actions inspire the trust of your troops, then you will be able to trust them to give their all for you.

**WAR TIP: Earn the loyalty of your troops by treating them with fairness, consistency and respect. Establish clear systems and routines so that every individual knows what is expected of them.**

# 地形篇

# CHAPTER 10

# THE SCROLL OF THE LANDSCAPE

# THE SCROLL OF THE LANDSCAPE

The title of Sun Tzu's tenth chapter uses the ideograms 地, meaning "earth" or "ground", and 形, meaning "shapes" or "forms". The chapter is divided into four main areas:

1 The six types of battlefield landscape
2 The six types of poorly commanded army
3 A military review for a leader
4 Rules and advice for "golden generals"

The first section itemizes the six types of terrain that a military force may find itself on and explains what to do in each of those situations. The second section outlines the six ways in which a leader can lose command and shows how to avoid this happening. The third section consists of a short review of previous teachings but with the addition of a lesson on when to disobey civil orders. The final section is a set of rules and advice for the highest level military leaders.

## SUN TZU SAYS

*We may distinguish six kinds of terrain, to wit:*

*1 Accessible ground*
*2 Entangling ground*
*3 Temporizing ground*
*4 Narrow passes*
*5 Precipitous heights*
*6 Positions at a great distance from the enemy*

*Ground which can be freely traversed by both sides is called accessible. With regard to ground of this nature, be before the enemy in occupying the raised and sunny spots, and carefully guard your line of supplies. Then you will be able to fight with advantage.*

*Ground which can be abandoned but is hard to re-occupy is called entangling. From a position of this sort, if the enemy is unprepared, you may sally forth and defeat him. But if the enemy is prepared for your coming, and you fail to defeat him, then, return being impossible, disaster will ensue.*

*When the position is such that neither side will gain by making the first move, it is called temporizing ground. In a position of this sort, even though the enemy should offer us an attractive bait, it will be advisable not to stir forth, but rather to retreat, thus enticing the enemy in his turn; then, when part of his army has come out, we may deliver our attack with advantage.*

*With regard to narrow passes, if you can occupy them first, let them be strongly garrisoned and await the advent of the enemy. Should the army forestall you in occupying a pass, do not go after him if the pass is fully garrisoned, but only if it is weakly garrisoned.*

*With regard to precipitous heights, if you are beforehand with your adversary, you should occupy the raised and sunny spots, and there wait for him to come up. If the enemy has occupied them before you, do not follow him, but retreat and try to entice him away.*

*If you are situated at a great distance from the enemy, and the strength of the two armies is equal, it is not easy to provoke a battle, and fighting will be to your disadvantage.*

*These six are the principles connected with Earth. The general who has attained a responsible post must be careful to study them.*

# LESSON 169

## THE SIX TYPES OF BATTLEFIELD LANDSCAPE

In this lesson we will look at the six categories of battlefield terrain. What are their characteristics and what should you do in each situation?

### 1 ACCESSIBLE TERRAIN

"Accessible terrain" (有通者) is land on which both armies can move with no difficulty. Supply lines and escape routes are both available.

In this situation you should move to higher and open ground (yang) to give your side an advantage.

### 2 NO-RETREAT TERRAIN

The problem with "no-retreat terrain" (有挂者) is that you cannot easily leave it the same way that you entered it, especially if you are under pressure from the enemy. Scrambling down a rocky slope in your own time may be easy enough, but climbing back up with the enemy on your tail is a different proposition. This applies to all situations and configurations of this type.

**ABOVE:** The army on the right can easily enter the battlefield, but they will find it hard to get out under pressure.

Doing battle on no-retreat terrain is feasible if you are certain that your force will win, because in that case you will not need to go back the way you came. However, if you are in any doubt, then do not engage the enemy here – your troops are likely to become trapped if they have to retreat. Check the battlefield and if your escape route is restricted in any way think hard before attacking.

## 3 STANDOFF TERRAIN

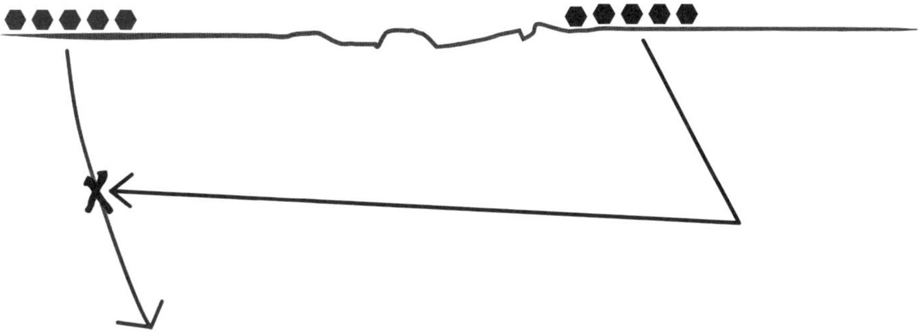

A battle area that is difficult for both armies to approach is known as "standoff terrain" (有支者).

In this situation there are various options. You could leave the area and reform elsewhere, starting afresh. Alternatively, you could lure the enemy away from its position and then strike them as they are in a phase of movement. This is the tactic of the black troops in the diagram above. The black troops are making as if to leave, which tempts the red troops to pursue them. However, when half of the red army is on the move, the black troops turn around and strike their centre.

Another option is to attack while the enemy is still forming up and before it has had a chance to take full advantage of the landscape.

## 4 SURROUNDED TERRAIN

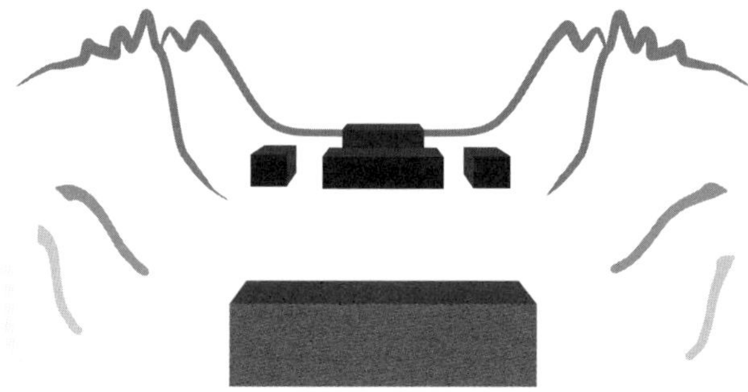

"Surrounded terrain" (有隘者) is an area that has obstacles around it, such as mountains, rivers and forests.

If you arrive on this type of terrain before the enemy, take up position ready for their advance. If the enemy is already there and in full formation, then do not enter. However, if the enemy is there but not yet in formation you can move forward.

## 5 STEEP AND DANGEROUS AREAS

"Steep and dangerous areas" (有險者) are mountain tops, tops of ravines and generally difficult high places.

When in rocky mountain heights and steep places, find the most open high place (yang). This is where your forces will be safest and it will give you a platform from which you can launch a downhill attack. If the enemy has taken the higher or more open ground, do not engage them. Leave and find a more advantageous position.

## 6 OPEN TERRAIN

"Open terrain" (有遠者) has no obstructions in any direction.

In this situation an enemy can easily chase you down if you retreat, because there is no hiding place. Therefore, make sure that you actually have enough strength to win the battle. Furthermore, when on vast, open land it is incorrect to make the first move; stay in formation and await the enemy attack.

Sun Tzu says that these six situations are all-encompassing and that any military commander who is worth anything studies them in great detail.

**WAR TIP: Accessible land is the same for both sides. No-retreat land should be entered with great caution. In a standoff area lure the enemy into movement and then strike. Only enter an area surrounded on all sides if the enemy is not already there. On great mountain tops take the highest and most open position. In vast, open, flat land only engage the enemy if you can win, because if you flee they will follow you and destroy you.**

## SUN TZU SAYS

*Now an army is exposed to six several calamities, not arising from natural causes, but from faults for which the general is responsible. These are:*

1 *Flight*
2 *Insubordination*
3 *Collapse*
4 *Ruin*
5 *Disorganization*
6 *Rout*

*Other conditions being equal, if one force is hurled against another ten times its size, the result will be the flight of the former.*

*When the common soldiers are too strong and their officers too weak, the result is insubordination.*

*When the officers are too strong and the common soldiers too weak, the result is collapse.*

*When the higher officers are angry and insubordinate, and on meeting the enemy give battle on their own account from a feeling of resentment, before the commander-in-chief can tell whether or not he is in a position to fight, the result is ruin.*

*When the general is weak and without authority; when his orders are not clear and distinct; when there are no fixed duties assigned to officers and men, and the ranks are formed in a slovenly, haphazard manner, the result is utter disorganization.*

*When a general, unable to estimate the enemy's strength, allows an inferior force to engage a larger one, or hurls a weak detachment against a powerful one, and neglects to place picked soldiers in the front rank, the result must be rout.*

*These are six ways of courting defeat, which must be carefully noted by the general who has attained a responsible post.*

# LESSON 170

## THE SIX TYPES OF POOR LEADERSHIP

The following are six types of bad leadership that can lead to the failure of an army. These have nothing to do with the terrain (Earth) or the weather (Heaven); they are purely down to incompetence.

### 1 RASHNESS

Do not rush into battle with a much more powerful enemy. Even if your army is evenly matched in technology, training and ability with that of the enemy, if the enemy army drastically outnumbers yours – say, by ten to one – your forces will flee no matter what you say or do.

### 2 PROMOTING WEAK OFFICERS

Choose officers based on merit, because if the troops are strong but the officers are weak and unsuited to leadership, discipline will be poor and the troops will lack direction and determination. The army will be lax.

### 3 POOR RECRUITMENT AND TRAINING

Recruit and train your troops thoroughly. Even if the officers are strong, well disciplined and correct, if the troops are not good enough or are unprepared, then the army will collapse from the bottom up.

### 4 TOLERATING ILL-DISCIPLINED OFFICERS

Never allow high-ranking officers in charge of their own sections of troops to push on independently. If officers ignore the ways and orders of the military leader, the leadership structure will crumble and the force will be in despair and confusion and will collapse.

### 5 AIMLESSNESS

Make sure that everyone understands the overriding goal of the army and their own role within it. Set clear objectives, assign useful tasks to all people, and keep the forces busy with correct procedure. Troops who do not know what they are supposed to be doing become restless and chaos is inevitable.

### 6 POOR DECISION MAKING ON THE BATTLEFIELD

Correct placement is paramount; the vanguard should have the most elite troops of the combined force so that they form a hard wedge to defeat the enemy. If the overall military leader makes all the incorrect decisions, does not know the enemy plans, attacks superior forces and does not deploy the correct troops to the correct places, then undoubtedly the army will flee at some point and the leader will not be able to maintain control.

These are the six ways in which bad leadership can destroy an army. A good military leader must understand all of them.

**WAR TIP: Never fight against a force that is too big no matter how good your troops are. Appoint strong officers. Make sure the troops are well trained. Do not let your officers act independently. Give everyone a clear role. Make sure the person in overall command – whether that be you or someone else – is up to the task.**

SUN TZU SAYS

*The natural formation of the country is the soldier's best ally; but a power of estimating the adversary, of controlling the forces of victory, and of shrewdly calculating difficulties, dangers and distances, constitutes the test of a great general. He who knows these things, and in fighting puts his knowledge into practice, will win his battles. He who knows them not, nor practises them, will surely be defeated.*

*If fighting is sure to result in victory, then you must fight, even though the ruler forbid it; if fighting will not result in victory, then you must not fight even at the ruler's bidding. The general who advances without coveting fame and retreats without fearing disgrace, whose only thought is to protect his country and do good service for his sovereign, is the jewel of the kingdom.*

# LESSON 171

## WORK WITH THE TERRAIN NOT AGAINST IT

Having explored the subject of poor leadership, Sun Tzu returns to the terrain and makes it clear how crucial it is to understand this aspect of warfare if you want to be a great leader:

- Know that terrain is the foundation of victory for an army.
- Understand all forms of terrain and know how to take advantage of them.
- Understand extreme terrain such as deep rocky areas and steep places.
- Analyse the enemy intent and situation.

**WAR TIP: Treat the terrain as your ally, but know that it can also be an enemy.**

# LESSON 172

## KNOW WHEN TO MOVE AGAINST ORDERS

To disobey an order seems like the last thing that would be promoted within the *Art of War*. However, Sun Tzu teaches that if victory is certain, yet you have been ordered not to fight, you should ignore the order. Similarly, if you have been ordered to attack, yet it is clear to you that this will bring about defeat, you should not attack.

This is a difficult lesson and should be followed only by those leaders who have the deepest understanding, the so-called "golden generals". It is wrong for a leader to disobey such an order without taking account of the complex politics behind a decision. Maybe there is a subtle reason for a retreat or an advance that on the surface seems like the wrong thing to do.

It is clear that Sun Tzu is talking about a master strategist, almost "god-like" in understanding, who has seen all avenues of war, been to the ends of all topics, including the political repercussions, and still knows the order is a mistake.

If this sounds like you, go ahead and disobey the order. But you had better not get it wrong.

**WAR TIP: Only the greatest leaders should disobey an order, and only when they are certain that to do so will bring victory or avert defeat.**

# LESSON 173

## ADVANCE AND RETREAT FOR THE CORRECT REASONS

Never advance just to gain fame or retreat to avoid personal danger or reprimand. A wise leader advances or retreats only when the situation dictates and not for any political or self-serving reason. The key considerations are always to protect the people and protect the state. Sun Tzu says that a leader whose only focus is practicality in advance and retreat is a national treasure.

**WAR TIP: Only ever advance or retreat for practical reasons. Never allow other factors such as personal advancement or political concerns to cloud your judgement.**

## SUN TZU SAYS

*Regard your soldiers as your children, and they will follow you into the deepest valleys; look upon them as your own beloved sons, and they will stand by you even unto death. If, however, you are indulgent, but unable to make your authority felt; kind-hearted, but unable to enforce your commands; and incapable, moreover, of quelling disorder: then your soldiers must be likened to spoilt children; they are useless for any practical purpose.*

*If we know that our own men are in a condition to attack, but are unaware that the enemy is not open to attack, we have gone only halfway toward victory. If we know that the enemy is open to attack, but are unaware that our own men are not in a condition to attack, we have gone only halfway toward victory. If we know that the enemy is open to attack, and also know that our men are in a condition to attack, but are unaware that the nature of the ground makes fighting impracticable, we have still gone only halfway toward victory.*

*Hence the experienced soldier, once in motion, is never bewildered; once he has broken camp, he is never at a loss. Hence the saying: If you know the enemy and know yourself, your victory will not stand in doubt; if you know Heaven and know Earth, you may make your victory complete.*

# LESSON 174

## TREAT YOUR TROOPS AS IF THEY WERE YOUR CHILDREN

This teaching does not mean that you should treat your troops like children, but that you should think of them as if they were your own offspring. Place pride in them, but discipline them in the correct way. Give them enough attention to show that you care about them, but not so much that you undermine your authority.

If the troops feel that you have their best interests at heart and that you would deeply mourn their deaths, they will follow you to hell and back. However, if you treat them too favourably they will become disobedient. You can show you respect your troops while still maintaining your distance.

**WAR TIP: Show troops the same respect you would show to a cherished family member to gain their trust and obedience, but never let them become unruly.**

# LESSON 175

## DO NOT ACT ON HALF AN UNDERSTANDING

Before any form of action, ask yourself: do I know all the facts? If not, you have only half an understanding. Here "half" should not be taken literally, it just means "incomplete". Knowing 90 percent of what you need to know is still only half an understanding. Sun Tzu gives three important questions you need to ask yourself:

- Can the enemy be attacked? The allied troops may be ready to attack the enemy, but what state is the enemy in?
- Are the allied troops ready to attack? The enemy may be vulnerable, but the allied troops need to be able to exploit this situation.
- Does the terrain allow you to attack? Even if the enemy is vulnerable and your troops are ready, if the terrain does not favour the attack it may be better to withdraw.

If you know all aspects then there will never be surprises and all blind spots will be illuminated. While it may be impossible to know everything, the point here is to be aware of what you do and do not know so that you are never taken off-guard.

**WAR TIP: Never move on insufficient information. In warfare surprises are rarely pleasant ones.**

# LESSON 176

## KNOW YOURSELF AND KNOW THE ENEMY

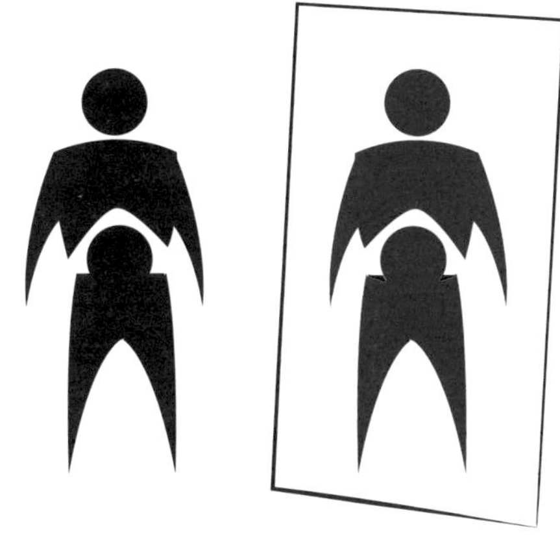

"Know yourself and know the enemy" is one of the most famous sayings from Sun Tzu, but it is more than just a slogan. It can be seen as a practical application of the previous lesson about fully understanding the situations of both sides. It means to have mirror information on both yourself and the enemy. Examples are as follows:

- What is the terrain like for each side?
- What is the morale of each side?
- What advantages does each side have?
- What disadvantages does each side have?
- What should each side do next?

The questions to consider will vary according to the situation, but the point is that you should always have two columns on your checklist: one for your side and one for the enemy.

The Chinese commentator Yuen has an alternative reading of this teaching. He says that it can also mean that you should cultivate your own mental harmony while destroying the mind of the enemy.

**WAR TIP: Make a checklist of key questions, answer them from your point of view and then answer them from the enemy point of view.**

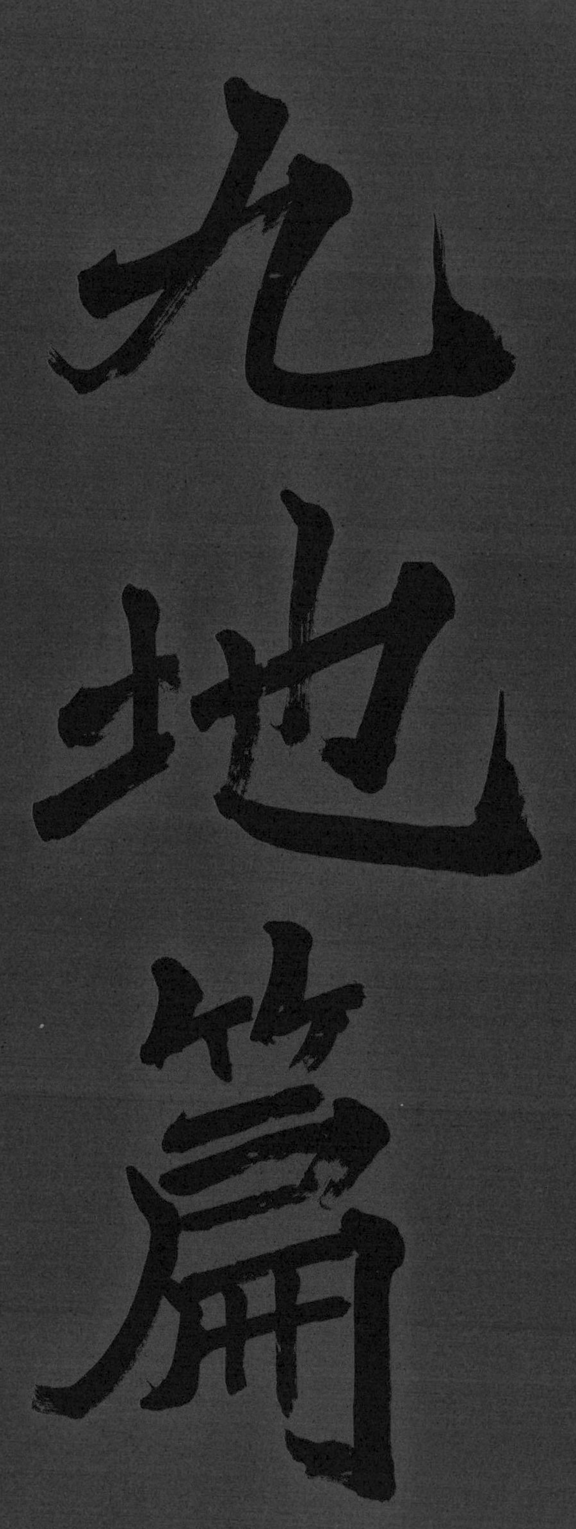
九地篇

# CHAPTER 11

# THE SCROLL OF THE NINE TERRAINS

# THE SCROLL OF THE NINE TERRAINS

The title of Sun Tzu's eleventh chapter uses the ideograms 九, meaning "nine", and 地, meaning "earth" or in this case "terrain". It is the longest chapter and contains teachings on a variety of subjects. The core theme is the nine types of landscape situation, but it soon deviates into all kinds of other subjects, which has led some commentators to believe that parts of the chapter have been moved from elsewhere in the book. The chapter can be divided into six main areas:

1 The nine types of landscape situation
2 Advice for leaders in the field
3 Emotions of the troops
4 Outlook and behaviour of the leader
5 Return to the nine landscape situations
6 Further advice for leaders in the field

The first section itemizes the nine types of situation within the landscape that an army may find itself in. This section has been rearranged from the original so that each situation is dealt with fully before moving on to the next. The second section gives advice for leaders in the field, such as how to divide the enemy or create disorder and how to move through enemy territory. The third section deals with the emotional and mental state of the troops and how to avoid them becoming exhausted, but it also contains advice on deciding when to fight to the death. The fourth section deals with how leaders should conduct themselves, including how they should behave toward their troops. The fifth section is a baffling and incomplete return to the nine landscape situations. It contains much of the same material as the first section, but in a less well-structured form, so it is possible that the text has become corrupted here. The final section offers a mixed selection of advice for leaders confronting the enemy. There are hints and tips for many different situations.

Although this chapter seems disorganized in places, it holds some of the core concepts of Sun Tzu.

## SUN TZU SAYS

*The art of war recognizes nine varieties of ground:*

1. *Dispersive ground*
2. *Facile ground*
3. *Contentious ground*
4. *Open ground*
5. *Ground of intersecting highways*
6. *Serious ground*
7. *Difficult ground*
8. *Hemmed-in ground*
9. *Desperate ground*

*When a chieftain is fighting in his own territory, it is dispersive ground. When he has penetrated into hostile territory, but to no great distance, it is facile ground. Ground the possession of which imports great advantage to either side, is contentious ground. Ground on which each side has liberty of movement is open ground. Ground which forms the key to three contiguous states, so that he who occupies it first has most of the empire at his command, is a ground of intersecting highways. When an army has penetrated into the heart of a hostile country, leaving a number of fortified cities in its rear, it is serious ground.*

*Mountain forests, rugged steeps, marshes and fens – all country that is hard to traverse: this is difficult ground. Ground which is reached through narrow gorges, and from which we can only retire by tortuous paths, so that a small number of the enemy would suffice to crush a large body of our men: this is hemmed-in ground. Ground on which we can only be saved from destruction by fighting without delay, is desperate ground.*

*On dispersive ground, therefore, fight not. On facile ground, halt not. On contentious ground, attack not. On open ground, do not try to block the enemy's way. On the ground of intersecting highways, join hands with your allies. On serious ground, gather in plunder. On difficult ground, keep steadily on the march. On hemmed-in ground, resort to stratagem. On desperate ground, fight.*

# LESSON 177

## THE NINE LANDSCAPE SITUATIONS

The number nine is one of the most important elements within Sun Tzu's *Art of War* and lays the foundation for understanding the landscape as a whole. In the previous chapter, six types of landscape were categorized in physical terms. However, here the teaching is about the nine situations that an army might find itself in within the landscape. The original text gives the information in three separate lists: the name of each situation; an explanation of each situation; and actions to take in each situation. I have put these three aspects together so that each situation is discussed fully before moving on to the next.

The Chinese commentators discuss any ambiguous points and offer their advice. The various modern translators have focused on correct translation of the ideograms instead of their meaning and context, leading to a need for clarification. Therefore, this will be an extensive lesson combining all translations, all instructions for each situation and all commentary, ancient and modern. The headings will be descriptive rather than literal translations of the original. It is hoped that the whole teaching will be easy to understand with everything in a logical order.

### 1 HOME GROUND FROM WHICH TROOPS CAN EASILY FLEE

Originally given as "scattering" or "dispersive ground" (散地), this is home territory or friendly areas where there is no real threat. It is called scattering ground because its proximity to home will persuade weaker soldiers to desert. Therefore, never fight on this type of ground because the army will break up.

Clements translates this as "compromised situation" on enemy lands, while the Denma Group considers this as "dispersed ground" and say that both parties involved in the battle consider it to be ground of importance but it is not easy to take. Therefore, leave it, or, in other words, scatter.

When this situation is revisited later in the chapter, Sun Tzu says to make sure to keep your people together, which favours the interpretation that this is an area where your troops find it easy to leave the army.

### 2 GROUND ON THE FRINGES OF ENEMY TERRITORY

Originally "light ground" (輕地), this means land situated just inside enemy territory. Here it is still easy for troops to leave the army and return to the safety of home territory and the soldiers' minds have not yet been sharpened and unified by a shared sense of danger. Therefore, pass through this ground as quickly as possible to avoid shedding numbers.

### 3 GROUND THAT HAS A FEATURE BOTH SIDES WANT

Originally "strategic ground" (爭地), this is land that offers an advantage to both sides. It might be a particularly good place to fight from, or it might be that capturing it will block off an important route for the enemy. Therefore, both sides will want to get here first. If you lose the race, do not attack the enemy when they have taken it. Instead, move away and lure them out.

Some commentators talk about using the "rear", but it is not clear what this means. Some say to take the rear of the enemy to defeat them, but later in the chapter when Sun Tzu revisits this section he advises bringing allied troops up from the rear. This point is not explained further and the translations do not match.

### 4 GROUND THAT ALLOWS FREE MOVEMENT FOR EVERYBODY

Originally "open ground" (交地), this is where there is total freedom of movement for everyone involved. In this situation there is no point in trying to block the enemy, because there will always be an escape route. However, do not allow sections of your own troops to become isolated, because they could become vulnerable to attack by a larger force. Keep your supply lines open and take a defensive position.

### 5 INTERSECTIONS AND BORDERLANDS

Originally "intersecting ground" (衢地), this is a place where the borders of multiple states come together. There is organized traffic here and often supply routes and trade networks. It is also an easily accessible place where reinforcements can reach you quickly. The first army to take this land will have a significant strategic advantage, as other forces will find it difficult to get past any blockades they put in place. On this type of land work hard to establish and maintain alliances with bordering states. By doing this you will be able to control all traffic and get the support you need.

### 6 GROUND THAT IS DEEP IN ENEMY TERRITORY

Originally "heavy" or "serious ground" (重地), this is a dangerous place to be. You will be surrounded by forts and citadels from which the enemy can strike out at you at any time. Your forces will be under constant threat. You will not be able to maintain supply lines this deep into enemy territory, so you will have to plunder. However, do not plunder heavily or you will incur the hatred of the enemy population. Civilians often judge an army by the way it treats them rather than by its origin. Therefore, by not "raping and pillaging", but focusing instead on winning hearts and minds and offering a better future, a good military leader can inspire the enemy population to turn on its own leaders.

You need provisions or your army will starve, but you also need the goodwill of the local population, so strike a balance between taking and buying from them. Get this wrong and you could end up being attacked from all sides.

### 7 GROUND THAT IS DIFFICULT TO PASS THROUGH

Originally "entrapping ground" (圮地), this is any type of land that slows your movement. This could be, for example, mountains, forests, cliffs, crags, marshes, fens or difficult roads. In such an area keep moving and get out as soon as possible. It is too difficult to set up fortified positions here and you can become trapped and be forced into a seriously dangerous situation.

### 8 ENCLOSED GROUND

Originally "encircled ground" (圍地), this is a place where your forces can be surrounded and captured or killed. Examples include gorges through high mountains, steep areas with narrow access points and areas riddled with twisting paths or bodies of water. It is any area that does not allow an army to move freely and in proper formation and restricts an escape. Larger forces can be easily attacked here by smaller forces and the advantages of guerrilla warfare are obvious.

If you need to take your army through such an area, first block off all access points with forward troops to stop ambushes. It will help if your army is responsive and agile and you yourself use ambushes upon the enemy. However, the Chinese commentator Liu Yin has an alternative view. He says that if you are attacking the enemy in enclosed ground you should not block the exits, because then the enemy will see the prospect of escape and so they will not fight to the death, which will make the battle easier.

In all cases do not enter this type of ground without plans for entry, traversing and exit. Therefore, scouts are needed more than ever here. Later in the original chapter, this section is revisited and it is said that manmade fortifications are another feature in the landscape that can cause a force to become enclosed.

### 9 GROUND THAT WILL TAKE HARD FIGHTING TO CLEAR

Originally "death ground" (死地), this is any place that you cannot get out of without a fight. You cannot flee nor can you retreat. On the positive side, this means that your forces will fight at their best and in unison. However, it also means that it will be a hard fight. Encourage your troops to fight to the end and fight hard.

**WAR TIP: There are nine types of situation within the landscape: (1) home ground; (2) the edges of enemy territory; (3) ground that has a point both sides want or can use; (4) ground that allows free movement for everybody; (5) borderlands between multiple states; (6) ground that is deep in enemy territory; (7) ground that is difficult to pass through; (8) enclosed areas with a narrow way in; and (9) ground that will take hard fighting to clear. Remember these are situations you may find yourself in.**

## SUN TZU SAYS

*Those who were called skilful leaders of old knew how to drive a wedge between the enemy's front and rear; to prevent co-operation between his large and small divisions; to hinder the good troops from rescuing the bad, the officers from rallying their men. When the enemy's men were united, they managed to keep them in disorder. When it was to their advantage, they made a forward move; when otherwise, they stopped still.*

*If asked how to cope with a great host of the enemy in orderly array and on the point of marching to the attack, I should say: "Begin by seizing something which your opponent holds dear; then he will be amenable to your will." Rapidity is the essence of war: take advantage of the enemy's unreadiness, make your way by unexpected routes, and attack unguarded spots.*

# LESSON 178

## DIVIDE THE ENEMY

There are multiple ways to divide an enemy:

### STOP THE FORWARD AND REAR SECTIONS FROM CONNECTING

When armies march over long distances they do so in divisions, and sometimes they have to filter onto the battlefield in sections before they form up for battle. Make sure to stop the vanguard from forming a connection with the rear of the train. This will mean that the forward troops will have no support and will be surrounded.

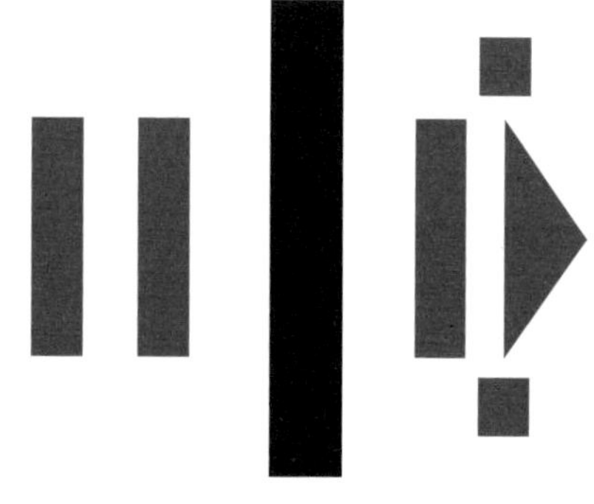

## STOP LARGE AND SMALL DIVISIONS FROM WORKING TOGETHER

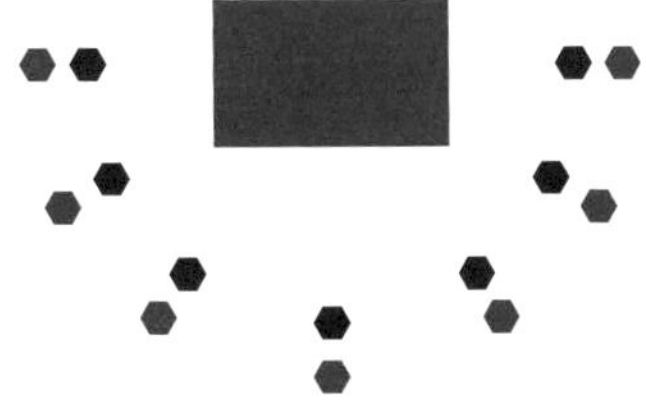

An army is made up of a large central force and various smaller peripheral divisions, which move around performing different functions, such as strikes, scouting and flanking manoeuvres. If you can stop them from working in unison with each other you will foil the enemy commander's plans and the main unit will be left to fight on its own.

## STOP ELITE TROOPS COMING TO THE AID OF POOR TROOPS

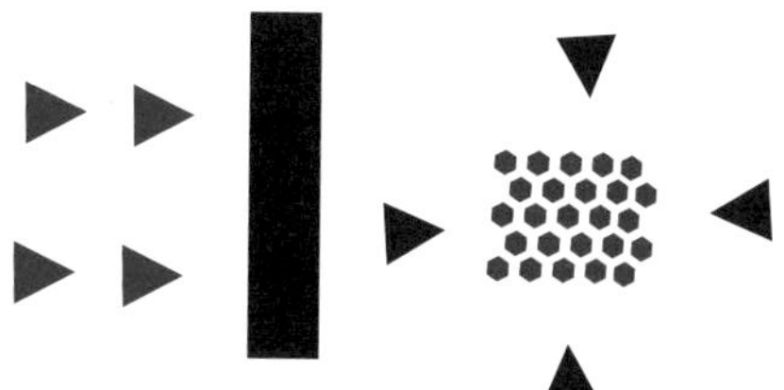

**ABOVE:** In this diagram the elite troops are represented as triangles.

Often elite troops are sent off to carry out certain specialist tasks. However, at the height of battle they may be brought back into the main force to give fighting courage to the weaker troops. Identify the battle-hardened troops and the weak troops, so that you can target the weak and block the elite. That is why some teachings say to mix troops of different ability levels in the main body of the army.

## DIVIDE THE OFFICERS FROM THE LOWER-RANKING TROOPS

If all troops are in accord they will fight together as one. Use spies, deceit and propaganda to drive a wedge between the lower classes and the upper classes so that the enemy cracks from within. This is the realm of the intelligence service.

### STOP THOSE WHO REUNITE FROM FORMING UP CORRECTLY

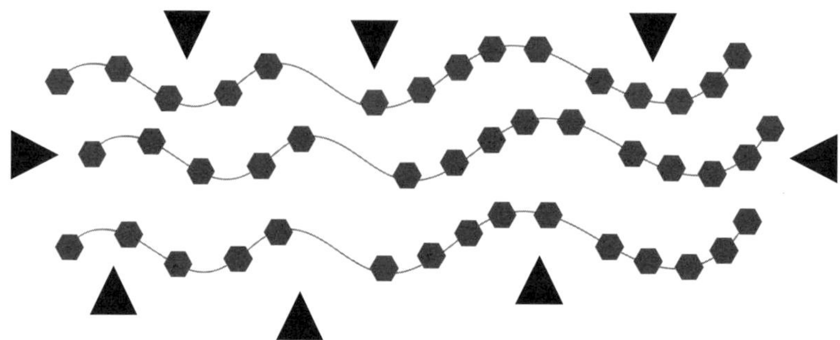

If the enemy divisions do manage to come together, stop them forming up in rank and file. The way to do this will depend on the situation and no examples are given in the text, but harass the enemy troops when they are trying to form up and keep the pressure on them so that they cannot fight as one even though they are in the same location.

**WAR TIP: Divide the enemy both physically and socially. Stop teams working together for a plan, spread dissension among them and never let a formation take shape when troops are getting together.**

# LESSON 179

## MASTER THE ART OF MOVEMENT AND NON-MOVEMENT

Movement

Non-movement

Knowing the terrain, knowing the enemy and knowing yourself are all aspects of great military leadership, but you must also know when to move and when to stay still. Remember that movement creates change, and change creates openings in your defence. The enemy will sometimes want you to move so you fall into a trap, but at other times they will want you to stay still so they can move freely. Only move when the advantage to be gained outweighs the disadvantage of opening up gaps in your defence.

**WAR TIP: Understand the concept of movement and non-movement. Move when the enemy does not want you to and be still when they want you to move. Also, block the enemy when they try to move and disturb them when they remain still.**

# LESSON 180

## UNSETTLE A SETTLED ENEMY

When the enemy is completely ready for you, its formations are formidable and to attack seems like madness, take something they need, want or love. The idea is to bring about change in the enemy and take advantage of that. Destroy their capital city or attack an ally, or choose a weak target so that they have to come to the rescue – anything that will force them to move from their strong position. When they have moved find gaps and destroy them section by section. Wang Xi says to cut off their supply lines; other commentators say that this lesson is about capturing cities. In either case, the point is that you should not attack a well prepared enemy directly, but find an easier target that will enrage the enemy and force them to move.

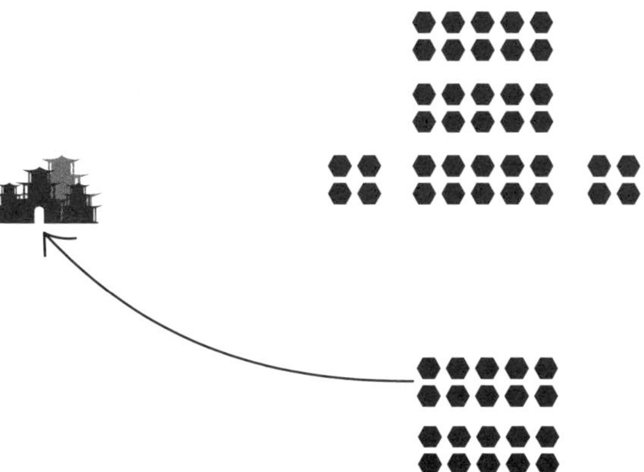

**WAR TIP: If the enemy is in perfect formation, target something they love or need to defend. Wait for their movement and attack them.**

# LESSON 181

## TAKE THE UNEXPECTED ROUTE AT SPEED

Drill your force so that it can move with absolute efficiency and speed. The enemy commanders will be trying to guess your next move in their command tent, trying to see the situation through your eyes. They will expect you to come by a certain route, calculating your speed based on the size of your force. That is why you need to have well trained troops who can exceed the enemy's estimations. Your task is to guess what the enemy has guessed about you and do something different. To appear where you are not expected, this is one of Sun Tzu's key lessons.

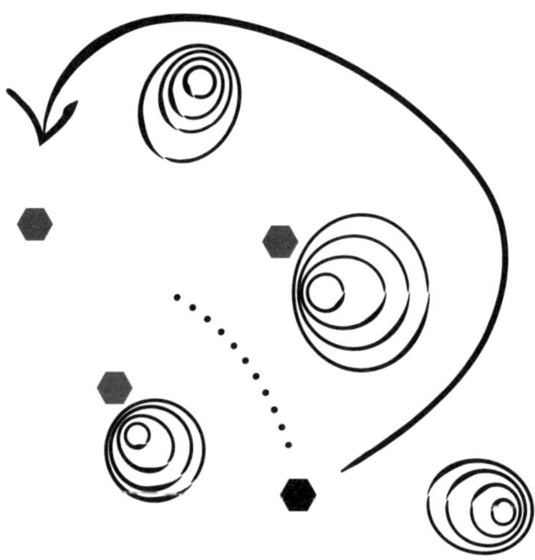

**WAR TIP: Always try to confound the enemy's predictions – arrive before they expect you to or appear somewhere unexpected.**

### SUN TZU SAYS

*The following are the principles to be observed by an invading force: The further you penetrate into a country, the greater will be the solidarity of your troops, and thus the defenders will not prevail against you. Make forays in fertile country in order to supply your army with food.*

*Carefully study the well-being of your men, and do not overtax them. Concentrate your energy and hoard your strength. Keep your army continually on the move, and devise unfathomable plans. Throw your soldiers into positions whence there is no escape, and they will prefer death to flight. If they will face death, there is nothing they may not achieve. Officers and men alike will put forth their uttermost strength.*

*Soldiers when in desperate straits lose the sense of fear. If there is no place of refuge, they will stand firm. If they are in hostile country, they will show a stubborn front. If there is no help for it, they will fight hard. Thus, without waiting to be marshalled, the soldiers will be constantly on the qui vive; without waiting to be asked, they will do your will; without restrictions, they will be faithful; without giving orders, they can be trusted.*

*Prohibit the taking of omens, and do away with superstitious doubts. Then, until death itself comes, no calamity need be feared. If our soldiers are not overburdened with money, it is not because they have a distaste for riches; if their lives are not unduly long, it is not because they are disinclined to longevity. On the day they are ordered out to battle, your soldiers may weep, those sitting up bedewing their garments, and those lying down letting the tears run down their cheeks. But let them once be brought to bay, and they will display the courage of a Chu or a Kuei.*

*The skilful tactician may be likened to the shuai-jan. Now the shuai-jan is a snake that is found in the Chung mountains. Strike at its head, and you will be attacked by its tail; strike at its tail, and you will be attacked by its head; strike at its middle, and you will be attacked by head and tail both. Asked if an army can be made to imitate the shuai-jan, I should answer, Yes.*

*For the men of Wu and the men of Yueh are enemies; yet if they are crossing a river in the same boat and are caught by a storm, they will come to each other's assistance just as the left hand helps the right. Hence it is not enough to put one's trust in the tethering of horses, and the burying of chariot wheels in the ground. The principle on which to manage an army is to set up one standard of courage which all must reach. How to make the best of both strong and weak – that is a question involving the proper use of ground.*

# LESSON 182

## INVASION STRATEGIES

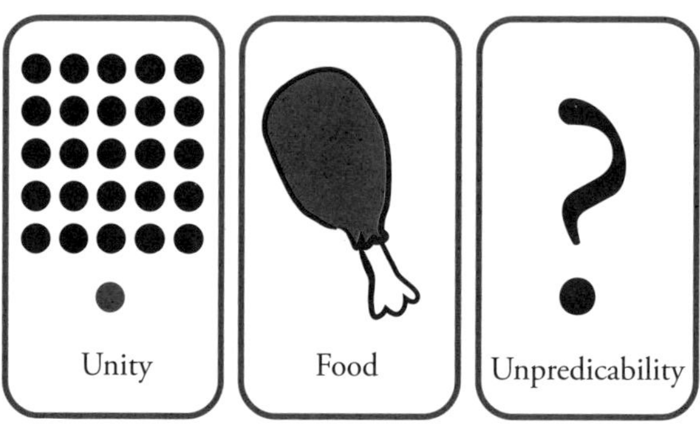


Sun Tzu gives the following principles for fighting deep in enemy territory:

• STAY TOGETHER. Do not dilute your threat by breaking up into small units. Become a unified machine of war moving relentlessly along its path.
• FIND FOOD AND CONSERVE ENERGY. Before entering enemy territory you may have urged your troops to march as quickly as possible. But now in enemy territory do not push them too hard, as they will need to keep some energy in reserve. This does not mean that you cannot move at speed or with intensity, it just means not to push your troops to the point of exhaustion. Give them time to rebuild their strength, then move on. Plunder fertile enemy lands for food, but remember that the Chinese commentators say not to over-plunder an area otherwise the population will turn against you.
• UNIFY THE TROOPS THROUGH SHARED DIFFICULTY. Danger concentrates the mind. Back on home soil troops may have been distracted by rivalries, minor gripes and plans to escape. Now that you are deep in enemy territory, such thoughts will have been forgotten. There will be an edge of fear and all troops will work as one formidable team because they want to get out alive. They will automatically: be prepared at all times; give their full co-operation; form strong bonds; fight to the extreme; and do what is needed without being told.
• REMOVE DOUBT. Doubts and fears can spread through an army like a virus. Soldiers have always been prone to superstition, which is why Sun

Tzu forbade practices such as augury and the reading of omens. A good military leader will identify the origin of any doubts and crush them at the source.

**WAR TIP: In enemy lands stay together, conserve energy and move to areas where you can obtain food. Know that troops will naturally become efficient through fear of the enemy and make sure to quash any doubts before they spread through the ranks.**

# LESSON 183

## MANAGE THE EMOTIONS OF YOUR TROOPS

At this point Sun Tzu discusses soldiers' attitudes to riches. He also alludes to troops shedding tears when they are ordered into battle. These words have been interpreted in various ways by the Chinese commentators. Some say that good soldiers do not care for material wealth; others say that soldiers should not be allowed to have wealth because it is too distracting. Some say that soldiers cry for fear of their lives; others say they do so because they are stirred up for war.

Sun Tzu finishes off this section with two examples of soldiers in desperate situations who achieved great things. Chu was an assassin who was sent to kill his uncle; while Kuei held a knife to the throat of an enemy leader to force the enemy to withdraw his army.

While it is not entirely clear what Sun Tzu is telling us here, the main point seems to be that soldiers are human beings with human emotions and different people react to events in different ways – with greed or honour, terror or excitement.

**WAR TIP: Do not assume that everybody thinks and feels the way that you do. Take account of the different emotional responses of your troops.**

# LESSON 184

## STRIKE LIKE A SNAKE

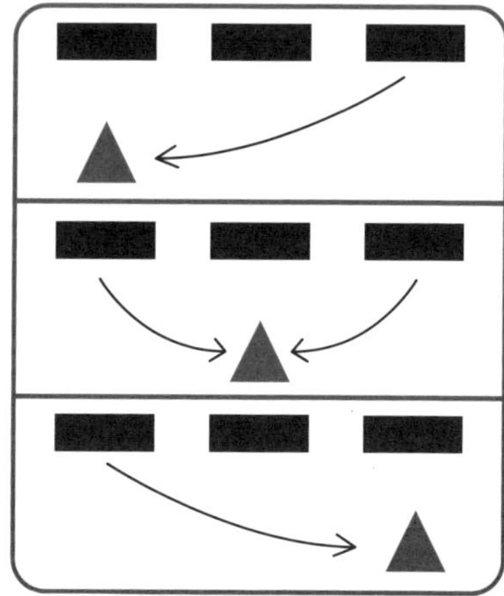

In this lesson Sun Tzu uses the image of a snake. When it is attacked at the head, it lashes out with its tail; when attacked at the tail, it bites with the head; and when attacked in the middle, both head and tail strike together. The point here is that no matter where an army is struck by the enemy, other troops will run to help and this help can be from any direction. It is important to note that Sun Tzu is not giving a specific formation here but a principle. It is also essential that by moving troops in response to an enemy attack you do not open up a gap elsewhere in your formation.

**WAR TIP: If the enemy attacks from one direction send troops from a different area to help defend – but do not weaken your formation in the process.**

# LESSON 185

## MAKE ALLIES FROM ENEMIES

The original text has a story about two enemies, one from Wu and the other from Yue, who are in a boat caught in a storm. Instead of carrying on fighting they work together to survive. In a single group, disagreements will take place and factions will emerge. However, when the group is under threat all the separate factions will face the danger together and will naturally become allies. Enemies do not stay enemies forever … but nor do allies.

**WAR TIP: Even the fiercest foes can unite to fight off a common enemy, but they will return to being enemies later.**

# LESSON 186

## BUILD UNITY THROUGH A SHARED GOAL

This lesson is a roundabout way of saying that forcing troops to be strong and unified will not work; instead you need to foster a central core of courage and unity of purpose. Sun Tzu says it is no use locking up or burying chariot wheels in the mud to stop troops from escaping – they must actually want to be there. (However, some translators see the image of the chariot wheels as meaning to unleash the full force of the army.)

The teaching builds on the point about a successful army being unified by a shared goal instead of being forced to work together. Internal rivalries hamper the war effort – each division must actively want to help any other division, because to do so benefits them, too.

**WAR TIP: Encourage your troops to have a deep love for each other so that they fight as one in perilous situations.**

# LESSON 187

## MATCH THE TROOP STRUCTURE TO THE TERRAIN

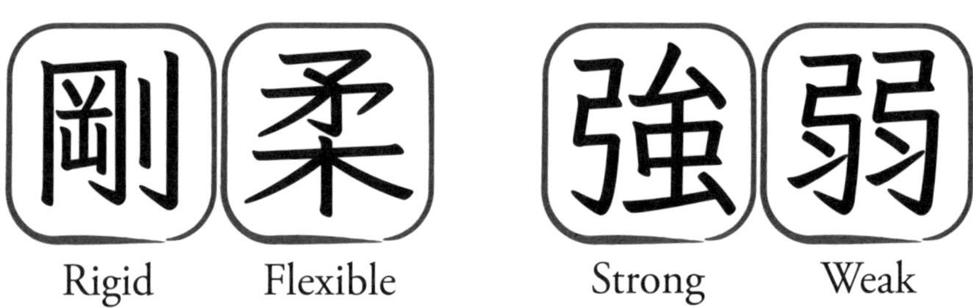


Sun Tzu says at this point to use rigidity and flexibility according to the terrain, but to understand this you first need to understand the "four ways". This is a staple in Eastern military classics and consists of two pairs – rigid and flexible, and strong and weak – which define the four types of troop structure in an army:

| | | |
|---|---|---|
| 1 | RIGID 剛 | – not moving and reinforced |
| 2 | FLEXIBLE 柔 | – adaptable to the situation |
| 3 | STRONG 強 | – a great force that can move forward with strength |
| 4 | WEAK 弱 | – quick to disperse, break up and move away |

The point is that it is no good using a rigid, unyielding structure on terrain where you need movement and adaptability. Similarly, flexibility will not help you on terrain where what you really need is to set up in a solid line. Some translators, including Giles, have mixed the two pairs up and used strong and weak by mistake, but the four ways is a precise system that extends through Asian military thought. Rigid and flexible is the pair that Sun Tzu intended here.

**WAR TIP: Know that troop structures can be static or mobile. Match the set up to the terrain for best results.**

## SUN TZU SAYS

*Thus the skilful general conducts his army just as though he were leading a single man, willy-nilly, by the hand. It is the business of a general to be quiet and thus ensure secrecy; upright and just, and thus maintain order. He must be able to mystify his officers and men by false reports and appearances, and thus keep them in total ignorance. By altering his arrangements and changing his plans, he keeps the enemy without definite knowledge. By shifting his camp and taking circuitous routes, he prevents the enemy from anticipating his purpose.*

*At the critical moment, the leader of an army acts like one who has climbed up a height and then kicks away the ladder behind him. He carries his men deep into hostile territory before he shows his hand. He burns his boats and breaks his cooking pots; like a shepherd driving a flock of sheep, he drives his men this way and that, and nothing knows whither he is going. To muster his host and bring it into danger – this may be termed the business of the general.*

# LESSON 188

## ASPIRE TO BE THE PERFECT LEADER

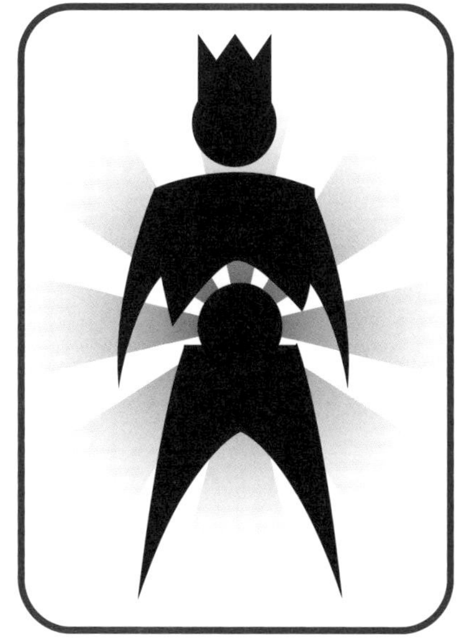

Sun Tzu rounds the last few lessons up by saying that an army must be commanded by a single person who makes each soldier feel as if they were being led personally by the hand. This is how to make the army work as one.

The perfect leader will have the following qualities:

• CALMNESS. A good leader is neither angry nor forceful. "Power" is not "force" and an army cannot be kept together for long through intimidation. Therefore, remain calm most of the time and only show your teeth when it is really necessary.

• UNPREDICTABILITY. Do not make the obvious move, and avoid leaving a pattern in your past activities. The enemy should not be able to identify what you will do in the future from what you did in the past. Do not take predictable routes, change your camp position, keep the enemy guessing.

• INSCRUTABILITY. You also need to be unreadable, so that even if an enemy spy succeeds in infiltrating your camp and observes you from close quarters they still cannot read your thoughts.

• SELF-DISCIPLINE. There is a difference between obedience, discipline and self-discipline. Many people are obedient, some have discipline forced upon them, but few are self-disciplined. While others rest and relax, the good leader works and only rests when it is the correct time.

• SECRECY. There is a delicate balance between keeping plans secret and involving your command team. Too much secrecy and the command team will be alienated; too little and plans will be leaked. It appears Sun Tzu prefers more secrecy and to keep his command team loyal in other ways.

• LEADING BY EXAMPLE. Always be there with your troops (but maybe not always at the front), be observable, and earn the respect of the soldiers by sharing their hardships. Sun Tzu uses various images here to back up his point that the commander is "with the troops". The first image he gives is of the commander leading the troops up a ladder that is then kicked away, allowing for no return. Alternatively, the army is represented as a great herd of animals moving as one with the leader in the centre directing them all in a way that cannot be predicted from the outside. Be with the troops in all dangerous situations, but remain unknown to the enemy.

• RESPONSIBILITY. As leader you must confidently assume responsibility for the whole force. Be at the centre of everything and use your troops in the most efficient way with the best results.

**WAR TIP: A perfect leader is calm, unpredictable, unreadable, self-disciplined, discreet, is in the thick of it with the troops and is in total command from the centre.**

### SUN TZU SAYS

*The different measures suited to the nine varieties of ground; the expediency of aggressive or defensive tactics; and the fundamental laws of human nature: these are things that must most certainly be studied.*

*When invading hostile territory, the general principle is, that penetrating deeply brings cohesion; penetrating but a short way means dispersion. When you leave your own country behind, and take your army across neighbourhood territory, you find yourself on critical ground. When there are means of communication on all four sides, the ground is one of intersecting highways. When you penetrate deeply into a country, it is serious ground. When you penetrate but a little way, it is facile ground. When you have the enemy's strongholds on your rear, and narrow passes in front, it is hemmed-in ground. When there is no place of refuge at all, it is desperate ground.*

*Therefore, on dispersive ground, I would inspire my men with unity of purpose. On facile ground, I would see that there is close connection between all parts of my army. On contentious ground, I would hurry up my rear. On open ground, I would keep a vigilant eye on my defences. On ground of intersecting highways, I would consolidate my alliances. On serious ground, I would try to ensure a continuous stream of supplies. On difficult ground, I would keep pushing on along the road. On hemmed-in ground, I would block any way of retreat. On desperate ground, I would proclaim to my soldiers the hopelessness of saving their lives.*

### COMMENTARY

The above section of the original text returns to describing the nine situations within the landscape and repeats itself, yet with less structure than before and with some elements missing from the list. It looks as if the text has become corrupted here. Any pieces of extra information found in this extract have been added to the relevant parts of lesson 177.

### SUN TZU SAYS

*For it is the soldier's disposition to offer an obstinate resistance when surrounded, to fight hard when he cannot help himself, and to obey promptly when he has fallen into danger.*

*We cannot enter into alliance with neighbouring princes until we are acquainted with their designs. We are not fit to lead an army on the march unless we are familiar with the face of the country – its mountains and forests, its pitfalls and precipices, its marshes and swamps. We shall be unable to turn natural advantages to account unless we make use of local guides.*

*To be ignored of any one of the following four or five principles does not befit a warlike prince. When a warlike prince attacks a powerful state, his generalship shows itself in preventing the concentration of the enemy's forces. He overawes his opponents, and their allies are prevented from joining against him. Hence he does not strive to ally himself with all and sundry, nor does he foster the power of other states. He carries out his own secret designs, keeping his antagonists in awe. Thus he is able to capture their cities and overthrow their kingdoms.*

*Bestow rewards without regard to rule, issue orders without regard to previous arrangements; and you will be able to handle a whole army as though you had to do with but a single man. Confront your soldiers with the deed itself; never let them know your design. When the outlook is bright, bring it before their eyes; but tell them nothing when the situation is gloomy. Place your army in deadly peril, and it will survive; plunge it into desperate straits, and it will come off in safety. For it is precisely when a force has fallen into harm's way that it is capable of striking a blow for victory.*

*Success in warfare is gained by carefully accommodating ourselves to the enemy's purpose. By persistently hanging on the enemy's flank, we shall succeed in the long run in killing the commander-in-chief. This is called ability to accomplish a thing by sheer cunning.*

*On the day that you take up your command, block the frontier passes, destroy the official tallies, and stop the passage of all emissaries. Be stern in the council chamber, so that you may control the situation.*

*If the enemy leaves a door open, you must rush in. Forestall your opponent by seizing what he holds dear, and subtly contrive to time his arrival on the ground. Walk in the path defined by rule, and accommodate yourself to the enemy until you can fight a decisive battle. At first, then, exhibit the coyness of a maiden, until the enemy gives you an opening; afterwards emulate the rapidity of a running hare, and it will be too late for the enemy to oppose you.*

# LESSON 189

## THE THREE NATURES OF THE TRAPPED ARMY

The following three characteristics are typical of a trapped army:

1. For the surrounded army the only options are to fight or give up. As giving up is generally not considered an option, the army must therefore fight its way out.
2. If the encircling is complete and the enemy persists in its attack, the trapped soldiers will fight ferociously to the death because they know the alternative is to face capture and torture. For this reason many strategists recommend that the attacking force leaves an escape route open. The fleeing soldiers will be easier to pick off later.
3. Cornered troops will not need to be ordered to do things but will concentrate in full to achieve (an albeit unlikely) victory.

**WAR TIP: If your forces are encircled, they will fight to get out or fight to the death. Know that everyone will join in unity, but be aware of false escape routes set by the enemy.**

# LESSON 190

## USE SPIES, SCOUTS AND GUIDES

The following are considered as essential practices of a military leader. Any leader unaware of these points should not be in command.

- Know all plans. All people and all sides are potential enemies or allies, so use spies to discover the true intentions of key players. This will enable you to form the best alliances based on an accurate reading of the situation.

- Scout all areas in detail. Your scouts should always be active – before, during and after war. Without a thorough understanding of enemy territory, including all the difficult areas, your troops will get into trouble.
- Use local guides. Local guides are a primary resource for scouting enemy territory. Use money or force to get someone from the local population to show your scouts around the area and then to guide the army. Be careful, though, of enemy spies who pretend to be guides.

**WAR TIP: Spy on everyone to help you decide who to side with, create detailed maps of enemy territory and use locals to guide you.**

# LESSON 191

## DO NOT ALLOW A POWERFUL ENEMY TO STABILIZE

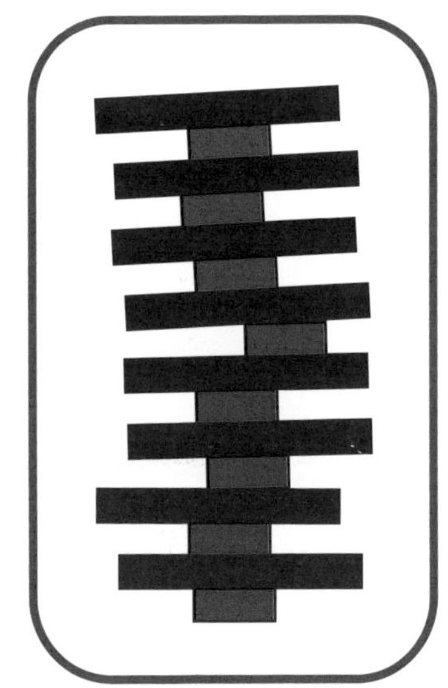

If you are in command of a high-functioning army but face a great and powerful enemy, make sure that you achieve the following:

- Prevent enemy troops coming together in a unified force.
- Disrupt enemy efforts to maintain alliances.
- Block off support troops.

A high-functioning army is an awesome force, with each section working at full efficiency and in unison. Its scouts know every inch of enemy territory, its spies know the details of enemy plans and alliances, its fast troops bait the enemy to distraction, and the main force remains unreadable. With all this in place even a powerful enemy will falter at the mere idea of your attack.

Be aware that there are alternative readings of this passage. Even in the time of the 14th-century Chinese commentator Zhang Yu it was debated. Some believe the lesson is about focusing on the stability of your own alliances or choice of alliances and knowing who to accept or not accept support from.

**WAR TIP: Do not allow the enemy to come together to form their full force and always disrupt their alliances.**

# LESSON 192

## REWARD ACHIEVEMENTS AS QUICKLY AS POSSIBLE

In ancient Chinese society the process for issuing rewards was long-winded and often the person due the reward was left empty-handed. On a military campaign, reward without delay and without care for correct protocol in normal times. To maintain morale and inspire excellence, troops must be recognized for their achievements as soon as possible.

**WAR TIP: Quickly reward those people who achieve so that others may see the profit of doing good.**

# LESSON 193

## DISREGARD CIVILIAN LAWS

The military should have its own regulations, not be restricted by civilian laws. The conventions of normal life do not always apply to the dark acts of warfare.

**WAR TIP: Do not be restricted by civilian rules within the framework of a military force.**

# LESSON 194

## CONSIDER THE WHOLE FORCE AS ONE PERSON

Do not view the army as a mass of individuals, but see its different sections as parts of a single body. Command it with simplicity and clarity, making all the different sections work together as one. Think of yourself as the brain and your orders as nerve signals.

Alternatively, Trapp translates this teaching as, "Treat all troops equally and with fairness."

**WAR TIP: Consider the whole force as a single entity and command it as you would command a single person and treat all people the same.**

# LESSON 195

## TELL THE TROOPS WHAT TO DO BUT NOT WHY TO DO IT

Give orders but do not explain them. If you tell the troops how you arrived at your decisions, this insight will leak to the enemy through any spies in your camp. It will also encourage your troops to believe they have a say in the process. Some will disagree with your conclusions, but they do not have enough information to see the whole picture. You cannot allow your authority to be undermined in this way. Good military commanders with victories to their name will gain the respect of the forces they command, who will come to trust their orders without question.

The Denma Group translates this teaching as, "Bind them with deeds. Do not command them with words."

**WAR TIP: Never explain your orders. That way nothing will leak out and your authority will remain intact.**

# LESSON 196

## ACCENTUATE THE POSITIVE

To boost morale always pass good news on to your troops, but keep bad news to yourself. Similarly, focus on the benefits to be gained from victory, be it financial profit or a move toward an even greater victory, but play down the potential dangers.

However, the Denma Group takes the opposite view in its translation: "Bind them with harm. Do not command them with advantage."

**WAR TIP: Sell the campaign to your troops by sharing positive developments and emphasizing what they will gain from victory, but gloss over any possible harm that may befall them.**

# LESSON 197

## TURN DEFEAT INTO VICTORY

Well trained troops will excel when they are fighting for their lives, so do not always try to shield them from harm. Obviously, avoid situations where there is no chance of victory, but do not be afraid to put your people in peril. They are soldiers and their job is war.

**WAR TIP: Get the best out of your troops by placing them in a "live or die" situation.**

# LESSON 198

## KNOW THE ENEMY'S NEXT MOVE

Knowing what the enemy will do before they have done it is a fundamental aspect of the *Art of War*, culminating in the final chapter on the art of spying. Here the original text could read "know enemy's details" or "know the deceptions of the enemy," but both mean to know what the enemy will do next. To know the plans of the enemy and how to counter them, this is considered the mark of a military commander of true quality.

**WAR TIP: Know where the enemy plans to move next and get there before them so you can take advantage well before events unfold.**

# LESSON 199

## SEAL YOUR HOME TERRITORY

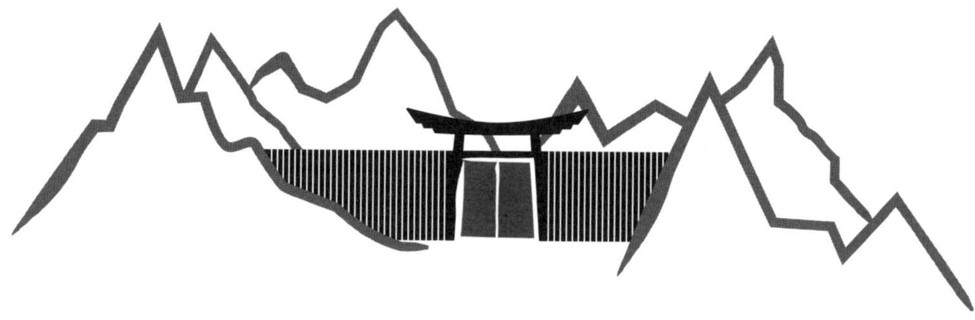

As you move out to war in enemy territory, make sure to seal the border of your home state. Leave frontier guards with orders not to allow any passage through, no matter what identification people have, especially enemy envoys. Enforce a total lockdown. Afterwards move your focus back to the command centre and work through the various situations in a war room, something originally done in a temple or other holy place.

**WAR TIP: Seal up your home borders so that no enemy can pass through.**

# LESSON 200

## LOOK FOR GAPS AND HOW TO EXPLOIT THEM

The next passage is difficult, because commentators differ in their interpretation of the key word. Some translate it as "gaps"; others as "spies". This is because the Chinese concept of spying is based on the idea of finding a gap. It is not known exactly what Sun Tzu meant, but the general point of this lesson is to be aware of gaps in your own defences and those of the enemy and consider how to make best use of them. This could involve the following strategies:

- When the enemy shows a gap take it.
- Do not have gaps within your own side.
- Offer false gaps to the enemy.
- Allow enemy spies to enter and use them to your advantage.
- Send spies into the enemy through gaps.

Note that it is not always essential to close up gaps in your defences – sometimes they can be kept open as bait. The important thing is to know where the gaps are and to monitor them carefully.

**WAR TIP: Look for gaps in your defences and decide whether to plug them or use them to tempt the enemy. Look for enemy gaps and go through them before the enemy has time to close them up.**

# LESSON 201

## FOLLOW THE BASIC STEPS OF WAR

Having covered preparations for war, Sun Tzu now summarizes what your next steps should be:

1. Attack what the enemy values. Armed with a clear picture of enemy plans and priorities, attack something they value so that it changes their plans.
2. Keep them confused and impose change on them. Having forced the enemy to move in response to your initial attack, do not make the place, date or time of battle obvious. Keep the enemy disorientated and neutralize their scouts and spies, either through secrecy or deliberate misinformation – or both.
3. Respond to their change and defeat them. Now that the enemy is in a state of change because of your unexpected attack and they are unaware of where to strike your forces or where to engage you, find the best place to attack them at their most vulnerable and go for the kill.

**WAR TIP: Know the enemy plans, attack something they value and force them to move. Keep them guessing as to the date and location of the battle and then strike them unexpectedly.**

# LESSON 202

## APPEAR TIMID, THEN STRIKE

This teaching uses the symbols of a maiden and a hare. First be as coy and unthreatening as a maiden to lure the enemy into a false sense of security, and then attack with the speed of a hare. Complacency leads to carelessness, which leads to gaps. Wait for these gaps to open up, then pounce.

Clements suggests that Sun Tzu uses the idea of a woman here to stand for timidity or indecision, or that it could be a lost phrase meaning "to show a less threatening side". Whatever the original intention, the message is basically the same.

**WAR TIP: Appear weak and wait for the enemy to open a gap, then attack that gap with speed.**

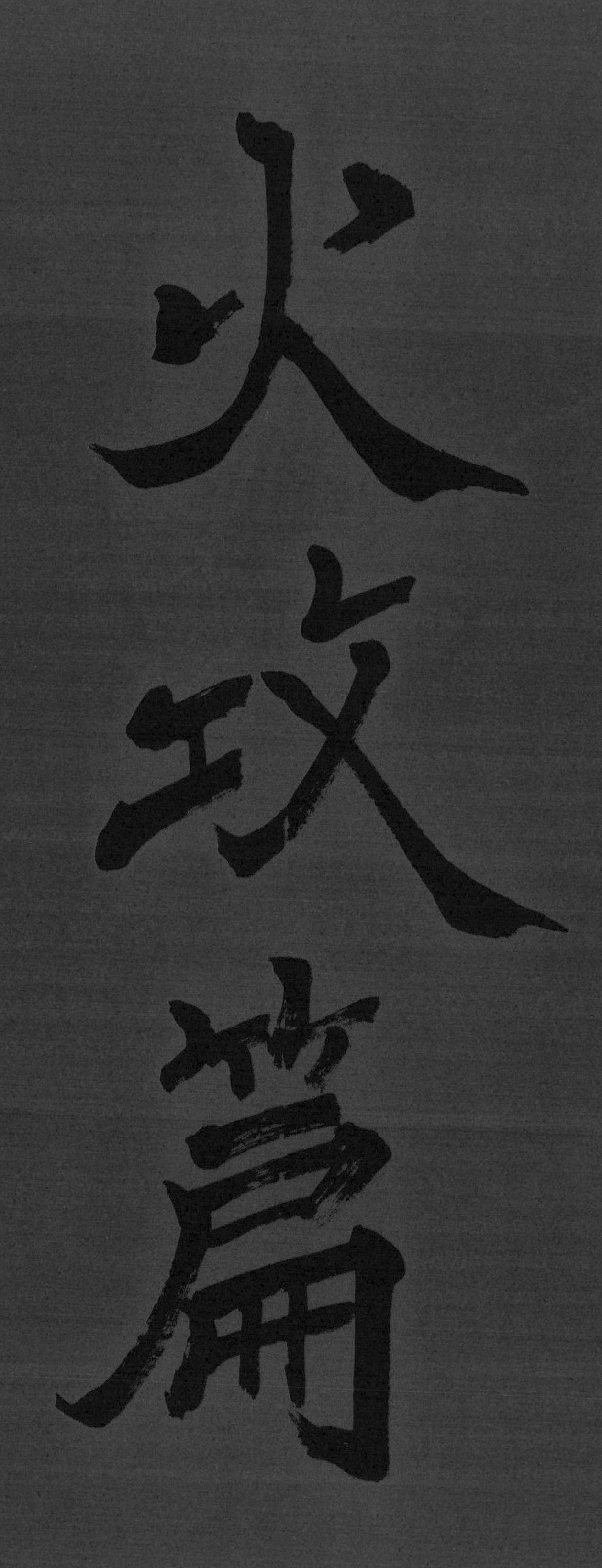
火攻篇

# CHAPTER 12

# THE SCROLL OF ATTACKING WITH FIRE

# THE SCROLL OF ATTACKING WITH FIRE

The title of Sun Tzu's 12th chapter uses the ideograms 火, meaning "fire", and 攻, meaning "attack". The chapter is divided into three main areas:

1 The five types of fire attack
2 The conditions needed to use fire
3 Emotional rage and "fiery" tempers

The first section deals with the five main targets that a military leader can strike using fire. The second section discusses the conditions and equipment you need to use fire and the situations in which fire will be most effective. The final section looks at fire in an emotional sense, warning of the dangers of anger and advising how to avoid having a fiery temper.

## SUN TZU SAYS

*There are five ways of attacking with fire. The first is to burn soldiers in their camp; the second is to burn stores; the third is to burn baggage trains; the fourth is to burn arsenals and magazines; the fifth is to hurl dropping fire amongst the enemy.*

# LESSON 203

## THE FIVE TYPES OF FIRE ATTACK

The following are the five ways to attack the enemy with fire, two of which target people and three of which target property.

### 1 TO BURN PEOPLE

Burning people with the intent to kill or maim them will instil fear in the enemy and reduce their numbers.

### 2 TO BURN STORES AND FOOD

Burn the enemy's food so that they will become weak and starve. The more you can burn, the less they will be able to function. Sometimes you will want to capture the supplies for use by your own army, but you will not always have enough time or troops to carry them away. If so, it is better to destroy the supplies than allow the enemy to continue to benefit from them. This kind of scorched earth policy is still used in modern warfare.

### 3 TO BURN SUPPLY TRAINS AND VEHICLES

Both equipment and food need to be transported, and when they are in transit they are particularly vulnerable. Therefore, attack enemy supplies when they are on the move.

#### 4 TO BURN ARMOURIES AND EQUIPMENT DUMPS

The enemy will have equipment dumps – strategic places to hide stores. These may be found close to the army, on their intended forward route or in a back-up position. When the locations of such places have been identified by scouts or spies, use fire to destroy the equipment.

#### 5 TO BURN FORMATIONS OF PEOPLE

When the enemy is in position and its formations are standing by, they are particularly open to attack by fire. Often troops in formation are less able to manoeuvre, which means that you will be able to kill more people, or if it causes them to flee it will create gaps in their defence.

This type of fire attack has many variants in its translations. Minford interprets it as burning lines of communication, while Giles, Griffith and Trapp see it as using incendiary missiles, which is based on the Chinese commentary by Tu Yu. Cleary translates it as burning weapons, while the Denma Group says this is about using fire in tunnels. I have gone with Sawyer's version, but be aware that there is no definitive translation.

**WAR TIP: Burn enemy troops when you can, scatter their formations with fire, destroy the food they have with them, burn any supply lines supporting them and hunt out all their back-up equipment dumps.**

## SUN TZU SAYS

*In order to carry out an attack, we must have means available. The material for raising fire should always be kept in readiness.*

*There is a proper season for making attacks with fire, and special days for starting a conflagration. The proper season is when the weather is very dry; the special days are those when the moon is in the constellations of the Sieve, the Wall, the Wing or the Cross-bar; for these four are all days of rising wind.*

*In attacking with fire, one should be prepared to meet five possible developments:*

1. *When fire breaks out inside the enemy's camp, respond at once with an attack from without.*
2. *If there is an outbreak of fire, but the enemy's soldiers remain quiet, bide your time and do not attack.*
3. *When the force of the flames has reached its height, follow it up with an attack, if that is practicable; if not, stay where you are.*
4. *If it is possible to make an assault with fire from without, do not wait for it to break out within, but deliver your attack at a favourable moment.*
5. *When you start a fire, be to windward of it. Do not attack from the leeward.*

*A wind that rises in the daytime lasts long, but a night breeze soon falls. In every army, the five developments connected with fire must be known, the movements of the stars calculated, and a watch kept for the proper days. Hence those who use fire as an aid to the attack show intelligence; those who use water as an aid to the attack gain an accession of strength. By means of water, an enemy may be intercepted, but not robbed of all his belongings.*

# LESSON 204

## MATERIALS AND CONDITIONS NEEDED FOR FIRE

To use fire effectively, there are certain materials you need and conditions that need to be in your favour:

### TOOLS AND EQUIPMENT FOR FIRE

Teachings on Chinese fire weapons are extensive and cover a huge variety of incendiary devices, from gas bombs to landmines and fire crackers to fire-throwers. Much of this detailed material is contained in manuals written after Sun Tzu, whereas Sun Tzu himself does not give any specific examples of the fire tools that he would have used. However, the basic elements are unchanging: flammable material and fuels, as well as containers and concoctions to make fire weapons safer for the attacker and more devastating for the target, all of which must be prepared in advance. The Chinese commentator Cao Cao mentions an important human resource that you also need: secret agents planted within the enemy camp to set fire.

### WEATHER CONDITIONS FOR FIRE

Setting fire should be done in the correct season and weather. It is useless to set fires in torrential rain or snowy conditions. While it is not impossible to burn a position down in bad weather, it is never a good idea to work against nature. When conditions are hot and dry, fire will be easy to start and quick to spread.

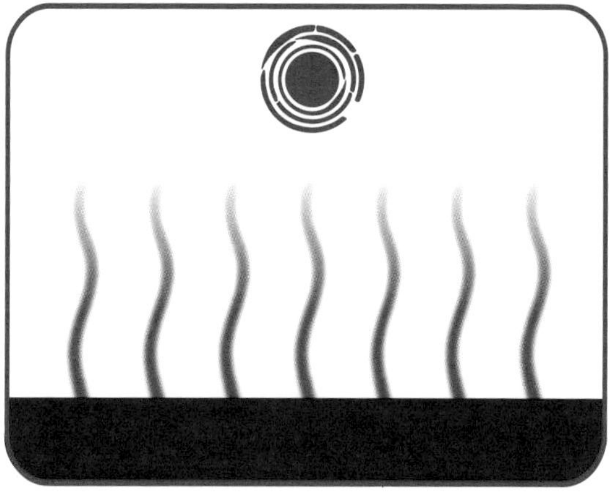

**WAR TIP: Only set fire when all the equipment needed is prepared and the weather is in your favour.**

# LESSON 205

## USE WINDY DAYS TO SET FIRE

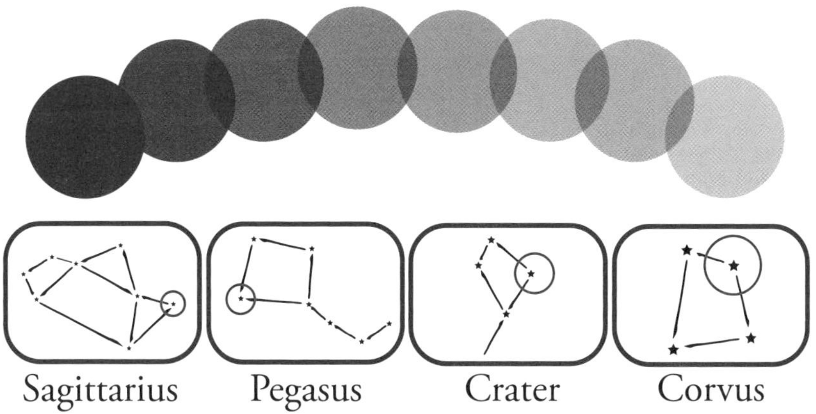


**ABOVE:** A stylistic representation of the moon crossing the four lunar mansions that Sun Tzu links to days of wind.

One of the only examples of pseudoscience and esoteric teachings within Sun Tzu is the mention of the lunar mansions, which supposedly enable you to predict days of wind. The ancient Chinese divided the constellations into 28 lunar mansions, imaginary lines that the moon crosses during its monthly journey around earth. Sun Tzu says that the days on which the moon crosses the four positions given in the following table will be windy:

| STAR NAME | CHINESE NAME | ENGLISH NAME |
|---|---|---|
| Gamma Sagittarii | 箕 | Winnowing basket |
| Gamma Pegasi | 壁 | Wall |
| Alpha Crateris | 翼 | Wings |
| Gamma Corvi | 軫 | Chariot |

Although this particular system of wind divination is now considered unreliable, the point that you should take account of forecasts of wind level and direction when setting fires is still vitally important.

**WAR TIP: Consider wind strength and direction when preparing to set fires.**

# LESSON 206

## THE FIVE PRINCIPLES OF INCENDIARY WARFARE

There are five basic ideas that Sun Tzu outlines in his discussion of using fire as a weapon. Note that while the original text states that there are five principles, the translators do not all agree how to divide them up. The list below is the closest fit to the consensus:

### 1 ATTACK WHEN FIRE BREAKS OUT IN THE ENEMY CAMP

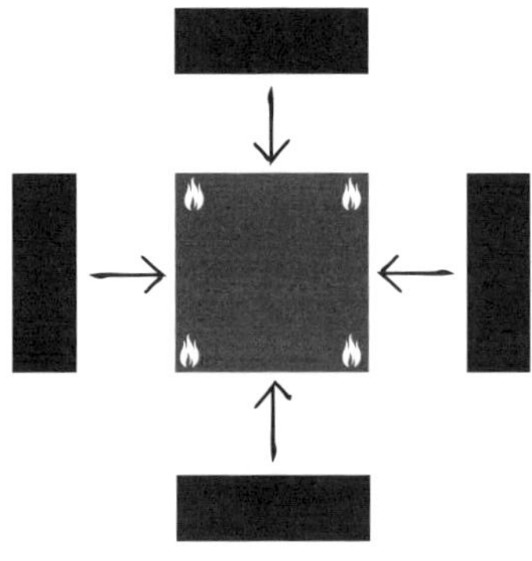

There are three reasons for a fire to break out in the enemy camp: it may have been started by an agent you have planted; it may have started by accident; or it may have been started by the enemy as a trick to lure you in. In the first two scenarios, you should attack because the enemy will have to divide its troops between fighting the fire and repelling your advance, which will make it easier to defeat them.

### 2 BE CAREFUL OF FAKE FIRES IN THE ENEMY CAMP

Do not fall for a fake fire deliberately lit by the enemy inside its camp. This is done to lure you into a kill zone inside the compound. If there is no sign of enemy troops rushing around, no orders being shouted and no obvious commotion, then you can be fairly sure it is a trap. However, beware of fake commotion designed to make the deception more convincing. As a rule of thumb, give the fire time to reach its full height, because at some point the enemy will have to put it out. If an opportunity presents itself then attack, but the core principle is not to rush in at the first whiff of smoke – unless, of course, you know for a fact that one of your agents has started the fire.

### 3 ATTACK FROM THE OUTSIDE

Fires set outside the enemy position do not always work very well, because the heart of what needs to be burned is well defended and on the inside. But always be on the lookout for an opportunity to start the fire from the outside if such a gap appears. They may be appropriate when the wind is blowing particularly strongly toward the enemy.

### 4 ALWAYS BE UPWIND WHEN SETTING A FIRE

When a fire is set, be it against an enemy camp or a formation, smoke and flames will blow with the prevailing wind. Therefore, never set a fire when the wind is blowing in your face when you look directly at the enemy. Ideally, the wind should be coming from behind when you observe the intended target, or at least blowing across from one side to the other. Remember wind can change direction without warning, so keep your troops back from the fire.

## 5 OBSERVE THE WIND

The wind is subject to change in direction, duration and intensity. Know that these changes can cause you problems if you have not prepared for them. The original text ventures into the esoteric, stating that wind that rises during the day will last for a long time, whereas wind that starts at night will die down quickly. This is not generally accepted to be the case.

Cleary – taking his lead from Chinese commentary – has an alternative interpretation of this point as: "Wind that starts in the day stops in the night, while wind that starts in the night stops in the day." So wind will not last more than 12 hours. The modern Chinese commentator Yang Ping-an (*see* footnotes in Ames) interprets this as: "If the wind is blowing in the day, then follow through with the attack. If it is blowing at night, do not attack."

After the teaching on wind at day compared to wind at night, Sun Tzu says that a good military leader must know these five ideas and apply them to their strategy. Giles and Sawyer both translate this part of the text to mean "observe the stars", meaning that you should calculate the best times to use fire.

Zhang Yu makes the important point that you should also consider how the enemy could use these principles against you. Vigilance is required whichever side of the flames you stand.

**WAR TIP: Take advantage of fire in the enemy camp, but do not be fooled by a fake fire trap. You can mount a fire attack from the outside the enemy camp, but never be downwind of the fire and make sure to check any changes in the wind.**

# LESSON 207

## KNOW THE DIFFERENCES BETWEEN FIRE AND WATER AS WEAPONS

There are substantial differences in the way this lesson has been translated, so we cannot be sure exactly what Sun Tzu is trying to say. However, the main point is that fire and water can both be used in warfare, but they need to be used differently. The various translations are given below:

- He who uses fire to aid the attack is powerful; he who uses water to aid the attack is forceful. (Ames)
- If an attack is to be assisted [by fire], the fire must be unquenchable. If water is to assist the attack, the flood must be overwhelming. (Calthrop)
- The use of fire to help an attack means clarity, the use of water to help an attack means strength. (Cleary)
- It is smart to use fire as an auxiliary attack. It is strong to use water. (Clements)
- One who uses fire to aid an attack is dominant. One who uses water to aid an attack is strong. (Denma Group)
- Those who use fire as an aid to the attack show intelligence; those who use water to aid the attack gain an accession of strength. (Giles)
- Those who use fire to assist their attacks are intelligent; those who use inundations are powerful. (Griffith)
- Fire assists an attack mightily, water assists an attack powerfully. (Minford)
- Using fire to aid an attack is enlightened, using water to assist an attack is mighty. (Sawyer)
- A general who attacks with fire is demonstrating his intelligence; one who uses water is showing his strength. (Trapp)

**WAR TIP: Use fire and water to help in your attacks either in combination or separately.**

# LESSON 208

## REDIRECT WATER

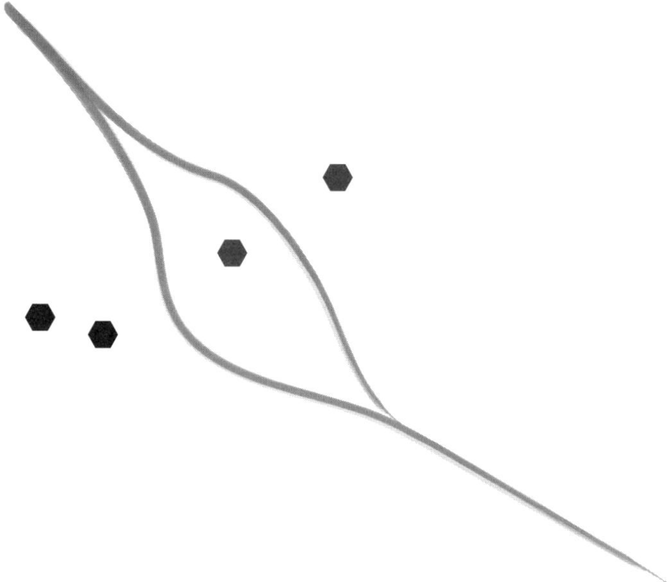

If you have the resources to carry out such a massive engineering effort, consider redirecting rivers, reservoirs or any large body of water to hamper the enemy by flooding their camp, dividing their troops or cutting off their operations base.

Sun Tzu points out that while water can cut the enemy off or flood them, it will not usually destroy their equipment – to do that you need fire.

**WAR TIP: Redirect large bodies of water to impede the enemy.**

## SUN TZU SAYS

*Unhappy is the fate of one who tries to win his battles and succeed in his attacks without cultivating the spirit of enterprise; for the result is waste of time and general stagnation. Hence the saying: The enlightened ruler lays his plans well ahead; the good general cultivates his resources.*

*Move not unless you see an advantage; use not your troops unless there is something to be gained; fight not unless the position is critical. No ruler should put troops into the field merely to gratify his own spleen; no general should fight a battle simply out of pique. If it is to your advantage, make a forward move; if not, stay where you are.*

*Anger may in time change to gladness; vexation may be succeeded by content. But a kingdom that has once been destroyed can never come again into being; nor can the dead ever be brought back to life. Hence the enlightened ruler is heedful, and the good general full of caution. This is the way to keep a country at peace and an army intact.*

## COMMENTARY

Strangely, at this point Sun Tzu stops giving teachings on fire and returns to the subject of wise and unwise leadership. There does not seem to be an obvious reason for this change of theme, but Clements points to the symbolic connection between anger, which is the focus of this section, and fire. Note, however, that fire and anger are not connected in ancient Chinese Five Element theory.

# LESSON 209

## BE THOUGHTFUL AND EFFECTIVE

Thoughtful leaders plan extremely well and all that they predict comes to pass, but leaders must also be effective. It is not enough to know what is going to happen, you also need to know what to do when your predictions come to pass. Therefore, plan ahead but also have the initiative to act when you see an opening.

**WAR TIP: Do not waste the accuracy of your planning and predictions by being indecisive when the crucial moment comes.**

# LESSON 210

## ACT ON REASON NOT EMOTION

The following section is an amalgamation of the next set of teachings on the danger of letting emotions influence your decision making:

- Move your force only if you will gain something from it. If there is no sure benefit then halt, because movement creates openings. Never make a move out of anger or any other emotion. Calm down and think.
- Raise or deploy an army only if you are certain of victory. The decision to form an army should be based on calm calculation, not an emotional reflex.
- Enter into combat with another force only when you are fully prepared and the odds are in your favour. It must be a battle you know you will win, not a battle you hope to win. Again, never enter combat out of anger. War should always be the last resort when all other options have been ruled out.

**WAR TIP: Emotions are constantly in flux. Anger can soon turn to calmness – do not make a life-or-death military decision just because you are in the wrong mood.**

# LESSON 211

## YOU CANNOT BRING BACK THE DEAD

When pushing counters around in the war room, it can be easy to forget that they represent real people whose lives depend on your decisions. Once people are dead they are gone forever, and once a civilization has been destroyed it cannot be rebuilt.

War is horrific and destructive, so to enter into it out of anger is not the way of leadership. A good leader takes time to decide what to do and when to do it. This is the foundation of statecraft and military leadership and also the path to peace.

**WAR TIP: Your choices can result in the deaths of vast numbers of people and the destruction of civilizations. Treat this responsibility with supreme respect.**

# 用間篇

# CHAPTER 13

# THE SCROLL ON THE USE OF SPIES

# THE SCROLL ON THE USE OF SPIES

The title of Sun Tzu's 13th and final chapter uses the ideograms 用, meaning "use of", and 間, meaning "spy" or "looking through a gap". The chapter is divided into four main areas:

1 Why spies are essential
2 The five types of spy
3 How to use spies
4 How to use information

In the first section Sun Tzu explains the essential role spies play in lowering the overall costs and devastation of war by providing information that brings the speedy downfall of the enemy. The second section outlines the five types of spy and their specific functions within the network. The third section talks about how spies are used and their relationship to the military leadership. The final section discusses the information gained via spies and how to use it against the enemy. The chapter concludes with a recap of the importance of spying and its relevance to all other areas of the military.

## SUN TZU SAYS

*Raising a host of a hundred thousand men and marching them great distances entails heavy loss on the people and a drain on the resources of the state. The daily expenditure will amount to a thousand ounces of silver. There will be commotion at home and abroad, and men will drop down exhausted on the highways. As many as seven hundred thousand families will be impeded in their labour.*

*Hostile armies may face each other for years, striving for the victory which is decided in a single day. This being so, to remain in ignorance of the enemy's condition simply because one grudges the outlay of a hundred ounces of silver in honours and emoluments, is the height of inhumanity. One who acts thus is no leader of men, no present help to his sovereign, no master of victory.*
*Thus, what enables the wise sovereign and the good general to strike*

*and conquer, and achieve things beyond the reach of ordinary men, is foreknowledge. Now this foreknowledge cannot be elicited from spirits; it cannot be obtained inductively from experience, nor by any deductive calculation. Knowledge of the enemy's dispositions can only be obtained from other men.*

# LESSON 212

## WAR IS HUGELY EXPENSIVE AND DISRUPTIVE

Even if you win, war is always expensive. For the losing side it can bring bankruptcy and ruin the population for generations. The figure Sun Tzu quotes of "a thousand ounces of silver" a day may not be entirely accurate but is representative of money beyond the imagination of normal people. He wants his readers to appreciate the drastic cost of war.

| | | |
|---|---|---|
| 1 | 2 | 3 |
| 8 | 9 | 4 |
| 7 | 6 | 5 |

**ABOVE:** In ancient China, land is believed to have been divided into nine sections but farmed by eight families, with the produce from one of the sections going to the government as a tax. If the son of one of those families went to war, the other seven families carried the burden for them.

As well as the direct costs of running and equipping an army, war entails other, less obvious costs. In old China, certain families had to provide sons for war, which took away a proportion of the farming workforce, resulting in less production for the next year and a greater burden for the people left behind. The figure of 700,000 families disrupted probably comes from a calculation based on an army of 100,000 using the ancient Chinese system of dividing land for farming explained in the above diagram. An army of 100,000 soldiers from 100,000 families meant 700,000 other families taking the strain.

Also, when an army marches out to war, it interferes with the routine of the local population. Admittedly, in some cases this can be financially profitable as farmers and traders rush to sell the army their produce, but it still creates disruption. Other authors translate this to mean "the army will be weary and fall by the wayside near the local population," or that "beggars and undesirables will be along the roadside following the army." The main point is that an army on the march leaves all kinds of disorder in its wake.

**WAR TIP: When war is taken up, it does not just cost the lives of soldiers but also the time and resources of the nation as a whole.**

# LESSON 213

## WAR CAN LAST FOR YEARS

The process of a war – including preparation, planning, the raising of an army, marching out, extended campaigns, sieges, shadowing and returning – can last for many years, even generations. Even the shortest of wars will bring great disruption, cost many lives and drain the nation's wealth.

**WAR TIP: Battles turn into wars and wars can last for an extended period, which is something a well governed state must take pains to avoid. So make conflicts as short as possible.**

# LESSON 214

## DO NOT BEGRUDGE THE COST OF SPYING

The previous two lessons lead up to this one. The cost of running a division as small as the intelligence service may seem comparatively high, but if spying hastens your victory it will pay for itself many times over. Information, such as the location of the enemy and foreknowledge of enemy movements is, quite literally, worth its weight in gold (or silver in the Giles translation).

In fact, according to the figures Sun Tzu quotes, information is worth ten times its weight – as the daily cost of running the army as a whole is ten times greater than that of running the intelligence operation. That is assuming the figure of 100 ounces of silver to pay for spying is a daily expense, rather than an occasional outlay (Sun Tzu does not make it completely clear).

**WAR TIP: Compared to other types of soldier, spies are expensive, but the game changing information they provide makes them incredibly cost-effective.**

# LESSON 215

## DO NOT BE AN INHUMANE LEADER

Sun Tzu concludes his point by appealing to the vanity of military leaders. He says that any general who would turn down the chance of a quick victory for a fraction of the total cost is lacking in humanity. Piles of bodies and heads, mass graves, famine, destruction are the results of war and any leader who does not wish to stop that is devoid of decency. He says such a person:

- Is not a competent military leader
- Is not a support to the government
- Does not understand war and will not have victory

To use spies is the way of a supreme leader.

**WAR TIP: To ignore the chance of a victory gained through spying is to be without humanity and is not the way of a true leader.**

# LESSON 216

## FOREKNOWLEDGE IS GOLDEN

**ABOVE:** Spying is like an arrow that points to where the enemy will be in the future.

When you march out to another country with your army, you can see only as far as the horizon ahead of you. Scouts will be able to see to the next horizon, but the information they glean will be getting old by the time it reaches you. In contrast, spies see far into the enemy territory and into the future. There is no comparison.

**WAR TIP: Only spies can tell you what the enemy will do before they do it.**

# LESSON 217

## DO NOT USE THE SUPERNATURAL

In Sun Tzu's day, the world was considered to be divided between the opposing yet complementary elements of yin (earth, darkness, water, female, stillness) and yang (heaven, light, fire, male, movement). From this came a complex system of divination, involving cloud formations, weather patterns, bird observation and many other early forms of augury. As we have seen, few if any esoteric elements have made their way into the *Art of War*, making it a remarkably practical text for its time. Sun Tzu warns against relying on divination and says to put your faith in spies instead.

**WAR TIP: Clouds may tell you when it will rain and birds may tell you when the season is changing, but only spies can tell you what the enemy is going to do next.**

# LESSON 218

## BASE YOUR ANALYSIS ON INTELLIGENCE NOT GUESSWORK

Asking yourself "what would I do if I were the enemy?" has an important place in military strategy, but only if it is based on something more concrete than blind analogy to your own situation. It is wrong to assume that the enemy leader will think in the same way as you.

First arm yourself with stacks of intelligence reports and a detailed understanding of the enemy and their military systems, and only then put yourself in their shoes.

**WAR TIP: Important military decisions must be taken using reliable, up-to-date intelligence. Do not bet the lives of your troops on a hunch.**

## SUN TZU SAYS

*Hence the use of spies, of whom there are five classes:*

1. *Local spies*
2. *Inward spies*
3. *Converted spies*
4. *Doomed spies*
5. *Surviving spies*

*When these five kinds of spy are all at work, none can discover the secret system. This is called "divine manipulation of the threads". It is the sovereign's most precious faculty.*

*Having local spies means employing the services of the inhabitants of a district. Having inward spies, making use of officials of the enemy. Having converted spies, getting hold of the enemy's spies and using them for our own purposes. Having doomed spies, doing certain things openly for purposes of deception, and allowing our spies to know of them and report them to the enemy. Surviving spies, finally, are those who bring back news from the enemy's camp.*

# LESSON 219

## LOCAL SPIES

*This is the first of the five types of spy.*

As part of your pre-war preparations, send out "living spies" (*see* lesson 223) into enemy territory to mingle with the general population. As well as gathering information, they will also identify, cultivate and recruit people they think will make good local informants. These could be farmers whose land looks onto a castle or merchants who supply the army. Clements translates this category as "native asset" and Calthrop as "village spy". They are not spies by trade but are useful because their situation gives them access and time to observe for you. The more local spies you have in play, the broader the picture of the enemy you will obtain.

Note that local spies are normal, everyday people and not to be confused with internal spies or converted spies, who work within the enemy's inner ranks.

**WAR TIP: Hire local people of no apparent importance to inform you of enemy movements and developments.**

# LESSON 220

## INTERNAL SPIES

*This is the second of the five types of spy.*

Target people who work directly for the enemy leader or within the enemy government, or go for people who have recently been dismissed from an important position and who are angry at the fact. Whereas local spies can give a broad picture of enemy movements and status, internal spies (or "inward" spies in Giles) can deliver specific information about the internal workings and plans of the enemy military or government.

**WAR TIP: Bribe people in key government and military positions to divulge important classified information.**

# LESSON 221

## CONVERTED SPIES

*This is the third of the five types of spy.*

The enemy will, of course, be spying on you at the same time as you are spying on them. It is the task of your living spies to discover who the enemy spies are. Once identified, they can be induced (with money, honours or other benefits) or coerced (through torture or threatened imprisonment) to convert to your side. A converted spy, also known as a double agent, is a "golden egg" in terms of intelligence – not only can they supply you with continuous information, but they can also feed the enemy false information and help you recruit internal spies. Capturing and turning an enemy spy is considered one of the highest forms of espionage, but the real problem is knowing which side they truly work for. Are they playing for you, or are they just playing you?

**WAR TIP: Discover enemy spies and use reward or punishment to convert them to your side.**

# LESSON 222

## DOOMED SPIES

*This is the fourth of the five types of spy.*

Deploying a doomed spy is a tactic designed to mislead the enemy. It involves telling one of your spies false information about your status or plans (the spy will generally be unaware that it is not true), then sending them on a dangerous mission in enemy territory. You need to make sure that the doomed spy gets captured – perhaps by instructing one of your internal spies to betray them. Under torture, the spy will confess all before being killed. If the enemy does not kill them but sends them back as a converted spy, then continue sending the spy back with false information in a double-sided spy game.

The point here is to make the enemy think they have obtained legitimate information. You can back up the deception by having your troops do some of the things mentioned in the doomed spy's report. The doomed spy can be an expendable low-level agent or they can be a high-level agent who volunteers for the task. The difference is that one of them knows they will probably be killed, the other does not.

The Clements version is subtly different: he suggests that the "doomed" or "dead" description refers to the information not to the spy. The spies are not necessarily destined to be killed, but the information they carry has no life in it because it is false.

**WAR TIP: Deceive the enemy by sending a spy to them with false information.**

# LESSON 223

## LIVING SPIES

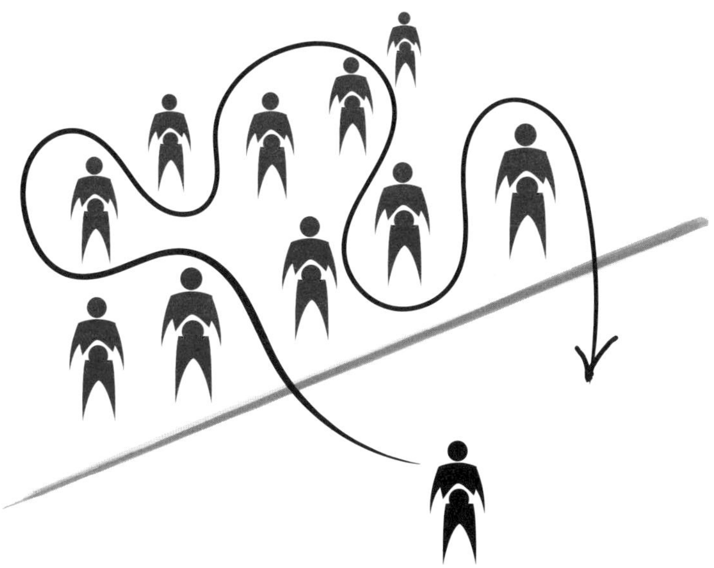

*This is the last of the five types of spy.*

Living spies (or "surviving" spies in Giles) are professional agents entrusted with all manner of missions, including information gathering, recruitment of local and internal spies and infiltration of the enemy base. They are considered the classic spy in action. With many of these operatives in play, you can gain detailed information on enemy movements and intentions. Living spies can be low-level agents undertaking lesser tasks all the way to the "perfect spy", who is expert in covert commando operations.

**WAR TIP: Use specialist spies to collect information, form relationships with the enemy and return with valuable information.**

# LESSON 224

## USE THE FIVE TYPES OF SPY IN COMBINATION

These five types of spy are the foundation of all espionage. Their use as a combined force is an in-depth subject, beyond the scope of this chapter. However, what can be said here is that the living spies are at the heart of the intelligence operation. They move around the enemy domain, recruiting and handling the other types of spy, infiltrating deep undercover and reporting back to the allied commander either in person or by other channels.

Based on tip-offs from internal spies, living spies also approach or capture enemy living spies and turn them into converted spies. The living spies then liaise with the converted spies, giving them false information to feed back to their original side and receiving genuine information about the enemy.

The role of the central intelligence staff is to collate the information from the various spies in the field. By mapping out the details they will be able to identify any false information, and so detect any allied living spies who have been turned by the enemy. Their findings and recommendations are presented to the war council where action is taken.

**WAR TIP: Think of your intelligence network as a single living machine. To get all the moving parts working in unison is "divine", the highest form of warfare according to Sun Tzu.**

SUN TZU SAYS

*Hence it is that with none in the whole army are more intimate relations to be maintained than with spies. None should be more liberally rewarded. In no other business should greater secrecy be preserved.*

*Spies cannot be usefully employed without a certain intuitive sagacity. They cannot be properly managed without benevolence and straightforwardness. Without subtle ingenuity of mind, one cannot make certain of the truth of their reports. Be subtle! be subtle! and use your spies for every kind of business.*

# LESSON 225

## CREATE A CLOSE BOND WITH YOUR SPIES

It is doubtful that Sun Tzu meant that the lord and master should be close to all spies serving the allied cause, as some of them are local spies in enemy territory and even internal spies inside the enemy base. So this teaching almost certainly applies to the relationship between the leader and the highest-level living spies, who, as we have seen, are the ones who link up the whole intelligence network. These people are rewarded with land, inheritance and gold, and are trusted to work on behalf of the leader without accountability for most of the things they do. Their relationship with the leader has to be close.

**WAR TIP: Form a strong relationship with your top spies that is based on mutual loyalty and trust.**

# LESSON 226

## PAY YOUR SPIES WELL

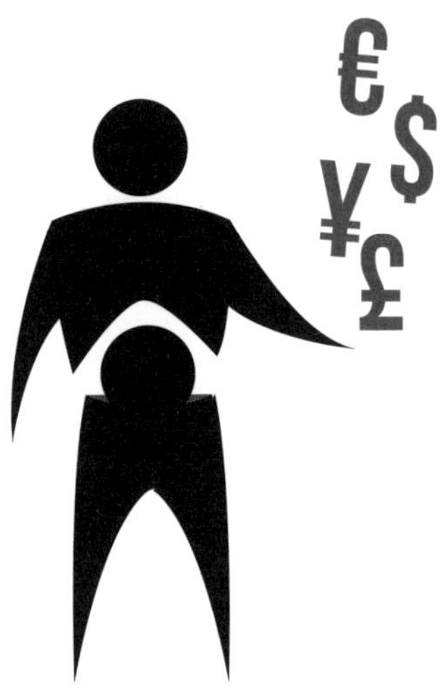


As well as trust and loyalty, which is formed by a close relationship with the military leader, spies must also receive well above the average pay and have access to an expense account that they are free to spend at will. In their line of work, they have to use money to bribe, smooth the way, create false identities and cover many expenses, from attending brothels to living the high life. By rewarding your spies generously and allowing them to do their work without restriction, you will make them less likely to be swayed by bribes from the enemy.

**WAR TIP: Spies need money for expenses in the field and a high salary to ensure their loyalty withstands enemy bribes.**

# LESSON 227

## MAINTAIN THE UTMOST SECRECY

All aspects of spy work must be secret. The spy must not reveal their role even to their closest friends and relations, under pain of the severest punishment. This means they must have a plausible cover story for their frequent absences. Spies must never be allowed to discuss their work with anyone but their handler or the military leader and they should not know each other's identity unless the operation requires it.

**WAR TIP: Enforce the strictest confidentiality and anonymity in your intelligence network so that nothing leaks out.**

# LESSON 228

## HANDLE SPIES WITH WISDOM, KINDNESS AND SUBTLETY

Managing a spy network is not a straightforward matter and requires particular qualities that only the most gifted leaders possess. Sun Tzu highlights the following three areas:

### INTUITIVE WISDOM

You will need to have a mind that can perceive the delicate strands of the "web of intelligence". This again is about predicting future outcomes from a small amount of seemingly unconnected information. Among the ideograms used in this section are 微妙, which have connotations of "small" and "mysterious" or "hidden things". Thus you are looking for the hidden elements within the whole, the clues that will unlock the mystery of what the enemy is planning to do next.

### KINDNESS

Show kindness to valued spies. This reinforces the idea that spies' loyalty comes not only from ample financial reward but also a close relationship with their leader.

### SUBTLETY

The ideogram for subtlety, 微, also appears in chapter 6 (lesson 83), but with a different ideogram for the exclamation mark (here the ideogram used is 哉, in chapter 6 it was 乎). Sun Tzu repeats himself, presumably for emphasis: 微哉微哉, "Be subtle! Be subtle!" There are various translations of this point: Trapp renders it as "Subtlety is the key," whereas the Denma Group goes for "Secret! Secret!" It involves more than just secrecy. It means handling your spies with sensitivity and deftness and also having the ability to read intelligence reports and see what does not appear to be there. Like spotting a trap many moves ahead in a game of chess, a military leader must be able to pick out the salient points and see the underlying patterns in a mass of information.

**WAR TIP: Understand the implications of intelligence reports, have the subtlety to deal with delicate matters and be kind and generous to develop spies' loyalty.**

# LESSON 229

## INVOLVE SPIES IN EVERYTHING

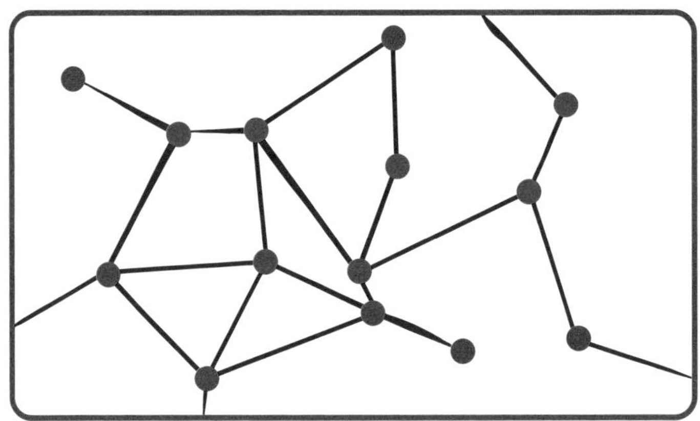

Espionage is like the thinnest of nets draping over the whole military campaign – barely visible yet covering everything. Spies are embedded in the enemy base, watch from without, are set as sleeper agents in potential threat territories. They also operate within your own camp, sniffing out enemy spies and disruptive elements from top to bottom. Spying is done everywhere at every level and in every branch of the armed forces from before a campaign starts to well after it has finished. Spies are everywhere at all times.

**WAR TIP: Intelligence is not a tap to be turned on and off. Maintain a constant flow of information by having spies in position at home and abroad during times of peace as well as war.**

## SUN TZU SAYS

*If a secret piece of news is divulged by a spy before the time is ripe, he must be put to death together with the man to whom the secret was told.*

*Whether the object be to crush an army, to storm a city, or to assassinate an individual, it is always necessary to begin by finding out the names of the attendants, the aides-de-camp, and door-keepers and sentries of the general in command. Our spies must be commissioned to ascertain these.*

*The enemy's spies who have come to spy on us must be sought out, tempted with bribes, led away and comfortably housed. Thus they will become converted spies and available for our service. It is through the information brought by the converted spy that we are able to acquire and employ local and inward spies. It is owing to his information, again, that we can cause the doomed spy to carry false tidings to the enemy. Lastly, it is by his information that the surviving spy can be used on appointed occasions. The end and aim of spying in all its five varieties is knowledge of the enemy; and this knowledge can only be derived, in the first instance, from the converted spy. Hence it is essential that the converted spy be treated with the utmost liberality. Of old, the rise of the Yin dynasty was due to I Chih who had served under the Xia. Likewise, the rise of the Zhou dynasty was due to Lu Ya who had served under the Yin.*

*Hence it is only the enlightened ruler and the wise general who will use the highest intelligence of the army for purposes of spying and thereby they achieve great results. Spies are a most important element in water, because on them depends an army's ability to move.*

# LESSON 230

## DEATH TO THOSE WHO SPEAK AND TO THOSE WHO HEAR!

Any spy caught leaking confidential information should be executed immediately, together with the person or people to whom they revealed it. No matter whether it is a deliberate act of betrayal or a casual conversation with a loved one or close friend, the consequences must be the same.

This action is both a remedy and a deterrent. Killing everyone who has heard the secret will stop any leaked information from spilling out further, thereby fixing the immediate problem. It will also make other spies fear talking to anyone – and that means anyone – in the future.

**WAR TIP: Keep your intelligence network watertight by threatening death to any spy who leaks classified information and anyone who receives it.**

# LESSON 231

## SEND SPIES TO DISCOVER THE NAMES OF ENEMY PERSONNEL

Sun Tzu gives examples of objectives that a military leader might use espionage to achieve:

- Striking an army
- Taking a city
- Assassinating a political figure

To achieve the above he says that first spies need to root out the names of certain significant people:

- 守將 Defensive commander
- 左右 Assistants to the above
- 謁者 General staff
- 門者 Gate guards
- 舍人 Attendants

Some of these are important because of their rank, others because of their role. Spies should find out as much as possible about these people so that they can understand enemy routines.

**WAR TIP: Before making any move against the enemy, use spies to identify key people. Use this information to form a plan of attack.**

# LESSON 232

## EMPLOY ASSASSINS

This lesson is inferred from the text and the previous lesson where Sun Tzu mentions assassinating enemy leaders. Therefore, train individuals to kill enemy targets. This can be their primary function or an additional skill for more general troops. Also, remember that anyone can perform an assassination if they have access to the target and the opportunity to make the kill.

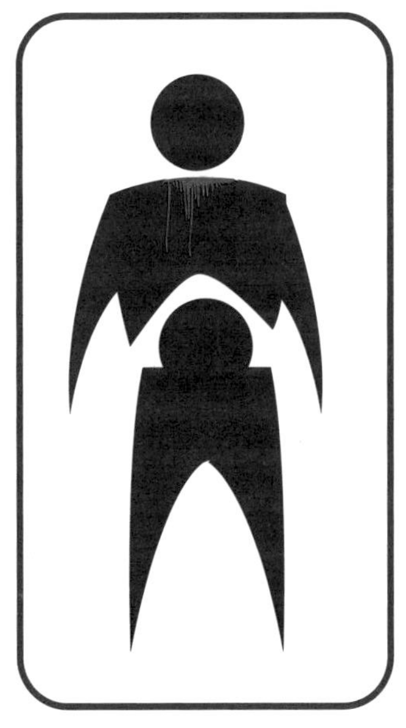

**WAR TIP: Make use of assassins to kill high-level enemy figures.**

# LESSON 233

## TREASURE YOUR CONVERTED SPIES

Sun Tzu at this stage reinforces the absolute need to convert enemy spies (*see* lesson 221). It is the task of living spies and internal observers to identify and approach enemy agents who have been sent to spy on your side. They should be bribed with rich rewards such as money, land, income, sex, wine – whatever their weakness may be. Alternatively, some enemy spies may respond to moral arguments explaining the inhumanity of the enemy cause. It is up to your living spies to work out what will persuade them to convert to your side.

Sun Tzu goes on to give the following explanations for the importance of converted spies, some of which have already been covered:

### THEY ARE A CHANNEL FOR FALSE INFORMATION

A fundamental aspect of warfare is to feed the enemy a false idea of your status. This is quite hard to do because the enemy will have multiple spies observing your movements. Therefore, if you can get enough converted spies to send back the same false information, the enemy will start to believe your version of the facts rather than the genuine reports of their unconverted spies. This is part of the skill of substantial and insubstantial.

### THEY CAN POINT LIVING SPIES TOWARD POTENTIAL LOCAL SPIES AND INTERNAL SPIES

Recruiting spies from among the enemy population, army and government is extremely dangerous. Your living spies need to be confident they are approaching the right people, otherwise they risk blowing their cover. This is particularly true of attempts to infiltrate the enemy base. With their inside knowledge of personal weaknesses, rivalries and grievances within the enemy inner circle, converted spies can identify the people who are most likely to consider changing sides. This is not a small point; its importance is immeasurable.

### THEY CAN ADVISE LIVING SPIES ON THE BEST WAYS TO INFILTRATE THE ENEMY

Living spies serve as the eyes and ears for the rest of the army, but when they go into the enemy they do so "blind". Converted spies can supply valuable information on the best times and places to infiltrate based on their knowledge of enemy routines and the internal layout of the enemy camp. If the converted spy has enough reliable information of this nature, it may even mean that the living spy does not have to infiltrate at all.

**WAR TIP: Converted spies are worth their weight in gold. They misinform the enemy, identify potential local and internal spies and help your living spies get into the enemy base.**

# LESSON 234

## USE HIGH-RANKING PEOPLE TO BRING YOUR ENEMY LOW

Sun Tzu quotes two old Chinese stories, one about the rise of the Yin dynasty and one about the rise of the Zhou. They both involve influential advisers who worked for the rulers who were in power before these dynasties rose. The first man worked for the Xia but changed sides and helped the Yin come to power. In the second story the Yin dynasty fell victim to the same move that had brought them power when one of their men conspired to help the Zhou replace them. It is only through informants that you can bring down an enemy from the inside.

**WAR TIP: By turning people in high places, one dynasty can collapse and another can rise. Such is the power of internal betrayal.**

# LESSON 235

## A WISE GENERAL AND INTELLIGENT SPIES ARE THE FOUNDATION OF ARMY MOVEMENT

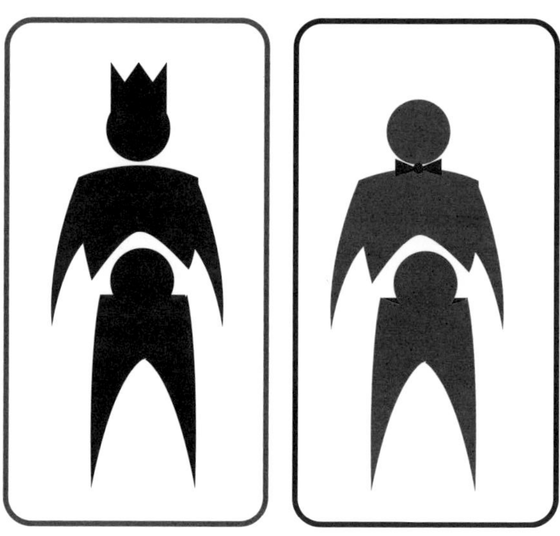

As Sun Tzu has told us throughout this book, the key to defeating the enemy is being steps ahead of them. This is only possible through spying. Observing enemy territory, the personality of the enemy leader and the make-up of their force, gauging their rations, supplies and morale, understanding their routines – all of this and much more is done by spies.

Therefore, value your spies above all other personnel, and from their reports predict enemy movements and plan your strategy.

**WAR TIP: The combination of an intelligent leader and skilled spies is the key to victory.**

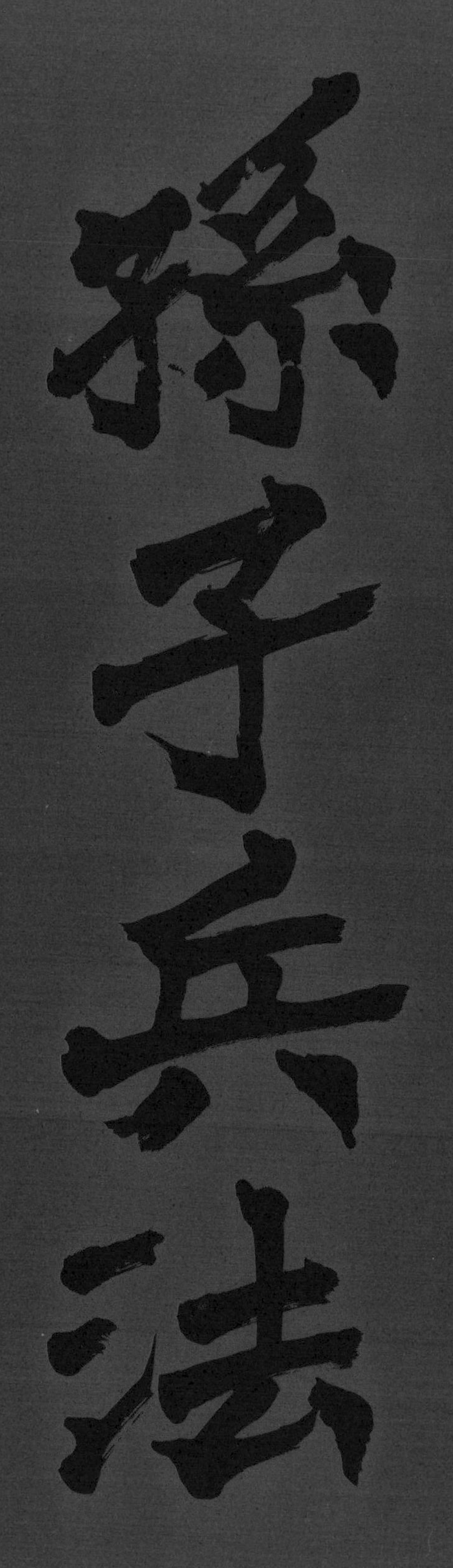
孫子兵法

ART OF WAR

# THE COMPLETE STRATEGY OF SUN TZU

# THE COMPLETE STRATEGY OF SUN TZU

Here you will find the teachings of Sun Tzu broken down into accessible points and rearranged into relevant subject sections under the umbrella of the five constant factors (*see* lessons 2–7):

### THE WAY

This section focuses on the state of mind of both enemy and allied troops, their welfare and their sense of unity. It contains all elements that can cause either harmony or disharmony within an army.

### HEAVEN

This section focuses on any aspects that deal with weather, wind, rain, the night sky and the moon and sun. It deals with everything that is above the land.

### EARTH

This section contains teachings that relate to the army's place in the landscape and how to use natural geographical features to your advantage.

### THE COMMANDER

This is the largest section. It focuses on the qualities required by a commander and gives the entire repertoire of practical military strategies.

### ORGANIZATION

In this final section you will find teachings relating to internal army structure, including advice on codes of conduct, rules and systems of punishment and reward.

This constitutes the *Art of War* in its totality but designed for ease of understanding and for use in personal training. It is also available as a download from the author's website: www.natori.co.uk

# 1 THE WAY

## THE HARMONY OF YOUR PEOPLE

- Always have a clear objective
- Consider the whole force as a single entity with movable sections
- Make the army feel like a family
- Know that war is very expensive and can disrupt the harmony of your people
- Have a reserve fund, rather than taxing the people again, if the cost of war rises beyond calculations
- Do not commit to a war that you know will be prolonged
- Never forget that war is horrific and disturbing
- Make sure all in the army understand the goals and have a unified purpose
- Understand the difference between swift, decisive action and hasty action
- Correctly estimate the number of troops needed for the war to avoid a second conscription
- Remember that an army will always disrupt the land and the people no matter where it goes
- Set clear rules and give your troops time to learn them
- Give rewards without delay
- Appoint commanders from military personnel not civilian ranks
- Allow no civil interference in military matters – civil leaders decide when to go to war, military leaders win the war
- Never succumb to social or political pressure
- Maintain unity by forbidding internal competition between your allied commanders
- Understand the physical and mental limits of your troops
- Establish solid bonds with your troops before giving out any punishments
- Know that soldiers who feel trapped will unify with intensity to fight their way out
- Keep the emotions of the troops in check
- Conserve the strength of your troops by allowing them to rest and feeding them well
- Share all good news but withhold bad news

- Unite your troops against a common enemy
- Demonize the enemy so that your troops feel no pity for them

## THE DISHARMONY OF THE ENEMY

- Provoke the enemy commander to unbalance them
- Create discord among the enemy in any way you can
- Treat enemy prisoners of war with respect and offer them a place in your own army
- Offer any enemy soldiers who fight for you the same rewards as your own troops
- Treat the enemy civilian population with fairness to gain their support
- Recognize problems in the enemy camp:
    - Dissension can be seen in troops being disrespectful to officers
    - Loss of discipline can be seen in enemy officers being overly aggressive toward the troops
    - Thoughts of revolt can be seen in troops gathering to gossip
    - Exhaustion and a breakdown in internal structure can be seen in the frequent giving of honours and awards that were once difficult to achieve
- Divide the enemy lower ranks from the upper ranks
- Starve enemy troops to unbalance their minds
- Attack enemy troops when they are exhausted and their morale is low
- When enemy troops call out encouragement to each other at night, know that they do this out of fear
- Know that enemy troops facing death are extremely difficult to defeat
- Recognize that if the enemy is silent and waiting it means they are unified and strong

# 2 HEAVEN

## WEATHER FORECASTING AND OBSERVATION

- Establish ways to predict the weather, including wind strength and direction
- Observe duration of the wind and the state of blowing and not blowing
- Study the effects the moon has on the environment
- Take account of the weather when planning a fire attack
- Be upwind of any fire in the battle

## SKY OBSERVATION

- Observe any strange behaviour in the flight of birds to identify enemy troop positions
- Understand what different kinds of dust cloud tell you about enemy activity:
    Vehicles moving at speed will shoot clouds of dust high into the sky
    An army marching slowly on foot will create a wide but low dust cloud
    Troops foraging create thin dust clouds in multiple areas at a similar time
    Troops setting up camp create thin dust clouds in a single area at different times
- Understand the night sky and all the constellations
- Record the rising and setting of the sun and moon
- Understand the lunar cycle and the position of the moon in the night sky

# 3 EARTH

## THE BASICS OF TERRAIN

- Treat the terrain as your ally
- Make plans for all types of terrain
- Know which types of troops match each type of landscape
- Obtain or create maps of enemy territory
- Locate your fortress in an isolated and extremely defensible position
- Beware of a third party along your borders attacking while your main force is away at war
- Replenish your supplies when you leave home territory and when you re-enter it
- Have the ability to move in all terrains from the lowest to the highest
- Take control of all major roads
- Secure position on easily traversable ground for better communication between sections
- Keep high ground to the rear
- Keep difficult ground behind the enemy
- Keep your troops in open places if possible
- Guard against troops deserting and returning while still in home territory
- When on the move stick to lower ground
- After war plunder enemy lands but do not devastate the people
- Divide any conquered land fairly among your troops

## IN ENEMY TERRITORY OR ON THE MOVE

- Just inside enemy territory, know that it is still quite easy for troops to desert
- Use a corps of professional trained scouts to move about the landscape and report
- Recruit local people as guides by either force or reward
- Take measurements of the enemy terrain
- Measure both mountains and valleys
- Make observations of all ground types and terrain changes
- Take your army the long way to a specific destination if it is safer than the direct route

- Never let the enemy decide the battlefield
- Be the first to the battlefield
- Avoid battlefields that cannot easily be exited
- Take measurements of the battlefield
- Lead the enemy into a position you want them to be in
- Force the enemy into difficult terrain
- If the enemy has set up on difficult ground that is hard to approach, do not attack them
- If the enemy has not yet set up on difficult ground, move in and attack as they are forming up
- Understand that if the terrain will force your army to break up and lose cohesion then it is sometimes better to turn and face the enemy
- If the enemy tries to tempt you to approach, it is because they are in a strong position
- If the enemy is in a secure position, coax them out to a new one
- Predict which types of troop the enemy will deploy by the landscape features
- Consider using a smaller force in certain landscapes even if more troops are available
- Be aware that in open and expansive terrain there is nowhere to run or hide and the enemy can chase you down and destroy you
- When deep inside enemy territory, come together and move as an unstoppable machine of war
- Send scouts to positions where ambushes and kill squads are likely to be stationed
- Block all possible ambush points before moving through them
- Trap the enemy in restricted places
- Search forests and tree lines for enemy troops
- If animals leave an area in a hurry, expect enemy troops to be coming from that direction
- In open terrain wait for the enemy to make the first move and exploit the gaps that creates
- If in the open do not allow any of your sections to become isolated from the main force
- When setting up position or preparing for combat, move to higher ground
- Do not attack uphill
- Do not ascend the steepest sides of hills – find an easier path

- Make camp in places that are easily defensible
- Move through dangerous areas as quickly as possible
- Establish set locations as rallying points

## BODIES OF WATER

- When preparing for battle move away from any form of water
- Be wary of gorges, ravines and places where water makes movement difficult
- Redirect vast bodies of water to flood the enemy
- Position yourself upstream of the enemy
- Do not cross a river when a flash flood is likely
- When you cross a river allow space on the opposite bank for the whole army
- When targeting an enemy that is crossing a river, allow half their troops to cross before attacking
- Cross marshlands with speed
- If you fight in a marsh, find higher ground with dense foliage

# 4 THE COMMANDER

## A PERFECT COMMANDER

- Know that the commander must be a fully trained professional soldier
- Understand that all things have a beginning, a middle and an end
- Know that situations are in constant flux and things can change fast
- Understand, adapt and move between the concepts of rigid and flexible
- Switch between orthodox and unorthodox tactics
- Have a mind of iron which is immovable
- Know when to advance and when to retreat
- Never react with emotion – take time to calm down
- Share in the hardships of the troops to gain respect
- Do not make decisions based on how they will affect your reputation

## THE FOUNDATIONS OF GOOD STRATEGY

- During times of peace maintain a position of strength as a deterrent
- Drill your troops to form up quickly
- Make best use of the talents of individual troops
- Set up systems for long-distance communication
- Know the aims and goals of all people of influence – both military and civilian and enemy and allied
- Prepare exhaustively and secretly, execute swiftly
- Have subtlety in your actions with multiple steps
- Never be predictable in your tactics and do not repeat what has worked for you before
- Know that there is a finite number of war strategies but that their combinations are innumerable
- Never engage in open battle with a larger enemy without tactics in place
- Attempt to capture the enemy position, territory, force and stores intact
- Steal the enemy's stores and provisions if you can; destroy them if not
- Aim to inflict as few casualties as possible to gain victory
- Create momentum and speed only at the correct time
- Disguise your gaps and weaknesses
- Avoid making the obvious move
- Prepare counter-measures for all situations before moving to action

- Be neither reckless nor over-cautious
- Let the enemy come to you – do not go to the enemy unless launching a surprise attack
- Never attack an enemy that is in perfect order
- Attack the enemy when they are weak and you are strong
- When war is declared seal the borders of your country
- Forbid any supernatural practices within the army

## ASSESSMENTS AND OBSERVATIONS

- Make an honest, informed assessment and comparison of the strengths, abilities and discipline of the enemy and allied forces
- Assess the gain versus harm in any upcoming conflict or section of battle
- Always consider alternative options
- Make sure to have the fullest information possible on all matters
- Predict enemy plans based on your knowledge of their movements
- Before attacking, ask yourself one of the following questions, depending on the situation:

    "I have the ability to attack the enemy, but is the enemy in a position to be attacked?"

    "The enemy is in a position to be attacked, but do I have the ability to attack them?"
- Accurately predict future outcomes from diverse fragments of information
- Calculate the size of the enemy by their own territory and by counting

## BATTLE WITH THE ENEMY

- Defeat the enemy by destroying them section by section
- Aim your strikes at the weaker sections of the enemy, not its strong points
- Know when and where to strike – timing is everything
- Create disorder in the enemy and then strike
- Present both truth and falsehood to the enemy to keep them guessing
- Start with direct attacks, but finish with surprise tactics
- Allow the enemy to think that your troops are further away or closer than they are

- Fool the enemy into thinking you are incompetent
- Never attack a superior army in open battle
- If the enemy is strong in numbers and power, go on the defensive
- If you outnumber the enemy ten to one, surround them
- If you outnumber the enemy five to one, attack and overwhelm them
- If you outnumber the enemy two to one, use both direct and indirect assaults
- If you are equal in number to the enemy, focus on excellent tactics
- If the enemy outnumbers your forces, move away and do not engage directly
- If the enemy appears to placate you when they are in a strong position, know that this is a trap
- If the enemy appears aggressive and bullish when they are in a weak position, know that they are stalling to give themselves a chance to retreat
- If the enemy unexpectedly offers peace, know that they have a problem with their internal situation or home territory
- If the enemy tries to move your troops, keep them in position
- If the enemy tries to keep your troops in position, move them
- Observe how the enemy makes its formations
- When the enemy takes up a formation, send extra scouts to check for reinforcements arriving
- Give enemy scouts something false to report
- Track and kill enemy scouts
- Attack before the enemy has a chance to form up
- Identify the types of troops and vehicles the enemy has in its force
- Observe the quality of the enemy's internal signals to assess their competence
- Make a move to test the enemy's initial response tactics
- Provoke movement in the enemy so as to create gaps in their formation or position
- Offer the enemy a target as bait
- Do not allow faster troops to rush ahead of the others
- Divide the enemy and do not let them reunite
- Stop any enemy external specialist sections from reuniting with the army
- Attack one side to force the enemy to move troops to defend, which weakens their other positions
- If the enemy abandons one section of the army as an easy target, know that this is a trap

- Appear as if you are not going to react to the enemy's movements, but then attack when it is too late for them to change their momentum
- Deplete the enemy's strength by keeping them on the move
- Focus attacks on the enemy's least prepared section
- Attack from a position and direction that the enemy does not expect
- Capture and reuse enemy vehicles by changing their insignia and mixing them with your own vehicles
- Do not dump equipment to increase your marching speed because it will create problems later on
- If you want the enemy to be static, destroy any sections that move
- Keep an observation on enemy flanking troops, which represent the boundary of the battlefield
- Pretend to leave the battleground, then when the enemy disbands to move off turn back and strike hard
- Harass the enemy as much as possible to keep them from being unified
- Have troops available to support any sections that are under attack (the teaching of the snake)
- Look weak before you attack
- Use false threat to occupy the enemy and stall for time
- If the enemy suddenly breaks its normal internal routine, know that they are making ready to launch a last stand or death charge
- Do not force the enemy to fight to the death, but give them an escape route

## INCENDIARY WARFARE

- Stockpile and maintain equipment for incendiary warfare
- Burn enemy personnel, food stores, vehicles and equipment (if you are not able to capture them)
- Burn enemy formations and take advantage of their break up
- If a fire breaks out within the enemy camp launch an attack, but be wary of false fires started to lure you into a kill zone
- Attack from the outside and burn down outer defences
- Use spies to attack with fire from the inside

## SIEGE WARFARE

- Have specialists who understand the construction and usage of siege equipment
- When besieging an enemy use movable walls
- Use movable shields to create defences
- Know that patience, not hasty and drastic action, wins a siege
- Create earthworks in the landscape

## ESPIONAGE

- Allow ample funds for the intelligence service
- Create a central command for the intelligence service and attach it to the main headquarters
- Ensure that all information about the enemy is based on actual observation
- Use the central command for intelligence to analyse all field reports
- Understand how spying works to get the best from spies and their reports
- Make sure any analysis of reports includes the hidden implications of enemy activity
- Maintain strict secrecy throughout the intelligence service
- Reward all spies generously to avoid the enemy bribing them
- Shut down any leaks immediately by killing all involved
- Do not rely on deduction from comparison to predict enemy movements – always use up-to-date internal information from spies
- Discover the names and profiles of all key people within the enemy, including lower-level people with internal access
- Use spies to bring a quick victory
- Employ local people to act as spies when in enemy territory
- Bribe members of the enemy military to spy for you
- Discover enemy spies and convert them – pay them very well to keep them loyal to your side
- Send doomed spies with false information to mislead the enemy
- Employ highly trained and professional permanent spies
- Create bonds of loyalty between full-time spies and the command group
- Target specific people for assassination by specialist operatives

## HIGHER-LEVEL TACTICS

- Recognize situations where orders from above should be ignored, but this is a delicate subject
- In certain situations, lose the first battle in order to lead the enemy into a position where you want them
- Do not lay out your troops in a set pattern – appear to be formless
- Divert the enemy by creating fake positions or defences, but be aware the enemy will do the same
- Understand and execute the tactic of false retreat, but do not fall for enemy false retreats
- Allow a retreating enemy to leave the battlefield
- For your troops to maintain the illusion of being disordered, know that they must actually be extremely well ordered
- For your troops to maintain the illusion of being cowardly, know that they must actually be extremely brave

# 5 ORGANIZATION

- Establish a central command headquarters whether you are in home or enemy territory
- Have a proper chain of command in place
- Maintain a clear distinction between lower and upper ranks, but ensure mutual respect between all soldiers
- Have excellent communications
- Give all troops proper training
- Ensure that all troops act with self-discipline and instantly move on command
- Value loyalty above all other virtues
- Promote troops based on merit not social position
- Establish a fair system of punishment and reward that is understood by all
- Give all combatants and non-combatants a clear role and set of tasks
- Break your army down into small sections that can separate and recombine with efficiency and speed
- Maintain strict secrecy in your army
- To avoid leaks and maintain your authority, do not give your troops too much information
- Ensure that your vehicles and equipment are maintained to a working standard
- Account for the cost of replacement vehicles and equipment
- Drill your troops to:

    March at speed like the wind
    Form up like trees in a forest
    Assume a defensive position as strong and impenetrable as a mountain
    Attack with the force of a raging fire
    Be as obscure to the enemy as darkness or clouds
    Strike as quickly as lightning
- Ensure that even your slowest troops are faster than the enemy
- In standard divisions mix the ability levels of the troops to help unify the energy of the army
- In specialist divisions hand-pick the troops with the right qualities for the task
- Follow military, not civilian laws

# INDEX

## A

# B



# C

# F



# G

# H



# I



# J



# K



# L

## M



## N

## S

# T

# U



# V

## THE BOOK OF SAMURAI SERIES

**ABOVE:** Antony Cummins, author of this volume, is also the project leader of the resurrected samurai school of war Natori-Ryu, whose teachings can be found in the Book of Samurai series (available from Watkins).

The *Art of War* has had a profound effect throughout the world, but nowhere more so than in Japan where it particularly influenced the samurai. The samurai school known as Natori-Ryu originated in the 16th century as the military branch of the Natori family, which was then serving the famous Japanese warlord Takeda Shingen. The school was redeveloped and expanded in the 17th century by Natori Masazumi, also known as Issui-sensei. Issui-sensei's extensive writings on military tactics drew heavily on the *Art of War*, and so Sun Tzu's work itself became a core text for all Natori-Ryu students.

The original school closed its doors in the late 19th century, but with the blessing of the Natori family it reopened on 5 May 2013 with Antony Cummins as the project leader. The original scrolls by Issui-sensei have been collected and translated into English in the Book of Samurai series (also published by Watkins), enabling students around the world to study these teachings for the first time. If you are interested in studying the way of the samurai, you can find further information at www.natori.co.uk

THE BOOK OF SAMURAI SERIES

## ABOUT THE AUTHOR

Antony Cummins is the Official Tourism Ambassador for Wakayama, Japan (和歌山市観光発信人) and an author on historical Asian military culture, particularly Japanese. His intention is to present a historically accurate picture of both samurai and shinobi (ninja) to the Western world and lay down the foundations for a better understanding of their teachings and ways. He has written an array of books on Japanese warfare, including translations of historical ninja manuals with his translation partners. Antony and his work can be followed on YouTube under "Antony Cummins" and "Natori Ryu", as well as on Instagram under @historicalninja and @natoriryu. For more information see his website: www.natori.co.uk

## ABOUT THE ILLUSTRATOR

Jay Kane (Kane Kong Illustrates) is a full-time graphic designer in the textile industry and a freelance illustrator based in Manchester, UK. Born in South Africa, he later moved to the UK and studied Art, Design and Print Making in Manchester. He has worked alongside Antony Cummins for over a decade on books including: *True Path of the Ninja* (cover concept designer), *The Secret Traditions of the Shinobi* (front cover designer), *Iga and Koka Ninja Skills* (internal illustrations), *The Book of Samurai: Samurai Arms, Armour & the Tactics of Warfare* (internal illustrations), *The Lost Warfare of India: An Illustrated Guide* (front cover designer), *Ninja Skills* (internal illustrations), *Old Japan – Secrets from the Shores of the Samurai* (internal illustrations) and *Ninja Warfare* (internal illustrations). He also created illustrations for *The Old Stones*, a field guide to the megalithic sites of Britain and Ireland.

# ABOUT THE CALLIGRAPHER

Yamamoto Jyuhō (山本寿法) was born in Wakayama city, Wakayama prefecture in 1967. He studied Buddhism Folklore at the Department of Buddhist Studies (仏教学科) in the Faculty of Buddhism (仏教学部), Komazawa University (駒澤大学), completed his religious education at the Sōtō-shū Daihonzan Eiheiji Temple (曹洞宗大本山永平寺), and was inaugurated as the 26th chief priest of Sōtō-shū Daihōzan Eunji Temple (曹洞宗大宝山恵運寺) in 2013. He is also director of Sōgenzan Daisenji Temple (曹源山大泉寺) and chief priest of Zenpukuji Temple (善福寺).

Yamamoto oversees the conservation and preservation of the grave, death tablet and death records for the Natori (名取) clan at Eunji Temple (恵運寺), which is home to the grave of the famous samurai strategist Natori Sanjūrō Masazumi (名取三十郎正澄), the author of the highly popular ninja scroll known as the Shōninki (正忍記). Natori Masazumi's grave is a key focus for tourism in Wakayama city. Yamamoto also established the Shōninki Reading Club (正忍記を読む会), which aims to spread the teachings of historical ninjutsu to the world. He lectures on the history of the ninja at various events.

Yamamoto is a well-known figure in the world of Japanese calligraphy and traditional seal engraving. He studied under Yamashita Hōtei (山下方亭) and is the director of the Zuifūkai group (随風会), as well as being a trustee of the Japanese Seal-Engravers Association (日本篆刻家協会) and the Yomiuri Shohōkai group (読売書法会). He is an examiner for the Nihon Shogeiin Nika Shinsa group (日本書芸院二科審査) and a member of the Zen Kansai Bijutsuten Mukansa (全関西美術展無鑑査会員) and Wakayama Calligraphy Association (和歌山書道協会). In 2018 he won first prize at both the Japanese Seal-Engraving Exhibition (日本篆刻展) and the Nihon Shogeiin Exhibition (日本書芸院展). His calligraphy has been published multiple times including in the Book of Samurai series.

The story of Watkins began in 1893, when scholar of esotericism John Watkins founded our bookshop, inspired by the lament of his friend and teacher Madame Blavatsky that there was nowhere in London to buy books on mysticism, occultism or metaphysics. That moment marked the birth of Watkins, soon to become the publisher of many of the leading lights of spiritual literature, including Carl Jung, Rudolf Steiner, Alice Bailey and Chögyam Trungpa.

Today, the passion at Watkins Publishing for vigorous questioning is still resolute. Our stimulating and groundbreaking list ranges from ancient traditions and complementary medicine to the latest ideas about personal development, holistic wellbeing and consciousness exploration. We remain at the cutting edge, committed to publishing books that change lives.

DISCOVER MORE AT:

www.watkinspublishing.com

Read our blog

Watch and listen to our authors in action

Sign up to our mailing list

We celebrate conscious, passionate, wise and happy living.

Be part of that community by visiting